D0142078

PALLADIUS
DIALOGUE ON THE LIFE OF
ST. JOHN CHRYSOSTOM

Ancient Christian Writers

THE WORKS OF THE FATHERS IN TRANSLATION

EDITED BY

JOHANNES QUASTEN   WALTER J. BURGHARDT

THOMAS COMERFORD LAWLER

No. 45

PALLADIUS

DIALOGUE ON THE LIFE OF

ST. JOHN CHRYSOSTOM

TRANSLATED AND EDITED

BY

ROBERT T. MEYER

Professor of Philology
Catholic University of America

NEWMAN PRESS
New York, N.Y./Mahwah, N.J.

COPYRIGHT 1985
BY
REV. JOHANNES QUASTEN
AND
REV. WALTER J. BURGHARDT, S.J.
AND
THOMAS COMERFORD LAWLER

Library of Congress
Catalog Card Number: 85-61570

ISBN: 0–8091–0358–3

Published by Paulist Press
997 Macarthur Boulevard
Mahwah, N.J. 07430

PRINTED AND BOUND IN THE UNITED STATES OF AMERICA

CONTENTS

NOTES

INDEXES

INTRODUCTION

"There was at Antioch on the Orontes a certain presbyter named John, a man of noble birth and possessed of such wonderful powers of eloquence and persuasion that he was declared by the sophist Libanius to surpass all the orators of his age."

SOZOMEN[1]

The historian goes on to say that as Libanius lay on his deathbed he was asked who his successor should be. "It would have been John," he replied, "had not the Christians taken him from me."

That was very good testimony, coming as it did from a man who was so strongly opposed to Christianity.[2] How fortunate that Chrysostom[3] left the rhetorical schools to save his soul. All Christianity is richer that he turned to the Church rather than to the law which he had once considered. Among all the Greek Fathers none left as vast a literary legacy as Chrysostom did.

We know little about St. John Chrysostom's early years. He never mentioned his parents' names in his writings, and it is only Socrates the historian who tells us that his father was Secundus and his mother Anthusa.[4] We are not even certain of the exact date of his birth, which must have been between 344 and 354. His father was an army officer and died when John was still an infant. His mother never remarried. The family must have been fairly well to do when we consider young John's good education. He showed from the very beginning the Roman quality of firmness and strength of will as well as the vivacious and versatile spirit of the Greeks.[5]

His education was first of all at Antioch, where he sat at the feet of Libanius, the famous rhetorician; then he betook himself to the study of philosophy under Andragathius. When he was but eighteen years of age he revolted against the pagan learning and decided to study Christian theology and Sacred Scripture. Meletius, bishop of Antioch, noticed his intellectual qualities and made him a lector. John, however, soon turned to the neighboring mountains. He spent four years as an ascetic living near an old hermit who advised him in spiritual matters. Then he retired to a cave for another two years of fasting and reading of the Scriptures, which was to serve him well in his later years. At the same time his excessive fasting and living in the cold laid the foundation for his later gastric troubles. Since he could not doctor himself, he returned to Antioch.[6]

In the year 381 he was ordained by Bishop Meletius as deacon, and about 386 he was ordained a priest by Bishop Flavian of Antioch. He was appointed to preach in the principal church in Antioch, and the period 386–397 was the time of his greatest homilies. That, however, came to a sudden end in 398, when he was consecrated bishop of Constantinople by Theophilus, who was patriarch of Alexandria. Bishop Nectarius of Constantinople had died and the emperor Arcadius forced the consecration on February 26, 398. Both the consecrator and the ordained were equally reluctant, Chrysostom because he did not believe himself worthy and Theophilus because he had another candidate of his own for the position. The two later became strong enemies.

John began a series of great reforms in Constantinople, where he soon gained the love of the people but found himself often halted by political intrigue and bribery. Proud and fearless, he offended many by his manner of speech. He criticized with veiled references the life style of the Empress Eudoxia. Theophilus was extremely jealous of John's good reputation; he probably felt that the more ancient primatial see of Alexandria was threatened by the upstart capitol of the Eastern world, Constantinople. In the conflict which erupted between the two ecclesiastics, the people sided with Chrysostom, but the Imperial Court was influenced by Theophilus. Appeals to Rome were unsuccessful.

John was exiled twice, and he died in Pontus when being taken to Armenia on September 14, 407. Remorse on the part of the Imperial Court was late in coming. Theodoretus tells us that Theodosius II, a son of Eudoxia, "laid his face upon Chrysostom's coffin and prayed that the sins of his parents might be forgiven for their ill-advised persecution of the bishop."[7] It was to Lausus, the royal chamberlain of Theodosius II, that Palladius had dedicated his *Historia Lausiaca*, and it is of Palladius we shall now speak.

LIFE OF PALLADIUS

Palladius of Helenopolis, the author of the *Dialogus de vita sancti Joannis Chrysostomi*, was born in 363 or 364 in Galatia. His parents as well were rather comfortable for he received a good classical education and was a pupil of the great Evagrius of Pontus, to whom he gives a long chapter in his *Lausiac History*.[8] He had at least one brother and a sister to judge from his writings. His father was still alive in 394, as we know from a reference in the *History*, and his brother and sister had both entered the religious life.[9] From the *Dialogus* we learn that the brother Brisson was a bishop, but probably because of the troubled situation at the time had resigned his see voluntarily and was supporting himself on a small farm.[10]

When he was twenty-three years old, Palladius went to live on the Mount of Olives with a certain ascetic named Innocent, who in all probability later on became Pope. After this he spent some time with Elpidius in a cave near Jericho. About 388 he went to Egypt to see the solitaries there in the so-called Solitudes not far from Alexandria. From there he went to Nitria and to Cellia, where he stayed for nine years. His health broke down and he went to Alexandria for medical aid; the physicians there told him that he must go to Palestine for the "better air" there.[11] It is quite possible that he met St. Jerome at that time. Somewhat later he went to Bithynia, where he was consecrated as bishop of Helenopolis, probably by St. John Chrysostom. He was shortly afterwards appointed to a commission to investigate charges against Bishop Antoninus of Valentinopolis. In 403 he was present at the Synod of the Oak, where Chrysostom was deposed by Theophilus. Palladius was himself accused of Origenism about that time, but modern historical criticism has cleared him of those charges. In 405 he went to Rome on an embassy to plead Chrysostom's case before Pope Innocent I, and on his return to Constantinople he was arrested with his fellow travellers by Emperor Arcadius and exiled to Egypt. There he probably wrote the *Dialogus* in Syene in 406 to 408. Then he went to Antinoë in the Thebaid for four years. With the death of Theophilus in 412, Palladius was free to return to Galatia, where he lived for a while with the priest Philoramus. It must have been about this time that he wrote the *Lausiac History*, a collection of biographies of the monks of the deserts of Egypt, Palestine, and Syria. We know from Socrates (7.36) that he was transferred from the see of Helenopolis to that of Aspuna, where he probably died before 431 as another bishop from there attended the Council of Ephesus convened that year.

There is one other work which is supposed to have been written by Palladius, the *Epistola de Indicis gentibus et de Bragmannibus*.[12] We know that Palladius was enough of a gyrovague to have made a trip to India to study the life and manners of the ascetics living there. If the composition is really by Palladius, it may have been written after his transfer to Aspuna. We are not convinced by the arguments that have been brought forward to prove Palladian authorship.

Dialogus de Vita Sancti Joannis Chrysostomi

The *Dialogus* was, as stated above, probably written in 406–408. This *vita* comes down to us in the form of a dialogue modelled on the *Phaedo* of Plato. It takes place between a bishop who is not identified as to name or see and a deacon of the Church of Rome, who is often addressed as Theodore. The locale of the exchange is Rome, and this is the bishop's first visit there. When Palladius refers to his own part in the dealings with Chrysostom he speaks of himself in the third person. Careful reading of the text reveals that the *Dialogus* extended over several days and several persons were in the audience. The deacon is anxious to hear the true facts of Chrysostom's exile and death. Many rumors have been circulating about Rome and now he has a chance to learn at first hand from one who had been in the company of John through those last years of his stormy career.

The immediate purpose of the *Dialogus* is to clear John's name of calumny. Theophilus had presumably written a letter which was loaded with falsehoods about John to Pope Innocent to clear himself in the matter of sending him into exile. Such a letter may never in fact have been written; it may have been a mere literary invention to justify the writing of the *Dialogus* so soon after John's death. The ultimate aim of the composition, as appears from the closing pages, is to point out Chrysostom as a model of what a true Christian bishop should be. Similarly the *Lausiac History* was written to teach moral lessons, not only to the chamberlain Lausus to whom it was dedicated, but to all who sought to practice the ascetic life. Chrysostom was not anxious to become a bishop because of the great responsibilities, but once he saw that it was God's will, he went ahead with all his powers to carry out His plan. He warned those who desired the episcopal office to consider whether they could bear the heavy burdens so fraught with dangers to body and soul. At the close of the *Dialogus* the deacon thanks the bishop and says he will lose no time in committing the whole account to new parchment so that it may not be lost.

The literary qualities of the *Dialogus* differ from that of the *Lausiac History*. Palladius was addressing a different kind of reader. He did not have the literary and rhetorical training that a reader of the *Dialogus* was presumed to have. The very textual tradition of the *History* with its numerous adaptations and versions in different languages shows how popular it was. The *Dialogus*, on the other hand, makes hard reading and requires constant application of the mind to follow the argument. The *History* runs on with a lively style, giving a panoramic view of the male and female ascetics in the desert. To be sure the Prologue and the Letter to Lausus at the beginning do show a certain amount of the rhetoric to be found in the *Dialogus*; but once we enter the main body of the *History* we find very good examples of Koine Greek. The *Dialogus* is addressed to an entirely different class of people, those who would appreciate long periods and classical allusions and occasional purple patches. This difference in stylistic treatment does not mean that Palladius did not write both works. The identical treatment of certain scriptural passages in both works establishes this beyond reasonable doubt. There are also groups of words which occur only in both these texts.[13]

HISTORICAL RELIABILITY OF PALLADIUS

Palladius was in close contact with Chrysostom for a great part of his public life in Constantinople. He was ordained by him as priest and probably also as bishop.[14] He made a journey to Rome to clear St. John of certain charges made by Theophilus. He was associated with him at Constantinople and also in his travels to Ephesus. He had seen him in all his activities: preaching, administering the sacraments, caring for the poor, managing church funds and properties, and in looking after the diocese generally. This is all apparent from even a casual reading of the *Dialogus*. Palladius also suffered persecution for this close connection to John.[15] This *vita*, then, is certainly not a work of fiction or hearsay. In one instance he blasts a tanner who dared make disparaging remarks about Chrysostom's way of life.[16] Another thing most noteworthy of the life thus depicted is the complete absence of the miraculous and the marvellous, which was the stock-in-trade of later hagiographers.[17] Furthermore, there are many passages where he quotes, accurately and reliably, from Chrysostom's works and homilies. When he quotes the canons of Church Councils, he is accurate.

There has recently come to light, however, some new evidence which would seem to challenge the reliability of Palladius.[18] A newly discovered manuscript, which unfortunately lacks both the beginning and end, proves to be a life of St. John Chrysostom. This anonymous *vita* gives us certain additional information about the charges which were brought against Chrysostom at the Synod of the Oak. One of the charges was that he had built a leprosarium within the confines of the residential district of Constantinople. Another, which can be ridiculed, is that Chrysostom had obtained power over the people by magic practices. More serious is one that he had gone beyond his canonical jurisdiction in making some ecclesiastical appointments, conducting ordinations, and censuring the clergy. Palladius doubtless knew of some of these infractions, but felt under no compulsion to present both sides of his hero's character. The charge that St. John ate alone may seem childish to us; Palladius explained why it was so, and he devoted a whole chapter (12) to defending his abstemious habits. The same is true of his outspoken manner of speech, which Palladius admits and exculpates with Scriptural texts in chapter 19. Palladius is the only one who claimed that John was exiled because he insulted Eudoxia publicly. This is not to be found in the other *vitae*. We do admit that Palladius was biased in favor of John and so may have glossed over intentionally or otherwise the weaknesses in John's character.

EDITIONS AND TRANSLATIONS

The editio princeps of the *Dialogus* was published at Paris by Emeric Bigot (1626–1681) in 1680.[19] It was based upon the Medici manuscript which he had copied at Florence. The text was accompanied by a new Latin translation alongside the original Greek. Bigot divided the text into twenty chapters of unequal length and all subsequent editors have followed that division. The volume of over 400 pages contains other texts as well. His textual apparatus and biblical citation references appear as marginalia. In 1738 Montfaucon the Maurist reprinted Bigot's text in his *Chrysostomi Opera Omnia*. He made some corrections and noted some biblical quotations which had escaped Bigot. In 1772 Galland included Montfaucon's edition of the *Dialogus* in his *Bibliotheca veterum patrum*. It is a mere reprint of Montfaucon. In 1839 a revised edition of Montfaucon appeared with slight changes in the text. Migne reprinted this revised edition with no changes in *Patrologiae cursus completus, series graeca*, 47.5–32 in 1858. In 1928 P.R. Coleman-Norton published his *Palladii Dialogus de vita sancti Joannis Chrysostomi* edited with revised text, introduction, notes, indexes, and appendices. This is the basis of the present translation.

TRANSLATIONS

Ambrogio Traversari (1386–1439) was a Camaldolese hermit who made a Latin translation which was not published until 1533,[20] still nearly a century and a half before the first printing of the Greek text. He substituted the proper names Palladius and Theodorus for the original Greek ἐπίσκοπος and διάκονος with no manuscript authority for so doing. His translation was reproduced in Du Duc's edition of the complete works of St. John Chrysostom in 1621. Bigot found the Latin translation of Traversari unsatisfactory and made a new one which was printed alongside the Greek texts. An English translation was published in 1921 by the Rev. Herbert Moore of Nantwich.[21] He based it on Migne, following any good emendations or conjectures found there without calling special attention to them. His translation was accompanied with somewhat fuller notes than are usually to be found in the S.P.C.K. series. He broke up the long chapters of the original into smaller subdivisions and these have been followed in the present translation. He acknowledged the help of P.R. Coleman-Norton, then a Rhodes Scholar of Christ Church who later produced the critical edition upon which this translation is based. A German translation by the Capuchin, Rev. Lothar Schläpfer, appeared at Düsseldorf in 1966.[22] It was the first translation based on the new edition of Coleman-Norton. I have made use of all these translations. I might add that the two Latin translations that I have used had both belonged to the late Coleman-Norton and were much utilized in his preparation of the critical edition for which we are so thankful.

Finally I must express heartfelt thanks to my colleague, Professor Thomas P. Halton, who read the first draft of my translation and gave me much useful advice. Thanks are due also to the late Rev. Edgar R. Smothers, S.J., who first encouraged me to undertake this task many years ago.

PALLADIUS:
DIALOGUE ON THE LIFE OF
ST. JOHN CHRYSOSTOM

AN HISTORICAL DIALOGUE OF PALLADIUS, BISHOP OF HELENOPOLIS,[1] WITH THEODORE, DEACON OF ROME, ON THE LIFE OF THE BLESSED JOHN CHRYSOSTOM, BISHOP OF CONSTANTINOPLE

Chapter 1

Bishop: My dear brother Theodore, it seems to me that God's gifts fall into three types. Some are common to all and not especially restricted. Others are common to all but restricted to a few. The third type are those which are neither common to all nor restricted, but are given to those to whom they are given by a special dispensation.[2]

Deacon: Your beginning leaves me puzzled; come now, please tell me the order of these kinds of gifts.

Bishop: The finest gifts without which life would be unbearable are common to all and they are not restricted.

Deacon: What is that, father?

Bishop: First there is the God over all, along with His only begotten Son and the Holy Spirit, common to all and unrestricted. Anyone who so wishes may possess Him in His wholeness by contemplation without recourse to material things.[3] After God there are the Holy Scriptures and the supernatural powers; in addition to these there are the heavens, the sun, the moon, the whole galaxy of stars, and the air itself, common to all without exception. Let that suffice speaking of unrestricted gifts. There was a time when land itself was common and unrestricted along with the streams of water. But from the time when[4] the insane lust for possession[5] came into the minds of the pleasure-loving mob, the heavier elements of earth and water became restricted.[6]

Deacon: Well said! Would you please complete your account of the second class, of the gifts which are restricted?

Bishop: It ill behooves us to leave the structure of our discourse unfinished. Take gold and silver and every kind of metallic substance, in addition to timber and such like taken all together—these are common to all, but nevertheless they are restricted. They do not belong to everyone who would like to have them.

Deacon: Your explanation of this is clear enough, but I doubt whether you will not be hard put in your demonstration of the third kind of special gift. You hold that there are some gifts that are neither common nor restricted, but are especially given to those worthy of the gift. End your speech, and tell us where you come from and explain[7] to us the truth we want to learn.

Bishop: Provided it is in my power and I have the necessary knowledge of these things which you ask, I will not hesitate nor would I hide them from you. I feel some obligation to pay off a debt[8] I owe you to the best of my ability, seeing that I have undertaken to do so.

Take virginity and the married state; you will not find them restricted. They are not of the class of the common or of the restricted. Now not everyone who desires to remains in the state of virginity, but he who is able. Many who are already married strive for virginity, but cannot practice it since they are already in the married state.

So it is in the Olympic games; the herald calls those who wish to compete, but the crown is only for the winner.[9] So it is in regard to chastity, as the Gospel tells us. Peter raises an objection to the Savior: " . . . if such is the situation of a man with his wife, he ought not to marry." The Savior answered him: "But it is not given to all to observe this precept, but to those to whom it has been given."[10] So you see that it is not intended for all, but for "those to whom it has been given."

Deacon: I thought you would be hard put to explain about those special gifts, but it appears that you have convinced us by your knowledge of Sacred Scripture and your powerful arguments.

Illustrations from the Old Testament

Bishop: If these things are clear to you, I shall enrich my argument with the rest of the proofs so that evil people are persuaded by them and cease to take what they cannot grasp. For we find in the Holy Scripture that the priesthood is not common nor appointed to all, but rather chosen by the worthy as the great-minded Paul says when admonishing the Hebrews: "For no one takes this honor upon himself, but he who is called by God, as was Aaron. He did not deem himself worthy to be a high-priest."[11] For there were six hundred thousand,[12] many of them very zealous, and one of them, Aaron, was publicly proclaimed to be the priest. The miracle of his rod sprouting forth nuts convinced many of them that he was chosen by God.[13] Some of them were unaware of the good and were wounded by the passion of vainglory;[14] they thought that this was one of the common or apportioned gifts, and they eagerly leaped upon the office, being self-ordained as it were. They received the reward deserving of their folly, making the ground itself where they stood bear witness to their recklessness. Dathan and Abiron longing for the dignity with covetous eye were overwhelmed and lost along with their followers; they found the assembly to be their rather unexpected grave.[15] And after these events Uzzah, unmindful of what had gone before and being swept away by passion, took the office of priest upon himself. One day as the Ark of the Covenant was being carried along the road on a wagon, the leader stumbled and that jolted the Ark. Uzzah was nearby and he grasped it with his hand, so the coffer might not be overturned. God took notice of this and was not pleased, lest it be a precedent for the proud, and He struck him dead. This taught a lesson to those who followed to refrain from such folly.[16]

Illustrations from the New Testament

Then a long time after Christ's coming Simon, the magician from the town of Gethae,[17] a man most learned in the things which are opposed to the truth, actually a man of dissolute life, hit on a subtle plan.[18] He feared the punishment dealt out to those of old, so that he sowed as they sowed but did not wish to reap as they reaped. He came then to the apostles with flattery, hiding the wolf[19] under the sheepskin, bringing them money and pretending not to be too anxious to grasp at what cannot be bought. He spoke just such words that such people mimic: "Take this money and give me the power of your office, so that the one on whom I lay my hands will receive the Holy Spirit."

Now he had been baptized in the name of Jesus, and the apostolic band gave him this answer: "Off with you, man, the grace of God is not purchased with money." But as he continued knocking at the door, beseeching them, they answered him a second time: "Why buy that which you may freely find by living worthily?"

Then as he considered the troubles of that way of life and the sluggishness of his own disposition as well as the uncertainty of the whole matter, he cleaned out his purse of all his money, having in mind to deceive the disciples of the Savior by a trick.[20] *But he who will catch the wise in their craftiness*[21] was angry at them and spoke through Peter: *Keep your money to yourself to perish with you, because you have thought that the gift of God may be purchased with money.*[22] He offered him the medicine of repentance, anointing him in his long-suffering and saying: *Do penance that perhaps this thought of your heart may be forgiven. For I see that you are in the gall of bitterness and in the bond of iniquity,*[23] for He wishes not the destruction of sinners in His love for souls.[24]

Now that I have explained all these things to the best of my ability, Theodore of the noble name, deacon of the mysteries of truth, ask us what you came to find out.[25]

The characters of the dialogue are introduced

Deacon: From where have you come to give us the benefit of your company?

Bishop: It must be clear enough to you that we are from the East. I am now seeing Rome for the first time.[26]

Deacon: What especially brought you here?

Bishop: It is our desire for your own peace.

Deacon: Is that any different from your peace?

Bishop: It is really nothing but the one and the same thing which our Savior gave from heaven when he said: *My peace I give you.*[27] And for the purpose of confirming this gift of peace, He seconded it: *My peace I leave to you.* Now the word "give" means it is from Himself, but the word "leave" refers to the Holy Spirit, so that they may reveal to the Gentiles in the Spirit through Christ the knowledge of the Father.

The unfortunate East has suffered just as in the case of one who has paralyzed limbs realizes that vital forces make their way to the healthier parts of the body. With her limbs entirely paralyzed the Church is unable to function properly since harmony has abandoned her.[28] Most of us who are her champions and adherents make ourselves exiles from our own country since we cannot live quietly and safely in our own land, as we love the truth.

We hope to pass the few remaining days of our life with you according to the teachings of the Gospel.[29]

Deacon: Reverend father, it would seem to me that you have been sent to us by divine Providence, for I find that your own troubles are in harmony with ours. I presume that you are of the company of John,[30] the bishop of Constantinople.

Bishop: It is as you say.

Deacon: You are requested, then, with God as a witness, to reveal to us a really true account of what happened there, for we are anxious to learn this in detail. You know full well that if you should speak an untruth, God shall be your judge and examiner, and you will be cross-examined by us, too, if we learn otherwise. For it is not one or two, or three, or ten, or even more, who have given us an account of the happenings in Constantinople. Some of these were bishops and priests and persons of a monastic order. And if you desire to learn in brief what the Church of Rome has done in this matter, I will inform you.

How the news reached Rome

The first to come to us was a reader[31] from Alexandria with letters from Pope Theophilus[32] which announced that he had deposed John of Constantinople.[33] When the blessed Pope Innocent[34] read this he was somewhat troubled. He condemned the rashness and the conceit of Theophilus, since he had written it on his own single authority and had not made it clear why he had deposed John, nor whom he had taken in counsel. He remained in a quandary in this circumstance, not wishing to answer because of the subtlety of the situation.

At that time a certain Eusebius,[35] a deacon of the church of Constantinople, happened to be in Rome on ecclesiastical business and he gave Pope Innocent petitionary documents[36] adjuring him to bide his time, to see the whole plot revealed.

Three days later four bishops arrived who belonged to John's company, highly revered men: Pansophius[37] of Pisidia, Pappus[38] of Syria, Demetrius[39] of the Second Galatia, and Eugenius[40] of Phrygia. They brought three letters; one from Bishop John, one from forty bishops in communion with John, and last of all a letter from John's own clergy. All three letters agreed in describing the disturbance made by ignorant people. The substance of the letter of John was as follows:

Chapter 2

Letter of St. John Chrysostom to Pope Innocent

"To my most esteemed and holy Bishop Innocent, John sends greetings in the Lord:[41]

"I think Your Reverence[42] has already heard even before our letters arrive of the lawlessness we have endured here. For the magnitude of these terrible deeds has left not a single part of the world ignorant of this tragedy. Rumor has carried these doings to the outermost bounds of the earth and has worked grief and lamentation everywhere. Now since it behooves us not only to lament this situation, but we should also correct it and look about to consider how this furious tempest within the Church can be remedied. We think it necessary to persuade our most honored and devout lords, I mean the Bishops Demetrius, Pansophius, Pappus, and Eugenius, to leave their local churches for the time being and brave the ocean deep for a long trip from home. We come then to Your Love to clarify everything as quickly as possible and thus arrive at a definite conclusion. We also send along with them the highly honored and beloved deacons[43] Paul[44] and Cyriacus.[45] They shall in a sense take the place of a letter, and they will inform Your Love shortly what has happened.

Theophilus reveals his hostility

"Now Theophilus into whose hands the government of the church of Alexandria has been entrusted was commanded to appear alone to our most pious emperor, because of charges which had been trumped up against him. Now he came accompanied by a crowd of Egyptians as wishing to show from the outset that he arrived for battle and conflict. When he had reached the great and God-beloved city of Constantinople he did not go to the church in keeping with the usual long-established custom, nor did he have anything to do with us in prayer, discourse, or communion. Upon leaving the ship he hurried past the very porch of the church, and leaving the city behind, he made camp outside.

"Now we kept inviting him and his followers to stay with us since we had all in preparation, including rooms and all facilities, but they refused our offer one and all. We were in a great quandary upon perceiving this, since we saw no cause for such enmity. Still we kept inviting them, doing the proper thing for them, trying to find out why he should start such a conflict and bring insult to a city such as ours. But since he was not willing to state his reasons and his accusers were pressing him, the most worthy emperor[46] commanded us to go over to his encampment and hear him regarding his case; for he was accused of violence and murder and other crimes too numerous to mention.

Chrysostom states his position

"But we had too much reverence and honor for the precepts laid down by the fathers[47] and even for the man himself, and we had his letter saying that 'one ought not to go beyond one's boundaries, but the affairs of each province should be dealt with in that province.'[48] We refused to judge the case, but no one even protested. But Theophilus, as though contending against former enemies, called my archdeacon in the manner of one having great authority, as though the church were widowed and did not have a bishop,[49] and so through him he won the whole clergy over to his own side. Then the churches were unsettled, the clergy were led astray[50] and were persuaded to present memoranda against us, and so they were trained to become our accusers.[51] This he accomplished and sent for us and called us to judgment, although he had not cleared himself of the charges brought against him—something which was against the canons and all the laws. But we knew full well that we were not about to come before a judge—one would willingly have appealed to a judge ten thousand times—but before an enemy and a dangerous one at that. Early and late his very actions showed this.

"We sent him bishops—Demetrius of Pisinum, Eulysius[52] of Apameia, and Luppicinus[53] of Appiaria, as well as the priests Germanus[54] and Severus.[55] We answered with the forbearance befitting us that it was not the trial we objected to, but to a trial by an open foe and enemy. He had not yet received the charges against us, yet from the very beginning he had cut himself off from the Church and Communion and prayer, and he was even bribing our accusers.[56] He transferred the clergy and emptied the churches; how could he rightly mount the judge's bench which in no way belonged to him? Nor was it even fitting for one from Egypt to act as judge in Thrace,[57] considering that he was answerable for charges and was an enemy and hostile besides. Still he was not put to shame by these circumstances but kept urging himself on to complete what he desired.

"When we made it clear that we were prepared to clear ourselves of the charges in the presence of a hundred or even a thousand bishops and to prove that we were guiltless, as we in fact are, he did not allow it. But when we were gone and even making an appeal to the synod and seeking a trial—we wished to avoid enmity, but not a fair hearing—he even admitted our accusers. He freed those whom I had put away and disregarding the charges against them he took their memoranda and drew up minutes. Now all of these things were against the laws and the canons and all regular procedure. Why should I speak any longer? He did not refrain from every sort of action until he had driven us from both city and church with force and all tyranny.

Chrysostom is expelled from Constantinople

"One evening when it was already late and I was being swept along with the whole populace, I was arrested by the chief spy[58] of the city. This was in the very center of the city. I was dragged off by force and put aboard a ship which set sail that night at the very time when I was calling a synod for a just trial. Who could hear of such things and remain dry-eyed though he possessed a heart of stone?

But just as I said before, this calls not only for lamentation but for setting things right again.

"I make an appeal to Your Love that you may support me and do all that you can do to stop these evils. For nothing has as yet put an end to their lawlessness; even more was added to the first.[59] After our most pious emperor expelled those who had so shamelessly and unrighteously attacked the Church, many of the bishops seeing the lawlessness of those against me, returned to their own homes so as to avoid their attacks as one would avoid an all-consuming fire. Then we were recalled to the city and to the church from which we had been unjustly exiled. Thirty bishops accompanied us and our most reverend emperor sent along a notary[60] for this occasion. Then Theophilus made off suddenly, and we know not why or for what reason.

The emperor himself convokes a synod

"When we entered the city we begged the most reverend emperor to call a synod to avenge what had happened. Theophilus knew his own guilt full well and fearing conviction once the imperial letters had been dispatched bringing in bishops from all quarters, he threw himself into a small boat and got away secretly in the middle of the night taking his adherents along with him.

"But we did not allow the matter to rest here, for we were fully confident in our own conscience. Once more we implored the most pious emperor and he fully agreed with us as was his custom. He sent off a messenger again to go speedily to Egypt commanding Theophilus and his whole party to return and give an account of what had happened. He was not to suppose that what he had unjustly faked, with only one side having been heard, in our absence, and in opposition to all the canons, could in any way serve to defend him.

Chrysostom exiled once again

"Now he paid no heed to the imperial letters, but he remained at home, putting forth the excuse of an impending uprising of the people and an untimely outburst of zeal on the part of some who supported him. Even before the emperor's letter came, these were the very ones who had vilified him.[61] However, we will not press this now, since we mention it only to show that his actions proved him guilty. After this we took no leisure but kept insisting that there be a trial with proper procedure of interrogation and response. We stood ready to assert our innocence and their disregard for law.

"Now there were some Syrians who had been with him and were left behind; they had played out this whole drama with him. We were prepared to go with them before a judge, and we kept insisting that either the minutes of the proceedings with the memoranda of our accusers should be given to us or that the nature of the charges or even the accusers themselves should be pointed out to us. We were not granted any of these requests, but were once more driven out from the church.

Acts of sacrilege at Constantinople

"How can I explain the following events which are greater than any tragedy? What description would express them fully? Who could hear them without shuddering? For while we were pressing those above-mentioned requests, a strong band of soldiers entered the churches on the Great Sabboth[62] as the end of day was approaching. They forcibly expelled the clergy who were with us and surrounded the sanctuary[63] with arms. Women members of the congregation were unrobed for baptism at that time, and they fled naked out of fear of this savage attack, not even being allowed to clothe themselves as womanly decency requires. Many of them received wounds before they were thrown out, and the baptismal fonts[64] were filled with blood and the holy water was dyed red from their wounds. Nor did the horrors cease here. Soldiers entered in where the sacred vessels were kept—I understand that some of them were not even baptized[65]—and they saw everything there and the most sacred Blood of Christ was poured out on the garments the women had left in their great consternation.

"Everything happened as in a barbarian captivity. People were driven out into the barren places and every layman fled from the city, and the churches were empty even during so great a festival. More than forty bishops who shared our own Communion were driven out along with the laity. There were cries everywhere, groans and lamentations, and fountains of tears in market places, in homes, and even in desolate places; the whole city was filled with these calamities. So great was their lawlessness that not only those who were directly concerned, but even those who did not suffer were sympathetic to us—this included fellow believers, heretics, Jews, and pagans alike. It was as though the city had been captured by force, such was the disturbance, confusion, lamentation. And all this was done against the desires of the most revered emperor, when it was nighttime, with bishops who were acting the part of soldiers who were not ashamed to have officers marching ahead of them instead of deacons.

The whole Church suffers injury

"When daylight came the whole city moved outside the walls and observed the feast under trees and bushes scattered about like sheep. It is up to you even to imagine the rest. Just as I said before, I cannot tell you everything in detailed argument. And this indeed is difficult, these great and manifold evils have not yet been resolved, nor is there any hope of their solution. It keeps getting worse every day and we have become a laughing stock to many. I should rather say that no one laughs. Even if one were ten thousand times more opposed to law and order, no one would laugh. All weep at the new type of lawlessness which is the very finishing point[66] of all evils.

"Who would tell of the confusion of the other churches? For it is not only here where there is trouble, but it has spread over into the East. Just as when something evil flows from the head, all the limbs will be corrupted; likewise seeing that troubles have had their beginning in this great city, confusion has made great inroads everywhere, just as water from a spring. The clergy are everywhere against the bishops. Speaking now of the laity, some groups are divided, others are bound to follow suit. We see the pangs of evil everywhere and the overthrow of the whole world.

Chrysostom asks for help

"Most honored and revered lords, you now know everything. Please show the courage and zeal which become you. We call upon you to put an end to this great outrage which has come upon the churches. If this custom should prevail, that anyone who wishes to go into other provinces no matter how far distant and drive out whomsoever they will on their own initiative, rest assured that everything will be ruined and a sudden war[67] will spread over the whole world, and there will be overthrowing on all sides. Now to keep so great a catastrophe from overtaking everyone under the sun, I beg you to state everything regarding these unlawful procedures taken against us in our absence, without any trial.

"These objections are all unfounded and have no binding force—and they cannot because of their very nature. We ask that those who have so acted against the law be subjected to the penalties provided by ecclesiastical legislation. Grant that we who have not been apprehended, or proven guilty, or convicted, may take advantage of your usual good services[68] and your love and aid in every way as heretofore.

He requests a trial

"But if these sinful lawbreakers even now wish to declare the charges by which they expelled us unjustly, then let the documents be given to us and let the memoranda of the accusers be brought forth. Once court convened without any prejudices against us, we could be tried and make our own defense, and we could show ourselves without guilt (as we surely are)[69] on all the charges preferred against us. For what they have been doing is entirely beyond all order and against every law and ecclesiastical canon.[70] [But why should I speak of ecclesiastical canons?][71] Something like this has never before been dared, whether in secular courts or even in those of the barbarians. Scythians and Sarmatians would never have judged a case having heard only one side, without hearing the accused. The accused did not object to a trial but this was due to personal hatred.

The accused asked for any number of judges, saying that he was blameless in this matter and was prepared to clear himself of fault in front of the whole world, and to show himself without any guilt whatsoever.

"Now I beg of you to review this whole question and thoroughly interrogate our most revered brother bishops, and then, having learned the truth, please proceed in the best possible way. In so doing you will please not only us, but the common good of all the churches, and you will have your reward from God who works continually[72] for peace in the Church. This has been written to Venerius,[73] bishop of Milan, and to Chromatius, bishop of Aquileia.[74] Farewell in the Lord."

Chapter 3

A synod convoked by Pope Innocent

The blessed Pope Innocent then sent an answer to this letter, informing each party that he was in communion[75] with both of them, and he nullified the judgment Theophilus supposedly made. He said another synod of bishops from the West and the East should be called and should be conducted without reproach. In order to obtain an unprejudiced verdict, first the friends and then the enemies of the accused must be barred from the proceedings.[76]

A few days later Peter,[77] a priest of Theophilus, accompanied by a deacon, Martirius[78] of the church of Constantinople, arrived with letters from Theophilus and minutes of the meeting. It seemed that John had been condemned by thirty-six bishops, twenty-nine of whom were from Egypt and seven from other regions. Pope Innocent read this document and, ascertaining that the charges were slight and that John was not himself present at the investigation, he continued in his denunciation of the madness of Theophilus in spewing forth a rash judgment against a man who was not even present. He sent him away with letters which reproved him, and he prayed to God[79] with prayers and fasting that the break in the Church would

be healed and that closer ties of brotherly love would be strength-
ened.

The gist of the letters was as follows:

Innocent's letter to Theophilus[80]

"Brother Theophilus: We know that both you and your brother
John share the same communion with us. This we made clear in our
previous letter. And now we write you again that we are not depart-
ing from our intentions, no matter how often you send letters telling
us that unless a proper judgment confirms what was done so flip-
pantly,[81] we cannot without reason cut off our communion with
John. If, however, you insist on your verdict, meet with a synod as
Christ commanded[82] and there openly state your accusation under
appeal to the canons of Nicaea[83]—for the Church of Christ admits no
other canon—and you will have an absolute guarantee of safety."

Bad news from Constantinople

A little time slipped by[84] and then a priest from Constantinople
named Theotecnus[85] arrived bearing letters from John's synod.
Twenty-five bishops or rather more advised us that John had been
expelled from the city by military force and sent into exile in Cacu-
sus, and that the church[86] had been burned. Pope Innocent gave him
letters of communion addressed to John and to those in communion
with him, and he begged them with much weeping to be long-suffering with him, for he was unable to be of any help to him because of
certain persons who could work harm for him.

A strange apparition

Then after a short while arrived an excuse for a man, ugly in
shape and hard to understand. His name was Paternus[87] and he
claimed to be a priest of the church of Constantinople. He was highly
agitated and certainly showed hostility by his conduct. He poured
out various abuses on Bishop John, and then he presented letters

from a few bishops—Acacius,[88] Paul,[89] Antiochus,[90] Cyrinus,[91] and Severianus,[92] and a few others—in which they freshly accused John of having set the church on fire. The whole story seemed so false to us that John made no defense for himself in a distinguished synod.[93] Pope Innocent treated it without concern and did not deem it worthy of a reply.

Chrysostom's party denounced

Bishop: Please be so kind as to lend me your ear, so that I may explain to you each single fact, for surely, as Elihu says to Job: . . . *the spirit of my belly constrains me.*[94] Here "belly" means metaphorically "his mind filled with words."

Deacon: Most reverend father, I must insist on this in order to make my account complete and accurate regarding everything that had happened so that I might begin to interrogate you. So after a few days there arrived Cyriacus,[95] the bishop of the Synnadi. He had no letter, but was qualified enough to give a harmonious narrative. He told us he had fled from Constantinople because of a threat contained in an imperial edict[96] which had as its burden that "if any one is not in communion with Theophilus and Arsacius[97] and Porphyrius,[98] he is to be excluded from his episcopal office; moreover, should he have money or property, it should be taken away from him."

More news to follow

After Cyriacus there arrived Eulysius, bishop of Apameia in Bithynia, bearing letters from fifteen bishops of John's synod, and the venerable[99] Anysius,[100] bishop of Thessalonica. They described the pillaging that had taken place and was still going on in Constantinople. Anysius said that he would abide by the ruling of the Romans, and Eulysius' own account agreed with that of Cyriacus.

A month went by and along came Palladius,[101] bishop of Helenopolis. He did not have a letter. He said that he also had fled to escape the fury of the rulers. He even made a point stronger in his account by producing a copy of the edict[102] which contained the order that "the house of anyone concealing or receiving into it for any purpose whatsoever a bishop or cleric belonging to the communion of John is to be confiscated."

After Palladius came Germanus the priest and Cassian[103] the deacon, both of the company of John, pious men who brought letters from all of John's clergy. They wrote that their church had suffered under violence and tyranny; their bishop had been forced out with military assistance and exiled through the intrigue of Acacius of Berea, Theophilus of Alexandria, Antiochus of Ptolemais, and Severianus of Gabala. Germanus and Cassian also showed a receipt to show that they had deposited with the magistrates under witness to Stadius,[104] the prefect of the city, Eutychianus[105] of the pretorian guard, and John,[106] the keeper of the treasury, as well as Eustathius,[107] chief of police and keeper of the records, the valuables in gold, silver, and clothing in order to clear Bishop John of the charges brought against him.[108]

After these there arrived Demetrius,[109] bishop of Pisinum, coming on a second journey a long way from the East. He announced that the Church of Rome was in communion with John according to letters of Pope Innocent and he brought letters from the bishops of Caria in which they rejoiced in their communion with John. He also brought letters from the presbyters of Antioch, who were attracted by the discipline and good order of the Romans, and they bitterly lamented the ordination of Porphyrius which had been so illegally and impiously performed.

After these came Domitian,[110] the priest who was steward[111] for the church of Constantinople, and also Vallagas,[112] the priest from Nisibis who told of the grief of the monasteries of Mesopotamia at seeing memoranda from a certain Optatus,[113] the prefect where it was stated that fine women from the upper classes, deaconesses of the church of Constantinople, were publicly paraded before him and forced either to be in communion with Arsacius or to pay up to two hundred pounds of gold to the treasury. What should one say then of the ascetics and virgins? Some of them pointed out evidence of the scraping of ribs upon a rack[114] and torture of their backs.[115]

Pope Innocent writes to Emperor Honorius

Since Pope Innocent could hold out no longer he sent a letter[116] to the pious Emperor Honorius,[117] in which he gave detailed information of what he had heard. His reverence was deeply moved by these things, and he ordered a synod[118] of the Western bishops to be convened and a unanimous decision to be reached and communicated to him. The Italian bishops met therefore and they requested the emperor to write his brother and fellow-emperor, Arcadius that he should command a synod to be held in Thessalonika. In this way it would be possible for both sides, Eastern and Western, to come together without difficulty and make it possible for a full synod, one not only in number but in understanding so that a binding resolution could be issued. His reverence was so inspired by this letter that he wrote in response to the Bishop of Rome that he sent five bishops accompanied by two priests and a deacon of Rome to carry his letter to his brother. The substance of this letter was as follows:

Honorius' letter to Arcadius

"I write now for the third time to Your Clemency, begging that you correct the affairs that led to the plot against Bishop John of Constantinople and, as it appears, nothing has been accomplished. Therefore I write you again on behalf of the bishops and priests, so eagerly do I desire peace for the Church, for it is only that peace by which our kingdom[119] also enjoys peace. I ask you then to consider making arrangements for the bishops of the East to come together in Thessalonika. Our bishops of the West have chosen messengers very carefully—men who are beyond evil or falsehood—five bishops, two priests, and a deacon of the greatest church, that is, Rome. Please treat them as worthy of all honors, so that either they may be convinced that Bishop John was rightly exiled, and you will tell me to separate from communion with him, or if they prove that the bishops of the East did evil deliberately, they will persuade you to break off communion with them. Now of all the letters I have received I am sending you two to show you what the bishops of the West think regarding Bishop John. These are letters from the bishops of Rome and

Aquileia; actually they carry the same conviction as the others. This above all else I beg of Your Clemency: that you demand the presence of Theophilus of Alexandria no matter how unwilling he may be to come. He is acknowledged as the ringleader of all the troubles. In this way the bishops assembled in synod will not meet with hindrance and will decide on a peaceful solution which our times desire."[120]

Chapter 4
The Bishop Takes Up the Dialogue

The deputation from Rome

So then the holy bishops, Aemilius of Beneventum, Cythegus, and Gaudentius, along with the priests Valentianus and Bonifacius[121] and the others, took the letters of Pope Innocent and the Italian bishops, Chromatius of Aquileia and Venerius[122] of Milan and the others. They also took a memorandum from the synod of all the West and went on to Constantinople at public expense. Along with them also went the bishops Cyriacus, Demetrius, Palladius, and Eulysius.[123] The memorandum made it clear that John ought not to come in for judgment unless his church and communion were rightly restored to him. In this way he would be taking his place in the synod freely and with no excuse for not attending.

Shameful treatment of the delegates

They came then to Constantinople, but they returned after four months with a description of Babylonian oppression.[124] They said: "We were carried along sailing the Greek coast and reached Athens, where we were held up by some miserable officer who immediately put us under guard of a centurion who did not allow us to go on to Thessalonika, for it was their purpose[125] to give over first of all the letters to Bishop Anysius there. Well, he put us aboard two ships and

sent us off. Then a violent storm from the south came up and we
were without food for three days, sailing the Aegean Sea and the
Narrows. On the twelfth hour of the third day we put to shore before the city near the environs of Fictor.[126] Here we were arrested by
the men in charge of the harbor and—we did not know by whose orders—were taken to the back parts of the city. Then we were locked
up in an isolated fort in Thrace named Athyra close by the sea, and
there we were tortured. The envoys from Rome were kept in a small
room, and Cyriacus and those in his company were kept in a different place, having not even a boy to wait upon us. Our letters were demanded from us, but we did not give them up, saying: How can we
delegates hand over the letters of the emperor and the bishops to be
given to anyone but the emperor himself? As we kept refusing there
came first of all a notary Patricius, then certain others, and last of all
a captain Valerianus,[127] a Cappadocian who broke the thumb of
Bishop Marianus[128] and made off with the sealed letter of the emperor along with the other letters.

"Then on the next day either the people of the royal court or else
Atticus[129]—we know not who it was but suspect the latter as he had
seized the throne of the church—sent us messengers who offered us
three thousand coins.[130] They thought we would accept them, communicate with Atticus, and give up urging the case of John. We
turned down the offer and remained in prayer, praying that, as we
perceived their savage fury, if we could not obtain peace we could at
least return unharmed to our own churches. That this was true God
the Savior clarified for them in various revelations, for there was seen
by Paul,[131] the deacon of the sainted Emmelius, a very holy and
gentle man, the Apostle Paul telling him while on the ship: 'Look
how you walk, not as fools but wise men, knowing that the days are
evil.'[132] The dream was given them to understand their manifold
treacherous attempts to persuade us to circumvent the truth by
bribes and flattery.

The delegates' return

"Valerianus the captain came back," they said, "and cast us into
a very untrustworthy vessel with a motley crew of twenty sol-

diers of various ranks. It was rumored that he had bribed the skipper to get rid of the bishops, and we were off in a hurry from Athyra. Thus we sailed along for quite a distance, narrowly escaping death when we landed at Lampsacus.[133] We changed there to a merchant vessel, and we were dragged into Hydrun[134] in Calabria on the twentieth day. They had found nothing to tell us of the whereabouts of the blessed Bishop John or of those bishops who had come along with us on our mission: Demetrius, Cyriacus, Eulogius, and Palladius."

The ringleaders of the opposition

Bishop: Now come, most reverend, give me your attention and listen to what I have to say. I shall tell you precisely of the whole tragedy, those most satyr-like public disturbances. I shall tell you from the very beginning even up to the point where they seemed to have stopped. But they have not stopped yet. Now the source or beginning of all the evils is, as one should say, the hater of good, the demon who is always opposed to the rational flocks of Christ, as a wolf tempting the experienced and tried shepherds with manifold torments. Just so the king of Egypt treated the male offspring of the Jews[135] and adorned those false shepherds with the allurements of earthly pleasures. Now the whole world knows that the sewer of the foul drainage are Acacius, Antiochus, Theophilus, and Severianus. They are given a name for what they are not, and they could not bear to be called by what they really are. Two of them are of the clerical order, priests, five of them are deacons, some of them of the unclean, some of them from evildoers. I do not know but that I run a risk in calling them either priests or deacons. Two of them, maybe a third, belong to the imperial household, and they are the ones who gave power to those in Theophilus' company by lending their military support.

Now as regards the women, you may add three more to those who are already well known, widows left rich by the death of husbands who made money by bribes and extortion to the loss of their own salvation. They are in fact husband-baiters and disturbers of the peace.[136] I mention here Marsa, wife of Promotus, Castricia, wife of

Saturninus, and Eugraphia,[137] an absolute maniac. Out of very shame I will mention no more.

These are the women and the men, indifferent in heart as regards the faith, gathered together as it were into a sort of drunken regiment, at one mind united in a hatred of Christian doctrine. They organized a deluge of destruction against the peace of the Church.

Theodore wishes to get to the truth of the matter

Deacon: Please be prepared, father, to tell us, having God as a witness, why did they hate John and what reasons did he have for so persistently vexing people in high place? Please tell us how he began his career and how he was brought to the episcopal see of Constantinople, and for how long he enjoyed that office; what was his lifestyle, and something, too, of the end of his life, if it is true, as we have heard, that he has already fallen asleep.[138] It is true that he was everywhere highly respected and his memory held in honor; but it is not my custom to believe too readily everything that rumor brings to me until its truth is established by those who have sufficient knowledge to give either blame or praise.

Truth is mighty and must prevail

Bishop: I praise your accuracy, most truth-loving man of God, Theodore, but I do not admit your distinction. For surely our own grey hairs, if I may refer to myself now, should have been guarantee that I spoke the truth; that as well as my high office. Since, however, you did not accept this you may judge me a second time, calling upon God, and promise that you will hear me without prejudice; only let not my double-piping of words fall on deaf ears. For I am fully aware of what is written in the divine law: *The Lord shall destroy all of them that speak lies,*[139] and in the Apostle John: *He who tells a lie is not of God,*[140] and once more from David: . . . *for the mouth of them that speak lies is stopped.*[141]

True it is that he who speaks a lie commits an injustice to the one whom he persuades; it is likewise true that he who believes a lie acts unjustly because he believes too readily.[142] Since both are equally guilty it ill behooves any of us to do wrong to his neighbor. For it is the virtue of the speaker to speak the truth, and of the listener to test unjust statements. For as Sacred Scripture has it: *Be you reliable money changers,*[143] casting out the spurious from the genuine coins. We are not to receive everything because it rings true,[144] but to weigh it by the testimony of the facts, whether it be spoken or written, with a good conscience and in the fear of God.

For this reason, then, God the Architect of what is beautiful has created the tongue guarded by two lips, for great is the danger from ears and tongue. He has fixed firmly the rampart of the teeth[145] within so that it would be a safe defense to moderate its activity, as has been written: *Place, O Lord, a watch before my mouth, a door of confinement about my lips . . . that I offend not with my tongue.*[146] For the ears he bored an opening spiralwise, hinting by this shape that words do not enter too quickly, so that going in more slowly the matter of falsehood along with the filth of evil might be more easily rejected and so left behind. And these were not the only bodily organs he carefully designed, not being the only ones that impede evil. He placed curtains ahead of the pupils of the eye as though they were doors so they would not accept deadly concupiscence. For the prophet gave witness to this when he said: *Death came up through the windows.*[147]

Grey hairs no guarantee of wisdom

Deacon: If our inquiry concerned ordinary events, most holy father, the mere fact of your appearance would have helped to guarantee your arguments. But since it brings no small blame now and thereafter when all the rulers and people are brought together for condemnation at the awful judgment seat and the truth is being sought, then pardon me, honored sir, if I do not accept your white hairs as ample testimony. Even the bad grow old and have hardly whitened their souls with virtue, but they have only their bodies wrinkled up by the passage of time. Such were the false elders at Babylon,[148] and take Ephraim in Jeremiah,[149] of whom the Word cries out in reproof: *Ephraim is a silly dove, having no heart; grey hairs have blossomed forth upon him, but he himself knows it not.*[150] Repeating it he speaks more oppressively: *Ephraim is a cake not turned, and strangers have devoured his strength.*[151]

And this I must now add, even though I seem long-winded. Who is whiter and more moderate than Acacius of Berea,[152] whom you and your company now revile as the leader of disorder and the chief of all those revolutionaries in their errors? Why even his very nostrils sprouted a crop of long white hairs when he came to Rome formally to announce the ordination of John.[153]

Bishop: Now I know of a certainty that you are a good money changer. You are not led astray by the skins of a tent, but you insist on really knowing the man who inhabits it. For the temples of the Egyptians[154] are very great and boast of the beauty of their stones, but inside them are apes, ibexes, and dogs, which are their gods. Our Lord God in warning Samuel about the appointment of a ruler for Israel exhorted him not to have regard for the condition and molding of a body made of clay, saying: *God sees not as man sees; for man looks upon the countenance, but God looks upon the heart.*[155] Hence those who are *imitators of God*[156] should examine more deeply into every action. Then I shall give myself over to you readily after I have tested that your balance is not leaning off to one side. Those two Babylonians mentioned above[157] were old in body but were really infants, wholly insensate, and had they only believed in the resurrection of the dead[158] they would have had the wisdom not to fall in love with Susanna, the wife of another man. Furthermore, if they had a fear of God they would not have mingled false testimony with their lust. Dishonor in old age is a sure proof of the misuse of youth.[159]

CHAPTER 5

The early years of Chrysostom

This John—yes, he has fallen asleep—was by birth of Antioch, the son of honorable parents, his father holding the rank of military commander of Syria.[160] He had an older sister born of the same father. He was highly gifted with a precocious mind[161] and he was carefully schooled in letters[162] for the ministry of the oracles of God.[163] When he was eighteen, a mere boy in years, he revolted against the sophists of word-mongering,[164] for he had arrived at man's estate and thirsted for living knowledge.[165] At that time the blessed Meletius the confessor,[166] an Armenian by nationality, ruled the church at Antioch. He took notice of the bright lad and was impressed by the beauty of his character so he had him almost constantly near him. He observed him with prophetic eye as it were, and he could envisage the young man's brilliant future. He was admitted to the mystery of the washing of regeneration,[167] and after about three years attendance upon the bishop[168] he was appointed reader.[169]

Chrysostom betakes himself to the desert

Being well aware of the fact that he could not be satisfied working in the city as his youthful nature was bursting within him[170] though his mind was perfectly sound,[171] he betook himself to the nearby mountains.[172] There he met up with an old man, Syrus,[173] who exercised great self-discipline, and John strove earnestly to imitate his austere lifestyle.[174] He spent four years battling it out with the crags of voluptuousness.[175] When he suppressed these temptations more easily, not so much by hard toil but by pure reason,[176] he retired to a cave all alone, eager to dwell in obscurity. There he stayed for twenty-four months, most of that time not partaking of sleep while he thoroughly learned the covenants of Christ[177] to dispel ignorance. He never relaxed for that two-year period, not in the days nor at night, and his gastric organs became lifeless and the proper functions of the kidneys were impaired by the cold.[178] Since he could no longer take care of himself alone, he went back once more to the haven of the Church. And this is a proof of the Savior's providence that he was taken away from the ascetic life by his sickness brought on by such strict habits, forcing him to leave his caves[179] for the benefit of the Church.

Chrysostom receives Holy Orders

Then after serving at the altar for five years he was ordained deacon by Meletius.[180] He had already become famous for his teaching and the people were sweetened from the bitterness of life when they met up with him, and he was ordained priest by Bishop Flavianus.[181] Then he spent twelve years at Antioch and shed great glory on the priesthood there by the strictness of his lifestyle. Some he salted by his moderation, others he illumined by his teaching, still to others he gave drink from the fount of the spirit.[182] It was all fair sailing with Christ as pilot[183] when the blessed Nectarius[184] fell asleep.

At once there rushed up certain people who were by no means sought for, who were actually craving the high office.[185] These mere men, hardly men at all, priests only by their office, but unworthy of the priesthood,[186] some of them battering down the doors of officials, some of them offering bribes, others still who went down on their knees to the people.[187] In addition to these the people of the orthodox sector kept annoying the emperor, demanding a priest of experience.

Chrysostom becomes bishop of Constantinople

At that time the eunuch Eutropius,[188] chief of the royal chamberlains,[189] was in charge of affairs. It was his desire to put John in charge of the city as he had become acquainted with his excellent qualities when some of the emperor's affairs had taken him to the farther East.[190] He managed to get the emperor to write a letter to the governor of Antioch[191] that he should send John quietly out of that city so as not to disturb the people. As soon as he received the letter he called on him to be at the shrine of the martyrs[192] outside the city close by the Romanesian gate. He put him on a public carriage and entrusted him to the care of the eunuch along with the magistrate's guard. In this way he was brought to Constantinople and ordained bishop of the church of Constantinople.

Theophilus makes trouble

Now Theophilus, bishop of Alexandria, observed his character and his blameless outspoken language, and he was from the very first strongly opposed to the ordination.[193] For Theophilus is clever at judging faces; the will and mind of a man are not so easy to read.[194]

Deacon: Hold on, father, I have a small objection.

Bishop: Yes, what is it?

Deacon: And if this Theophilus is so sharp of eye, why could he not realize that if he expelled John he would stir up the whole world?

Bishop: There is nothing strange about that, my dear man. For even the demons, fully aware of the coming of the Savior, still did not realize that they would be rendered powerless by a single breath of those who believed in Him.

Deacon: Where did they acknowledge His coming?

Bishop: When they cried out: *We know You, who You are, the Holy One of God! Why did You come to torment us before the time?*[195] You see that they knew not only that He is holy, but also that He is Judge.
  What shall I say about demons? Those evil-bent despicable prostitutes recognize continent men from the look in their eyes, and they do not solicit them. In much the same way the diseased eye turns away from the bright rays of the sun[196] or the vulture avoids perfume. Why is it that "Godliness is an abomination to sinners,"[197] if we do not recognize godliness? So it came about that Theophilus did not find in John's face something similar to his own eyes, or what was in his mind, and he inferred from that a certain degree of hostility very shrewdly but he did not carefully ascertain it.

Deacon: What you have said is astounding, father. But why was he opposed to the ordination?

Bishop: This was his custom all along not to ordain good and shrewed men lest he make a mistake. He wished to have them all weak-willed men whom he could influence. He thought it better to control the weak-minded than to give attention to the wisdom of the prudent. But nevertheless, whether he was willing or not, he had to yield to saving providence.

Chrysostom begins by reforming the clergy

Now that he was ordained John began the proper care of his affairs. First of all he tried his flock by playing them the pipe of reason. Sometimes he used the staff of correction as well.[198] He reprimanded very strongly that way of life that went under the fictitious name of 'living together as brother and sister.'[199] He called it by its right name, evil life, when referring to the so-called *subintroductae.*[200] He pointed out that if a choice were to be made between the two evils, the brothel-keeper was a better man. For such live far from a surgeon's help and keep the disease for those who willingly desire it. But the clergy live in the very workshop of salvation and invite healthy people to contract the disease.[201] This distressed that portion of the clergy who were without love of God and on fire with lust.

Chrysostom reforms the laymen

After this he began to speak about injustice, condemning avarice, that metropolis of evil,[202] with the intent of building a firm foundation for righteousness. For it is a characteristic of good builders[203] to pull down first of all the structure of falsehood and to erect later the firm foundation of truth, as it was said by the prophet: *I have set you this day over nations, and over kingdoms, to root up and to pull down, and to waste and to destroy and to build*[204] (the one case refers to him as a farmer, the other, as a builder). Then he stirred up the party of purse watchers[205] and he called attention to their way of life. He begged them to be satisfied with their wages and not be forever chasing after the savory odors[206] of the wealthy. He admonished them not to regard smoke as the torch-bearer, whereby they gave themselves up to the fire of intemperance, following the life of the parasite and the flatterer. Next the gluttonous were uprooted and enmeshed with those clever ones who bear false testimony.

He reforms the church's finance

Next he examined closely the accounts of the steward, and he found expenditures that were of no benefit to the church. He ordered all unnecessary spending to be stopped at once. Then he also questioned certain expenses of the episcopal household. Here again he found an over abundance of funds and he ordered the larger portion of them to be shared with the hospital.[207] He built more hospitals and over these he delegated two devout priests in addition to doctors, cooks, and other workers from the unmarried state to look after them. In this way strangers coming from afar to the city and becoming ill could receive proper medical care [most often for what we call epilepsy].[208] This hospital was not only a good venture, but it served for the glory of God as well.

He reforms the order of women

Then he called together the order of widows[209] and he made a thorough investigation into those who were not making the proper readjustment. He discovered that some of them were too sensual, and he advised them to undertake to fast and to avoid the public baths.[210] He also counselled them about too great a nicety in the matter of dress. He strongly advised some to enter upon a second marriage so the law of the Lord would not be lightly cast aside.[211]

Chrysostom calls for public prayer

After this he called on the people to persevere in the nocturnal litanies,[212] since the men did not have the leisure during the day. The women were counselled to say the prayers at home by day. This was a cause for grief with the more careless clergy, who were accustomed to sleep the whole night through.

Next he applied the sword of correction against the rich, lancing the abcesses of their souls, and he admonished them to be humble and considerate of the rest of mankind, persuaded by the precept of the Apostle to Timothy: *Charge the rich of this world not to be high-minded, nor to trust in the uncertainty of riches.*[213]

The benefits of these reforms

Because of all these reforms the church was flourishing more excellently from day to day. The very color of the city was changed to piety; everyone looked bright and fresh with soberness and Psalm-singing. But the hater of good, the demon, could not bear the flight of those whom he had once enslaved, those whom the word of the Lord had snatched from him by the teaching of John. As a matter of fact those horse-crazed men and theatre fans[214] have abandoned the courts of the devil and hastened to the fold of the Savior out of love for the piping of the Shepherd who loves His sheep.[215]

Chapter 6
The Beginning of Trouble

The plot against Chrysostom

Because of this, envy took possession of the minds of the hireling shepherds[216] who had been convicted, at least by implication. Since they were not able to take advantage of him because they did not invoke the Savior who is the destroyer of envy, they trumped up various calumnies against John. They pretended that certain homilies were really making sport of the Empress and of others of the royal court.[217]

Now it so happened at this very time that Acacius, bishop of Berea, was visiting him and, as he said, John failed to give him good lodging. He was much put out at this and he became infuriated in his anger, as though he had been slighted. He was overpowered by unruly feelings and he spoke a silly joke *out of the abundance of his heart*, worthy of his mind.[218] For in the presence of John's clergy he said: "I am going to season a pot for him." He at once joined company with Severianus, Antiochus, and Isaacius Syriscus,[219] that street idler, the guide of the false monks who wandered about saying bad things about the bishop. They looked about to arm themselves against John, but actually it was against the glory of the Savior. First of all they sent off to Antioch to look for any offences of his younger days. But as *they that seek failed*[220] they found nothing, and they sent messengers to Alexandria to the reckless Theophilus who is known as weathercock,[221] one who was very clever at engineering such projects as those. He opened up the books of his mind at once with all his stealthy thievery and kept looking about and searching for any kind of chance pretext.

Canon Law violated

Deacon: Stop the torrent of your words, father, before I forget so I may tell you of the charge that reached us from Alexandria. It has been generally accepted as true. For they say that John received into communion some clerics who had been deposed by Theophilus. This improper action was a source of grief to Theophilus, who as a result fell out with John and brought action against him.

Bishop: Even if we admit that the report of what they say is true, does it behoove a bishop to cure evil with evil? What then of the gospel saying: *Let not the sun go down upon your anger.*[222] What of the Apostle's own injunction: *Overcome evil by good?*[223] What of the prophet: *If I have rendered to them that repaid me evil?*[224] Would he not have been less obstinate when dealing with pious bishops to have said: "Brother John, have you not done this or that without due consideration?" And then John, in excusing himself, could have said that he was unaware of having done wrong.

Deacon: Truly spoken, if he had acted out of good and was not merely covering up for those clergy to satisfy his own private animosity.

Bishop: Then by the fear of God who rules over fears without limit, I tell you I speak nothing else but, as the matter stands, regarding those clergy of whom you speak.

Of Isidore and the gift for the poor

Now there was a certain Isidore[225] who had been ordained by the blessed Athanasius the Great[226] who was still alive in his eightieth year of age. (Most of the people at Rome knew him since he came there often on ecclesiastical matters, being the guest-master[227] of the church of Alexandria. You know the man yourself as he came along with Acacius to announce the communion between Flavianus and Theophilus[228] after a twenty-year interruption. This was due largely to the efforts of the blessed Evagrius, who fought many a good fight[229] on behalf of the Church.)

Now a widow of one of the nobles of the city gave Isidore one thousand gold pieces,[230] and she bound him by oath on the table of the Savior[231] that he would purchase clothes for the poorer women of Alexandria and that he must not share this knowledge with Theophilus lest he take the money and squander it on stones. Now Theophilus like Pharaoh[232] has a mania for stones[233] for building, but the Church does not need them—let that for another time; listen to what I have to say about Isidore. Well, he took the money and spent it on the poor and widowed women, and somehow Theophilus found out. Nothing escapes him, whatever is done or said, as he has everywhere spies and listening-posts—not to call them anything else. He called Isidore in and asked as mercifully as you please if that was true. Isidore confessed and did not deny the account of the whole matter. When he heard this, Theophilus shed his patience, and he who was a moment before most kind and courteous became swollen in body in his anger. His whole appearance changed entirely when he heard this from Isidore.

Theophilus accuses Isidore

He kept quiet for a short while like a dog that bites you when you least expect it, but after two months he produced a document when the clergy were convened. Then when Isidore had entered he spoke up: "I received this charge against you, Isidore, over eighteen years ago. Since I was very busy at the time the matter escaped me. As I was searching for some other papers just now I came across this document concerning you. Please speak for yourself."

The document contained a charge of sodomy. Taking up his own defense Isidore then spoke to Theophilus: "We will agree that you really did receive the document and that you forgot all about it. Did not the man who brought it remain for another inquiry?"

Theophilus answered: "But the lad did not stay; he was a sailor."

Then Isidore spoke up: "He did not appear at the time, as you say, Holy Father? Did he come back after sailing in the following year, or the second year, or even the third year? And if he is here now, command the man to stand up."

Theophilus excommunicates Isidore

Since Theophilus saw that he was going to be despised when the truth of the matter came out, he delayed action in this case for another day. He begged one of the young men with many promises[234] and he encouraged him to accuse Isidore, and gave him, so some say, fifteen gold coins which he entrusted to his mother. But she refused to take them because of the steadfast eye[235] and she was further prevented by the fear of the laws, thinking that if Isidore was falsely accused he might have recourse to the magistrate of the people. She came and confessed the story to Isidore, and showed him the coins which she said she had received from Theophilus' sister as a *bribe against the innocent*.[236] The mother paid the penalty for her many sins and especially for this last one mentioned, for she died during breast-surgery.

Meanwhile Isidore remained at home praying to God. The young man, fearing in part the laws and in part the anger of Theophilus because he had failed, fled to the protecting ramparts of the church and clung to the altar. So it was on a revolting charge which was never given a proper hearing that Theophilus declared Isidore to be expelled from the Church, pretending a solemn hearing to cover up his own wickedness. Isidore feared that Theophilus in his increasing fury should press upon him so as to affect his safety—they say he was really worked up to such a high pitch—and he went swiftly to Mount Nitria,[237] to an establishment of monks where he had spent his youth practicing the ascetic life. Here he sat in his own cell and prayed to the long-suffering God.[238]

Theophilus turns against the monks

Now Theophilus was fully aware that his victory was both unbecoming and ignoble, and he sent letters to the nearby bishops with orders that some of the monks who were in charge of monasteries were to be expelled from the mountain and the Inner Desert. Now he gave no reason for this action. Certain monks went down to Alexandria with their priests to ask Theophilus to state the reason why they were condemned to be cast out. He regarded them like a dragon with bloodshot eyes. He glared like a bull.[239] With his temper beyond control he was at first livid, then sallow, and then smiling sarcastically. He snatched the pallium[240] from the aged Ammonius[241] and twisting it around his neck he inflicted blows upon his jaw, making his nose bleed with his clenched fists, and kept crying out: "Anathematize Origen,[242] you heretic!"

Now the only point under consideration was in regard to Isidore's petition. So it is with the foolhardy: like dogs which bear their young blind and bark-less. So they went back again, bloodstained, and brought no answer to those on the mountain. They kept up their regular life of austerity, exercising their natural powers by which salvation is gained.[243]

CHAPTER 7
THEOPHILUS AND CHRYSOSTOM

Theophilus brings action against the monks

Not satisfied with this, Theophilus sent for all the neighboring bishops to concoct a synod against the monks. He did not call them together to make a proper defense. He gave them no chance to speak a word, and he denounced three of them of the highest rank as outlaws. (He feared to bring punishment upon them all at once) and he pretended there had been a perversion of doctrine. He was not ashamed to call impostors those very men whom he had often honored as teachers over and above bishops for their lives, their speech, and their long service—just because they supported Isidore. After he had announced this he bribed five monks; yes, men from that mountain, mannikins who never sat in the chapter house of the elders of the desert, miserable wretches hardly fit even to keep the gates, if you know what I mean. One of them he ordained a bishop, and since there was no city for him he placed him over a small village. (He fearlessly initiated new policies, calling himself a second Moses.)[244] He ordained another one a priest and three of them deacons. They were not Egyptians but of different places. One was a Libyan, another was from Pharanda, another was from Paralus. They fell in quite readily with his ridiculous operations, since they had no hope of any pledges from their own countries.

They appeal to outside help

Then he prepared them to bring memoranda against the three excommunicated bishops. He actually dictated the words of the accusation himself; they merely added their signatures. Once this was done, he accepted the memoranda from them at the church, and he went to the Augustial prefect[245] to lodge with him a representation against them in his own person as archpriest[246] of the diocese of Egypt. He also had with him the falsely concocted memoranda demanding that the men be expelled with military assistance from all of Egypt.

The monasteries are attacked

He took the army as a pretext along with an edict from the emperor and he gathered a crowd of ruffians who had no respect for dignity. He plied the lads with wine and fell upon the monasteries in the dead of night. First of all he ordered their sainted brother, Dioscorus,[247] the bishop of the mountain, to be dragged from his throne, and this was done by some Ethiopic slaves, most probably not even baptized.[248] He took his see[249] away from him, which since the coming of Christ had belonged to the city of Dioscorus. After that he raided the mountain and gave what little property he found to the young men. After he had shaken down their cells, he searched for the three bishops, whom they had lowered into a cistern with its mouth covered by a mat of rushes.[250] When he did not find them, he set their cells on fire with faggots and burned all the sacred books of Scripture as well as other serious books.[251] Some say they saw them burning up a boy and the symbols of the mysteries as well.[252]

The monks flee to Palestine

When he had ceased from his insensate fury, he returned to Alexandria and so gave those holy men a chance for escape. They at once took up their sheepskin habits[253] and set out for Palestine, making for Aelia.[254] Three hundred worthy monks they were, along with priests and deacons with them, and they were spread in different directions.

Theophilus pursues the monks

Now the *crooked serpent*[255] could not bear the freedom of action of the monks and again stirred up Theophilus against them. He was boiling with anger and wrote a letter to the bishop of Palestine: "You should not have received such men into your cities against my opinion, but since you were not aware of it I grant you pardon. But be sure in the future not to grant them any ecclesiastical or personal position."[256]

In his overweening pride Theophilus not only spoke as a god, but even imagined he was a god.

The monks approach John at Constantinople

The monks then were forced by necessity to change about from place to place, and they finally reached the capital,[257] where Bishop

John had been installed by God's hand for the spiritual guidance of our rulers. They fell down at his knees, imploring him to help souls plundered and abandoned by those more accustomed to this action than to doing good. John arose and beheld fifty sincere men with habits worn grey with their holy labors. Stung to the quick by his feeling of brotherly love as was Joseph,[258] he burst into tears and asked them: *"What sort of boar of the wood . . . or singular wild beast has been doing mischief to this fruitful vine?"*[259]

Then they said: "Please be seated, father, and bind up the horrible wounds we have suffered because of Pope Theophilus' madness, if indeed you can heal our swollen wounds. For if you cannot speak up for us either out of respect or fear of Theophilus, so is the case with other bishops. Then the only thing left for us to do is to approach the emperor and acquaint him with the man's evil actions, thereby bringing ill fame to the Church. If you have any interest in the well-being of the Church, then, consider our petition and please persuade Theophilus to allow us to go to our home in Egypt. We have done no wrong against the law of the Savior or against him."

Chrysostom intercedes for the monks

John thought he could easily change Theophilus' bad feeling towards the monks and willingly took up the matter. He called them together and instructed them for the love of God they should not reveal the reason for their presence "until I send word to my brother Theophilus." He gave them quarters in the Church of the Resurrection[260] for sleeping, but did not provide for other necessities of life. Some pious women brought their daily sustenance, and they themselves helped to some extent by the labor of their own hands.[261]

There happened at that time to be some of Theophilus' clergy in Constantinople, who had come to buy offices from newly appointed officials in the Egyptian province. Some of them were courting favor with him by helping to destroy those who were harassing him. So John called them in to ask if they knew the ascetics who were present. They willingly gave a good report of them, saying: "We know them and they have suffered great violence. But if it please you, master, do not allow them communion in the spiritual feast as it will annoy the Pope (Theophilus), but be considerate of them in every other respect. That would be more fitting for you as bishop."

Chrysostom writes to Theophilus

So John did not receive them into communion,[262] but did write a letter to Theophilus beseeching him: "Please do me the favor as your son and your brother and take these men in your arms."[263]

Theophilus did not grant them that favor, but he did send along certain men well practiced in verbal disputation—we spoke about them above—and he had prepared them to present requirements which he had laid down as was his custom. These contained false statements including every sort of accusation regarding their spiritual life,[264] since he found nothing wrong in their lives outwardly. Thus he prepared the way for them to be pointed out at the palace as frauds.

Chrysostom finds Theophilus implacable

The ascetics then saw they not only could not correct his view but actually incited him to greater anger, and they sent him a delegation of worthy men declaring that they had anathemized all false doctrine. Then they gave a petition to John which explained the various forms of tyranny from which they suffered along with certain subjects I should be ashamed to speak of before young people. I fear that in so doing I should shake their faith in the veracity of my statements. I am sure that even more advanced souls might not even believe me.

Then John himself and through other bishops called on them to drop their accusations against Theophilus because of the mortification of such a trial. He wrote to Theophilus: "The men are driven to such a degree of distress that they are filing a formal indictment against you. Answer them as seems best to you, for they refuse to leave the capital for me."

Theophilus was greatly incensed at this. He suspended the

brother of the monks from his own church, namely Bishop Dioscorus, who had grown old in the service. Then he wrote to Bishop John: "I believe that you are not aware of the order of the Canons of Nicaea where they declare: 'A bishop may not judge a case beyond his boundaries'; if so (and you know it full well), drop these charges against me. For if it were necessary for me to be judged, it should be by Egyptian judges, and not here with you at the distance of a seventy-five days' journey."[265]

CHAPTER 8
FIRST EXPULSION OF CHRYSOSTOM

The monks appeal to Empress Eudoxia

John received the letter and read it, but kept it to himself, and the matter of peace was discussed with the ascetics of both parties. Both sides were exasperated at hearing him, the one because they had been subjected to tyranny, the other because they could have no power to enforce peace without Theophilus. It had been at his orders that they brought forth the petitions of false accusation. John had given his answer and had then put the whole matter out of his mind.

Then the monks of the aggrieved party withdrew and brought up a long petition charging the other party of monks as being guilty of libel—and all the rest about Theophilus—lest I say any more of what everyone knows full well already. They came and made an appeal to their majesties in the Shrine of Saint John.[266] They approached the Empress and begged that the case of the defendant monks be thoroughly investigated by the prefects. They begged that Theophilus be judged before John, whether he was willing or not. The petition was made and this was the decree: "Theophilus is to be summoned by the magistrate and must appear, willing or unwilling, to stand trial before John; furthermore, Theophilus' monks should prove the charges made against the holy old men or pay the penalty for falsely accusing them."

Theophilus summoned to Constantinople

So it was that Elaphius,[267] lately of the captains,[268] was sent to Alexandria to bring Theophilus. The prefects were carrying out the rest of the empress' reply. The preliminary trial was held and resulted in a doubtful decision, and the laws lying over them illuminating the sword.[269] The wretched monks, fearful of the decision, awaited the arrival of Theophilus as he had suggested the petitions and actually dictated them. The military put them into prison until Theophilus should arrive and bail was not given them under such conditions. Some of them spent a long time in prison and died because Theophilus was long delayed in coming.[270] He eased the matter along by bribes, and some of the monks were sentenced to be transported to Proconnesus for malicious accusation at the final inquiry.

Theophilus arrives at Constantinople

So Theophilus arrived like a beetle[271] overladen with the dung of the best that Egypt or even India for that matter produces. He exuded a sweet fragrance to disguise the bad odor of his jealousy. He entered Constantinople at the sixth hour of the fifth day of the week[272] and was greeted by a mob of sailors.[273] This was the dishonorable glory he bore of which the Apostle said furiously: *whose glory is in their shame;* and he added: *who mind earthly things.*[274] He was entertained in the tents of the unjust.[275] He was disdainful of the Church, forgetful of that saying of David: *I have chosen to be an object in the house of my God, rather than to dwell in the tabernacles of sinners.*[276] He was excluded from the Church by his own conscience.

Theophilus the schemer

He stayed on for three full weeks and never had any conversation with John as is the custom among bishops. He never approached the church, but kept plotting by day and by night, joining his new hostility to the old, to thrust Bishop John not only out of the Church but from very life itself. For this purpose he was buying off those superstitious people[277] whom he conquered by a lavish expenditure of money to bear witness against the truth. He enslaved the gluttonous ones by his well-laden table, and others he won over by flattery and promises of promotion, instigating his fellow imposters among the clergy. Once he had all these in bonds, not of rope, but of pleasure, he was like some kind of a seducing demon bewitching the critical faculty of their souls. He sought for some diabolical person to serve him in this drama,[278] and he came upon such a one.

The renegade deacons

Two deacons had been expelled from the Church by Bishop John for immoral conduct. Theophilus took advantage of their weakness and persuaded them to present memoranda against John, assuring them that he would restore them to their office. (The offenses were murder and fornication, respectively.) This he promptly did once John was sent off into exile. He restored them to their places and it was only too clear that the memoranda which they had presented had been written by Theophilus himself. They contained not the slightest particle of truth, with the possible exception that John did advise everyone to take a little water or a small particle of food after Communion lest they might accidentally spit out part of the element with saliva or phlegm. He was the first to do this himself, to teach reverence to those willing to learn.[279]

The meeting at Eugraphia's house

After he received the memoranda a meeting was held at the house of Eugraphia in company with Severianus, Antiochus, Acacius, and any others who had a grudge against John for his moderate counsels. For the blessed John used to expound a more dignified behavior *both publicly and from house to house*,[280] and especially he harped upon such as those women: "You gray-haired old women! At your age, why do you compel yourselves to make your bodies young again, wearing curly locks of hair upon your foreheads like common whores? You outrage the rest of the free women, beguiling all you meet, some of you even widows to boot."

The Synod of the Oak[281]

As soon as they were convened they sought what way they should begin the action against John. One of them suggested they present the petition to the emperor and insist that John appear before the synod even if he were not willing to do so. This then was done and, as it is with the Jews,[282] money made everything easier for them.

Chrysostom addresses the synod

We were seated,[283] forty bishops with Bishop John in the dining room of the bishop's house. They were astonished how one who was an outlaw as it were and commanded to appear at court by himself on such unpleasant charges should have arrived with such a company of bishops. How could he have changed the thinking of a crowd of those in power and perverted most of the clergy? We were completely at a loss for words, but John was inspired by the Spirit and spoke to us all: "Pray for me, brothers, and if you love Christ, let none of you leave your own church for my sake, for that would be like the one saying: *For I am even now ready to be sacrificed; and the time of my dissolution is at hand.*[284] As I see it, I shall endure many tribulations and I shall depart this life. For I know the cunning of Satan; he can no longer put up with the annoyance of my invectives against him. And thus may you have mercy. In your prayers, be mindful of me."

Chrysostom shows great calm in his distress

We were so affected by an indescribable helplessness that some of us broke into tears and others left the gathering. They kissed his eyes, his venerable head, and his eloquent and holy mouth, weeping, and with spirit bowed down in despair. But as we were flying about hither and yon like bees buzzing about a beehive he invited us to come back to the gathering and said:

"Be seated, brethren, and do not weep and give me more pain. *For to me, to live is Christ, and to die is good.*[285] It has been frequently said that I ought to have my head cut off because of my rash speech.[286] And if you remember, look back into your memory, I always kept telling you: 'This present life is a journey; its joys and its sorrows are always passing on. What we see before us is a bazaar. We finish our buying and selling and we move elsewhere.'[287] Are we better than the patriarchs, or the prophets, or the apostles, that our present life should remain for us without death?"

Then one of those present sobbed aloud and said: "But we mourn because we are orphans and the church is a widow; likewise, because of the confounding of laws and the love of high place of those who fear not the Lord and groom themselves for the episcopal office. We bemoan likewise the defenselessness of the poor and the barrenness of teaching."

John tapped the palm of his left hand with his right forefinger, for the Christ-loving bishop was in the habit of doing this when deep in thought, and he addressed the speaker:

"That is enough, brother, speak no more! But mind what I said: Do not desert your churches. For the teaching office did not begin in me nor does it end in me. Did not Moses die? Was not Joshua found?[288] Did not Samuel die? Was not David anointed king?[289] Jeremias left this life; was not there Baruch?[290] Elias was snatched up; did not Elisha become prophet?[291] Paul was beheaded;[292] did he not leave Timothy,[293] Titus,[294] Apollo,[295] and many others?"

After this speech Eulysius, Bishop of Apameia in Bithynia, spoke: "Even if we keep our churches we shall be forced to communicate with them and to sign against you. That is a foregone conclusion."

Then blessed John spoke out: "You must communicate with them or you will split the Church; but please do not sign. I am not at all aware of any thinking of my own that deserves my being forced into exile."

John is summoned to the Council of the Oak

Meanwhile, there appeared the messengers from Theophilus. John ordered them to enter. When they had done so they were asked to what order they belonged, and they said they were bishops. He asked them to sit down and tell their business, to which they replied: "We have only a written message to be read aloud. Please let it be read."

John commanded that this be done, and they ordered the young protégé[296] of Theophilus to read the compilation, which he did. The gist of the communication was as follows:

"The Holy Synod gathered at the Oak" (that is, the so-called place beyond the sea, the suburb of Rufinus[297] in which they were gathered) "to John" (omitting what he really was, the bishop; the darkened soul never sees things in order, but it loves to imagine what passion dictates). "We have received memoranda concerning you which contain many evil things. Appear, therefore, at once and bring the priests Sarapion and Tigrius[298] along with you, for they are needed."

Those who came to him were Dioscorus[299] and Paulus,[300] young men who had only recently been consecrated in Libya.

Chrysostom's friends reply

After the message had been read John's fellow bishops prepared a reply addressed to Theophilus. There were first of all the three bishops, Luppicianus, Demetrius, and Eulysius, along with two priests, Germanus and Severus, all of them saintly and honorable men.

"Do not overthrow the estate of the Church and do not rend the Church for whose sake God from on high entered human flesh.[301] It would appear that you are acting in a disorderly manner in breaking the canons of the three hundred eighteen bishops at Nicaea in attempting to 'judge a case beyond your boundaries.' Come across to us now, to a well ruled city, and do not be like Cain when he invited his brother out into a field.[302] Let us first hear what you have to say. For we have seventy distinct memoranda against you plainly accusing you of unlawful deeds. Besides, we are stronger in numbers in our synod, brought together by the grace of God, not for the dissolution of the Church, but for peace. But you are only thirty-six and all of those from but one province; now we are forty from various provinces and have seven metropolitan bishops amongst us. It follows, then, that the lesser body should be judged by the larger number and the more honorable according to the canons. For we have from you the letter in which you inform our colleague in the ministry John that he ought not to entertain cases which lie outside his own boundaries. Then please be observant of the laws of the Church and call upon your accusers either to drop their charges against you or to end their attack on John."

Chrysostom writes to Theophilus

John was deeply moved at this answer and he spoke to his bishops: "Write what seems best to you. I feel it incumbent upon me to make my own statement in answer to their charges."

He sent the following reply to Theophilus and those in his group: "As for myself, I can only say that if any one had anything to say against me up to now, I do not know what it is. But if anyone would speak against me and you desire me to come before you, please put out of your assembly those who are my enemies and evilly inclined toward me. I do not argue about where I am to be tried, but the most fit place should be in the city. There are those whom I do avoid, Theophilus for one, whom I reprove for having said both in Alexandria and in Lycia: 'I go to court to depose John.'[303] I fully realize this since he had nothing to do with me when he arrived here. If he acted in such manner before the hearing as my enemy, what would he do after the trial? Likewise, I charge Acacius with saying: 'I am seasoning a pot for him.' And what shall I say of Severianus and Antiochus, whom the divine judgment will soon bring to grief? Why should I speak about them when even the worldly theatres are making up songs of their newfangled notions?[304]

"Therefore, you are requested, if you really wish me to come, to remove these four if they come as my judges. If they come as accusers, put them on the witness stand. Thus I may know how to regard them, as my opponents or my judges. And I shall come by all means, not only because of your love, but before any synod of the whole world. Be aware now that no matter how often you may send for me, you shall hear no more from me."[305]

The emperor summons the trial

When they had gone, a notary arrived at once with a letter from the emperor in which they demanded[306] that John come to be judged, even if unwilling, bidding him to come without delay.

After the reply had been given to the notary, two priests of John were announced, and Eugenius,[307] who had been given the see of Heraclia as payment for plotting against Bishop John, and Isaac, the monk sworn to secrecy, not to call him anything else, and they said: "The synod made this clear to you; come with us and defend yourself against the charges."

Chrysostom refuses to appear

To this John answered in reply through other bishops: "By what kind of procedure do you judge a case, first by not excluding my enemies from the court and then by sending my own clerics for me?"

They seized the bishops and beat the one, they stripped another, and around the neck of the third they put the irons they had intended for Saint John. They had planned to cast him into a ship and send him to some unknown place; the devil made them into savage lions. And the holy bishop, knowing their shameful plan full well, held himself aloof. But these worthy gentlemen[308] made up some puny charges, really more fragile than a spider's web,[309] to belittle him. They bore witness against the blessed man whose face they had never seen and whose voice they had never heard. So in a single day they concluded the evil which they had been fabricating[310] for a long time. (For no one can restrain the onslaught of the demon; it awaits no introspection.)

Chrysostom accused of treason

Then they sent off a report to the emperor as follows: "Since John is accused of various offenses and has refused to appear,[311] knowing his guilt full well that the laws degrade him—and this so stands. The memoranda also include a charge of high treason.[312] Your Piety, therefore, will command that he be expelled from his office, whether he is willing or not, and that he pay the penalty for treason, since we have no power to investigate this case."

Oh thrice miserable wretches![313] What are you thinking about? What are you doing? You should be ashamed to perform such deeds with no reverence or fear of men or God. The treason was a reproach to the empress, as they insist, because he called her a Jezebel.[314] These wonderful people! How they longed to see John dead by the sword! How they acted! But God revealed their innermost intent of evil and softened the hearts of the rulers, just as it was in the case of Daniel at Babylon.[315] For there the lions were subdued and spared Daniel,[316] but the men turned wild and did not spare the prophet. However, God conquered the wild nature of men once the nature of the beast was subdued.

CHAPTER 9
INTRIGUES AND VIOLENCE AT CONSTANTINOPLE

Chrysostom is exiled but returns

In this way John was exiled[317] from the Church and a high official along with armed forces as though going off on a foray against barbarians. When he was exiled he went to the country area of Praenetus[318] in Bithynia. But scarcely had a single day passed when a calamity occurred in the royal bedroom[319] This caused such an alarm that a few days later they called John back through a house notary, so he was brought back to his own throne.[320] Then Theophilus and his Egyptian bishops took to flight for his own safety (for the people in the city sought to drown him).[321] Two months passed, and they regained their spirits and rose up once more against John. Since they found no auspicious opening they sent a message to that man in Alexandria who was so clever at these things:[322]

"Either return to initiate proceedings against John or, if you fear reprisals from the people, at least suggest to us some means by which we can at least make a beginning."

Theophilus trumps up new charges

Now Theophilus did not come forward, fully knowing how he had been put to flight, but he sent three wretched bishops, Paul,[323] Poimen,[324] and another one newly consecrated. Along with them he sent certain canons which the Arians had composed against the blessed Athanasius. They thought that by the use of these canons they could devise a judgment against John, because he had returned to his see after being deposed—and that was on his own initiative. (You must realize that Theophilus is by his nature an impetuous person, rash, bold, seeking a quarrel above reason—anything he sees he rushes at in great haste without consideration and allows himself no time for reflection. So he proceeded with mad fury, confident in regard to the verdict declared about him. He vigorously opposed all who desired to make a cross-examination; he was always anxious to demonstrate that his own judgment and decision should carry the day.)

The bishops plot against John

This is what they did, knowing full well his custom. For they called together the metropolitans and bishops from Syria, Cappadocia, the whole province of Phrygia, and Pontus, to a conference at Constantinople.[325] They communicated with John according to the canons, so they would not fall into the same error they did in the first instance. This by no means pleased those who were in power. Theodorus,[326] bishop of Tyana, a man highly respected, was aware of the knavery from what had reached his ears, and rather than go along with Theophilus' reckless haste he left them all as though he were an outcast and went back to his own church, bidding a long farewell to the court. He kept his own province safe by the rampart of his piety and he remained to the very end in communion with the Roman faithful, to whom Paul gave witness, saying: *Your faith is spoken of in all the world.*[327] But Pharetrius[328] of Caesarea, close by Mount Argaeus, was frightened above measure just as children are terrified by a hobgoblin.[329] He never left his own city but carried on a correspondence with John's enemies, although he had not actually been sent for and knew no better, being entirely unaware of a bishop's duties. Leontius[330] of Ancyra in Galatia was involved with Ammonius[331] of Burned Laodicea[332] in burning the church.

Both of them submitted to the authorities and were led astray by the hope of gifts from the emperor. At the second session they made a vile suggestion to those on the side of Acacius and Antiochus that Theophilus' judgment, which was in fact no judgment at all, should be carried out: John should be given no chance to defend himself, and they appealed to the canons Theophilus had sent.[333] The forty bishops who held communion with Arius[334] had legislated that "if any bishop or any priest who has been deposed, justly or unjustly, should reenter his church on his own initiative, without permission of a synod, such a one shall have no opportunity of defense, but shall be absolutely excluded." Now that canon was declared null and void as being illegal and passed by illegal persons at Sardis[335] by the Roman, Italian, Illyrian, Macedonian, and Greek bishops (as you know full well, my dear Theodore) when Liberius[336] or rather Julius[337] in the reign of Emperor Constans received Athanasius and Marcellus[338] of Galatia into communion. That canon had been expressly passed against them.

A matter of Canon Law

At any rate this wonderful pair, Ammonius and Leontius, joined company with Acacius and Antiochus as well as Cyrinus[339] of Chalcedon and Severianus, and they approached the emperor with a proposal that ten bishops of John's party, of whom there were more than forty, should be summoned in order to keep the authority of the canons. Some of them affirmed quite confidently that the canons were orthodox, but others thought they showed an Arian origin. They came in then around Elpidius,[340] bishop of Laodicea in Syria, a man old in spirit and with white hair, and Tranquillus.[341] They persuaded the emperor that John should not be refused admission without cause.

"John was not previously deposed, but it was by a civil tribunal; nor did he enter the city except by order of Your Piety and a notary was along with him. Moreover, we are going to show you that the canons to which they appeal are of heretical origin."

Now the opponents of John continued in disorderly fashion, some of them shouting at the top of their voices, others strutting about in a pompous manner, shaking themselves with a movement of the chest before the emperor. Then Elpidius, most skilled in canon law, spoke to the emperor meekly in a moment of silence:

"Emperor, let us not annoy Your Gentleness any further, but let this be done. Let those who are in the company of Acacius and Antiochus subscribe to the canons which they claim to be the work of orthodox persons, that 'we are of the same faith as those who drafted them,' and so our whole quarrel will be solved."

The plot fails

The emperor was impressed by the simplicity of the problem and he spoke to Antiochus, smiling: "Nothing would be better than that." In all these proceedings the emperor was entirely blameless; others kept changing about his most excellent decrees. Those in the company of Severianus whirled and swirled[342] against each other like water in a mighty flood; they were stupefied at the bishop's prudent answer and at the emperor's judgment. They were rendered speechless and their bodies took on a more livid color. They were forced to restrain themselves in the emperor's presence and they signed the canons, however unwillingly, and left. They did not keep their promise, given as it were unwillingly, and they feared for the worst, but they did devise a means by which they could depose John.

Well, nine or ten months passed in various and sundry operations, and John gathered with his forty-two bishops and the people were following his teaching with much good will. (For the mind free from vainglory always expresses itself with greater grace and power in difficult circumstances.)

The emperor turns against John

In the meanwhile there occurred the Lord's fast[343] like the spring coming back again year after year. Again Antiochus and his party came privately before the emperor and they told him John had been deposed. They begged him to order that he be expelled at the approaching Paschal tide. But the emperor was of necessity tricked by them as he believed bishops. (For the true bishop or priest knows not falsehood. These names belong to a higher realm, for there is nothing more priestly or more episcopal than God who is the overseer[344] and He beholds all things.[345] Therefore, the bishop or the priest, as partaking of these names, ought also to be partaker in these deeds.)

The emperor said to John: "Depart from the church!"

But he replied: "I have received this church from God our Savior for the care of the salvation of my people and I cannot abandon her. But if you desire this (for the city belongs to you) then expel me by force so that I may defend myself on the grounds that I went by your command rather than that I abandoned my charge."

The emperor expels Chrysostom

Then men were sent from the palace, and they expelled him with a certain respect for him. They expected the wrath of God would overtake them, and they commanded him to stay on in the bishop's quarters for a time. Should any misfortune attend them, John could be restored to the church and the divine power would be appeased. Should nothing happen, they could proceed further against him as Pharaoh did against Moses.[346]

Happenings on Holy Saturday

In the meanwhile the day of the Great Sabbath was at hand in which the crucified Savior harried hell.[347] Again they told John:

"Leave the church!" and he made a suitable reply. Then the king with all respect for the most holy day and the disturbance in the city sent for Acacius and Antiochus and asked them: "What should be done? See to it that you do nothing rashly."

Then these gentlemen and exceedingly high-minded persons spoke to the emperor: "Your Majesty, the deposition of John is on our heads." As a last refuge the bishops siding with John, as many as the days of the holy fast,[348] approached the emperor and the empress in the shrine of the martyrs, weeping and begging them to spare the Church of Christ, especially in the Paschal Season and because of those who were about to be reborn in the mysteries, and for the Church to take back her prelate once more. But they did not hear, even when the blessed Paul[349] of Crateia pled with them with fearless bravery: "Eudoxia, fear God, have pity on your children, do not outrage the feast of Christ by the *shedding of blood*."[350]

The Easter Vigil

Now the forty bishops returned and spent a sleepless night in their rooms, some in tears, some grieving, and others with no fight left in them at all, so immersed in torpor of body and mind, just as the tragedy affected each one. However, the God-loving priests of John led the laity into the public baths named after Constans and they spent the night, some in reading to the people from the Holy Scripture, others in baptizing the catechumens as is the custom at Easter. Now those mind-corrupters and deceivers of the party of Antiochus, Severianus, and Acacius reported these doings to their own leaders, demanding that the people be prevented from gathering there.

But the magistrate answered them: "It is night and there are great crowds of people; let there not be some dreadful accident!"

Acacius and his party objected to this, however. "No one has remained in the churches. Our fear is that the emperor might enter the church and finding no one there he will realize the feeling of the people towards John and condemn us as slanderers, especially since we said there is really no one kindly disposed to him as if he were an outlaw."

Then the magistrate, being warned by them in regard to what

was about to take place, appointed Lucius,[351] a Greek, accompanied by armed men, sending him to tell the people gently to go to the church. He went but they did not listen, and he went back to Acacius, informing him of the zeal and dense crowd of people. After this they entreated him earnestly with golden words,[352] winning him over by promises of further advancement. In this way he could hinder the glory of the Lord; he told him either to bring the people to the church, persuading them in his speech, or else to excite them and by anger prevent the celebration of the feast.

Tumult in the church

Lucius set out then at once, taking along with him some of the clerics of the party of Acacius in the second watch of the night (for in our parts they keep the people at prayer until the first cockcrow). He had four hundred newly enlisted swordsmen from Thrace, the same number that Esau had.[353] They were exceedingly ruthless and he rushed out suddenly by night with some clerics and some soldiers who showed the way. He tore through the crowd of people with his flashing sword, headlong as wolves do. He came forward to the blessed waters within and hindered those who were about to be initiated into the Resurrection of the Savior. He hurled himself boldly against the deacon and spilled out the symbols of the mysteries. He beat up the priests, men who were well on in years. Their heads were bruised with cudgels and the baptistery was spotted with blood. Only to regard that angelic night when even the demons fell in terror, that night turned into a labyrinth.[354] Here were naked women running along with their husbands in fear of being killed or of being disgraced. One with his hand badly mangled was going away weeping; another was dragging away a maiden whom he had despoiled; all of them were making off with precious booty they had stolen.

The faithful continue to multiply

So the priests and deacons who were arrested were cast into prison; the more worthy citizens were expelled from the capital.

Various and sundry commands were issued, one after another, containing threats against any who would not renounce communion with John. Despite all that had happened, those bishops mentioned above devoted themselves to their duties. And the assembly of those who love good teaching, rather, I should say, the love of God was not abolished, but as was said in Exodus: *But the more they oppressed them, the more they multiplied and increased.* [355]

Tragedy of the newly baptized

On the very next day the emperor went forth to take exercise on the plain near the city and beheld the untilled land around Pempton[356] clothed as it were in white. He was astonished at the sight of the flowering of the newly baptized (for there were about three thousand of them) and he asked his bodyguards: "What is that crowd of those gathered there?"

And they lied to him and said they were the heterodox in order to bring them under his wrath. The agents of this affair and the champions of envy learned of this at once and sent to the suburb the most ruthless and unsparing of their followers to disperse the audience and lay hold of the teachers. They rushed upon them and once again they laid hands on a few of the clergy and many more of the laity.

Blessed are the poor in spirit

And Theodore spoke:

Deacon: Oh most blessed Father, how was it that so many, that the newly baptized alone numbered three thousand, and that only a few soldiers could overpower them and dissolve the assembly?

Bishop: This does not indicate small numbers here, nor is it a sign of lack of zeal, but rather it shows the fullness of piety and is a demonstration of their devotion to their teachers who constantly urged them to cultivate a peaceful turn of mind.

And Theodore spoke:

Deacon: Well spoken! Surely it would not have been fitting that they learned prudence and constancy from the holy John only to act against him by showing a senseless and turbulent manner.

CHAPTER 10
CHRYSOSTOM DEPARTS FROM CONSTANTINOPLE

The prison becomes a church

Bishop: You are satisfied on this point then. I beg you, please do not interrupt my speech born of such sad events. (For it so happens that it is events which give birth to more words.)[357] Along with the clergy and the laity who were taken, the wives of some of the foremost men were also arrested. Some of them had their veils[358] torn off along with the lobe of the ear. A very wealthy woman, wife of one Eleutherus,[359] when she perceived this removed her veil and rushed into the city in the guise of a serving girl. (She did this to shield her modesty, as she was endowed with beautiful features and a fine form.)

Thus it was that the prisons of the different magistrates were filled, but they changed into churches. Hymns were sung and the offering of the mysteries was performed in the prisons. But in the churches there were floggings and torture and horrible oaths to force them to anathematize John, who had contended against the evil works of the Devil even to the point of death.

Appeal to the emperor

The feast of Pentecost[360] had gone by and five days later Acacius, Antiochus, Severianus, and Cyrinus approached the emperor and said: "Your Majesty, by God's grace you are not subject to our authority, but you do have power over all and you may do whatever you wish.[361] Do not be milder than the priests or holier than the bishops. We told you in the presence of all that the deposition of John is on our heads. Please do not be merciful to one man, but unmerciful to the rest of us."

So they persuaded the emperor using the same arguments, and even more so, the same deeds as had the Jews.[362]

Chrysostom ordered to leave the church

Then the emperor sent Patricius the notary with a message to John: "Those in the company of Acacius, Antiochus, Severianus, and Cyrinus have taken your condemnation on their own heads. Place your own affairs in the hands of God and leave the church."

Bishop John then came down from the bishop's palace along with the bishops, and he admonished them all in a clear rally and said: "Come, let us pray and bid farewell to the angel of the church."[363]

He took delight at what had happened but he was grieving at the mistreatment of his people.

Chrysostom bids farewell to his friends

At once one of the God-loving officers signaled to John. "Since Lucius, a wild and hardened man, is ready in the public bath with his own soldiery to drag you willy-nilly from the church and expel you, the people are in a tumult. Hurry up and leave unnoticed, lest the people come to grips with the military trying to save you."

Then John kissed some of the bishops weeping the while (his grief prevented him from kissing them all), and he withdrew, saying to others in the vestry:[364] "Stay here for a while yet; I must go to rest a short time."

He went into the baptistery and called Olympias,[365] who never departed from the church, along with the deaconesses Pentadia[366] and Procla,[367] and Silvina,[368] wife of the blessed Nebridius[369] who adorned her widowhood by an exemplary life, and he addressed them:

"Come here, my daughters, listen to me. I see that the things concerning me have an end.[370] *I have finished my course*[371] and perhaps *you shall see my face no more.*[372] This is what I ask of you. Let no one prevent you from the good will you have had towards the Church. And if any one be brought forward for consecration as my successor, provided he comes willingly and at the will of all, bow down to him as if it were to John (for the Church cannot exist without a bishop). And thus you will find mercy. Remember me in your prayers."

Chrysostom departs

When these women made a great commotion with their crying and they rolled about his feet, he made a motion to one of the reverend priests and said: "Take them away so they do not stir up the crowds of people."

So they were subdued for a while and finally they seemed to have settled down. And John moved off to the eastern part of the church. (There was nothing in him that smacked of the West!)[373] He had ordered a mule which he generally rode to be standing at the west portal of the church to mislead the people who were waiting for him there. And the angel of the church accompanied him as he left, not able to bear the deserted place which evil powers and principalities[374] had promoted, making of it all a theatrical performance.

"So it was as in a theatre, the hooting and the whistling of the ungodly, the mockery and overpowering shouting by Greeks and Jews alike. There were blows and bodily wounds inflicted by soldiers as though this were in a prison; every faculty of the soul was tortured because the teacher had been taken away and because there is blasphemy against God."[375]

For where we expect *remission of sin*[376] there was instead an *outpouring of blood.*[377]

The church is burned

After this unutterable and inexplicable darkness there appeared a flame in the middle of the throne where John used to sit. It was just as the heart situated in the middle of the body controls the other members and communicates the oracles of the Lord. The flame looked for the expounder of the Word and not finding him it consumed the church furnishings. Then it took shape like a tree and grew up through the rafters to the very roof and like an adder it consumed the belly and crept up on the back of the church buildings.[378] It was as though God were paying *the wages of iniquity*[379] for the penalty assigned, to chide and warn those who would not be warned except by the sight of these calamities sent by God Himself. Not only that, but leaving a monumental memorial[380] of the violent synod itself.

The conflagration spreads

But the burning of the church was as nothing compared to that of the building known as the Senate House, which is opposite the church many paces to the south. The fire as though endowed with intelligence leaped over the people in the street like a bridge and it destroyed first of all the part closest to the church, but the part on the side of the royal palace. So we cannot say that it really burned because of the proximity of the structures, but it showed that it was only too clear that it had come from heaven. (One could see people going about their regular business between two mountains of fire without any harm.) So the fire was whirling and seething like the sea, stirred up by a strong wind as though proceeding under signal. The buildings all around were seized without mercy, but the fire left unscathed a small house in which most of the sacred vessels were kept. It was not that the fire respected gold and silver, but this was to give no opportunity for John's accusers to make false charges against the pious bishop, saying he had appropriated any of the church valuables.

Then the fire after causing all this disaster drew back[381] to the suburbs of the city, searching out the malice of the evildoers to expose the madness of Theophilus, because he had been preparing to cast John out on the plea that he had embezzled the treasures of the Church. In that whole crowd there was no loss of life, not of man nor of beast. But the dirt of those who had carried on in such foul fashion was cleansed by the force of the fire, which in three hours of daylight, from six until nine, destroyed the work of a long time.[382]

CHAPTER 11
EXILE AND DEATH OF CHRYSOSTOM

Chrysostom exiled to Armenia

Deacon: Then where was John, father, and the rest of the bishops while this was going on?

Bishop: The remaining bishops were either imprisoned or swept out of the city, and some even went into hiding. John together with Cyriacus and Eulysius was bound and carried off to Bithynia by soldiers of the prefect,[383] and they were threatened with various sorts of punishments for setting the church on fire. Afterwards Cyriacus and Eulysius along with other clerics were bound and brought to trial, but they were declared innocent and set free. The holy John with his usual boldness of speech sent them a last message, saying: "Even if you did not give me a chance to defend myself in other matters, you could at least listen to what pertains to the church if I am guilty as you say, of burning it."

He was not given a hearing in this matter but was sent under military custody to a very out-of-the-way small town in Armenia called Cucusus.[384] This was a place constantly raided by the Isaurians by night and by day, and it was possibly with the hope that John might be killed there.

Arsacius succeeds Chrysostom

Arsacius,[385] brother of the blessed Nectarius, was substituted in place of John, that teacher of sacred wisdom. He was in contrast less powerful in speech than a fish and about as effective in action as a frog. (Now there are times when action speaks, the more so when it

is directed to good.) However, he survived but fourteen months.[386]
He had perjured himself on the Gospels, swearing to his brother
Nectarius that he would never be consecrated bishop; his brother
had chided him for refusing to become bishop of Tarsus on the
grounds that he was expecting death shortly. Now it was vainglory
that was really the first reason for his perjury; he was in a manner of
speaking actually wooing his brother's wife,[387] and shame followed
that. His brother's reproach turned out to be prophetic.

Edicts against the Johannites

One of the priests, Atticus,[388] was chosen to succeed Arsacius;
he was the chief ringleader against John. Once he realized that none
of the eastern bishops were in communion with him, not even the laity of Constantinople, because of the illegal and uncanonical proceedings, he prepared to force those who were not in communion
with him, being himself ignorant of Holy Scriptures, by rescripts instead.[389] The edict against the bishops contained this threat: "If any
of the bishops is not in communion with Theophilus and
Porphyrius[390] and Atticus, he should be expelled from the Church
and his private property should be confiscated."

Some of them, weighed down by the circumstances, did communicate, however unwillingly; the poorer ones, less strong in their
faith, were inclined to communicate when they were enticed with
the promises of bribes. But there were those who looked askance at
high birth, possessions, pride of country, glory which vanishes, or
even bodily harm; they kept their integrity by flight, ever mindful of
the message of the Gospel: *And when they shall persecute you in this city,
flee into another.*[391] They were also thinking over that passage in Proverbs: *Riches shall not profit in the day of revenge.*[392] Some went to Rome,
others went to the mountains, still others betook themselves to the
monasteries of the ascetics, saving themselves from the Jewish fury.

The edict against the laity urged that: " . . . dignitaries are to be
demoted from their high position, soldiers are to lose their girdles,[393]
the rest of the civilians, including the craftsmen, are to be heavily
fined and then banished."[394]

Nevertheless, the prayers of the faithful continued to be offered up in the open air[395] and they suffered much since they were friends of the Savior[396] who said: *I am the Way and the Truth;*[397] and again: *Have confidence, I have overcome the world.*[398]

Chrysostom transferred to Arabissus

The blessed John lived at Cucusus for a year and he fed a good many poor of Armenia[399] during a great famine; I mean not so much with grain but with spiritual discourse.[400] The fratricides were filled with jealousy at him because of this and they transferred him to Arabissus,[401] exposing him to various discomforts so that he might depart this life. Here once more he shone not a little by reason of his virtues (for *a city set on a hill cannot be hid,*[402] nor can a clearly burning lamp be concealed under a measure).[403] He stirred up the whole surrounding country from the sleep of ignorance and from the depths of unbelief to the rays of the Word.

The persecution of Chrysostom continues

The adherents of Severianus and Porphyry were consumed with an even greater fire of iniquity, and some of the bishops of Syria laid plans to have John transferred again to some other place. For he was troublesome to them not only under conditions considered as prosperous, but much more so when he fell into evil circumstances. They were foolishly disposed to acknowledge the nature of trials, not remembering the divine message to the Apostle when he was overcome with tribulations: *My grace is sufficient for you; for my power is made perfect in infirmity.*[404] For they perceived the Church of Antioch being transplanted to the Church of Armenia and the pleasing philosophy[405] of John chanted there was wafted back again to the Church of Antioch, and these wretches sought to cut off his life.[406] They were stung by these reports as by a cutting whip (evil-loving hatred operates at such a high pitch); their followers noticed this and said in amazement:

"Only look at this powerful dead man throwing fear into the living, especially the rulers, as hobgoblins do with children! Great wonders! Look at these men endowed with all worldly power and supported by the wealth of the Church, with authority and control of affairs in their power, filled with fear and trembling, and becoming pale and even writhing at the priest who is all alone, exiled, sick, and deprived of all power!"[407]

Chrysostom goes to Pityus

Finally they could keep the serpent hidden in their tent no longer,[408] so they sent off to the capital and produced another rescript, one more violent than the earlier one: John was to be transferred to Pityus, a deserted place in Tzane lying on the shore of the Black Sea.[409] The soldiers of the praetorian prefect guarded him and rushed him along at high speed, saying that those were their instructions. Should he die on the way before arrival, the officers would receive a promotion. One of the soldiers who thought less of success in the present thought that he might secretly show John a certain kindness. But the other was so uncouth and ill-tempered that he considered it as acts of insolence if anyone approached him asking for special consideration of the saint. He had but one desire, to bring about John's death as miserably as possible. For example, he started out without consideration in the midst of a tempestuous rainstorm, so that streams of water ran down his back and chest. On another occasion the extreme heat of the sun must have been the occasion of delight to this man who knew full well that John suffered from it, because he was bald like Elisha.[410] Should they come to a city or town where there was the refreshment of a bath, the wretched man would not allow even a moment's delay. Thus it was a most difficult journey of three months.[411] But John kept on like a shining star despite these hardships, his emaciated body being as though it were an apple turning ripe in the sun on the topmost branch of the tree.

John dies in exile

They neared Comana,[412] but they bypassed it using a bridge and they stayed outside the wall in the shrine of a martyr five or six miles from the city. And that very night there appeared the ghost of the martyr of the place, Basiliscus[413] who had been bishop of Comana and was martyred under Maximianus[414] in Nicomedia along with Lucianus,[415] a priest of Antioch in Bithynia.

The vision spoke:[416] "Have courage, brother, tomorrow we shall be together."

They say that he had first called to the priest who was staying with him: "Make ready the place for brother John, for he is coming."

John accepted this as a reliable oracle for the morrow and calling them together he bade them remain until the fifth hour. They did not believe him and marched on, and when they had gone about thirty stades[417] they returned to the martyr's shrine they had left as John had an acute attack. Once arrived he asked for white clothes[418]—something more becoming his life—and taking off what he had previously worn he calmly[419] changed everything except his shoes. What was left over he gave to those present.

Then having taken the communion of the Lord's dispensation[420] he offered his last prayer using his usual formula: "Glory to God for all things." Then he signed himself at the last Amen. *He raised up his feet*,[421] those beautiful feet[422] that hastened for the salvation of those who choose repentance and for chastising those who cultivate sin so freely. (If measures of reproof were of no benefit to the wicked, it was surely no fault of him who had spoken out in such downright fashion,[423] but rather it was the fault of those who did not heed his words.)

Chrysostom buried in a martyr's shrine

So John was *gathered to his fathers*,[423a] shaking the dust from off his feet[424] and passing over to Christ, as is written: *"You shall come to your grave in ripe old age, as a shock of grain comes up to the threshing floor in its season,*[425] *but the souls of the trangressors shall die before their time."*[426]

There was such a crowd of virgins and ascetics and those who gave witness by their holiness of life from Syria, Cilicia, Pontus, and Armenia that many thought they had been brought together by warrant. He was buried then with appropriate ceremony.[427] His poor body was buried, victorious athlete that he was, in the same shrine as was Basiliscus.

CHAPTER 12
CHRYSOSTOM'S HABITS OF LIFE DEFENDED

The 'Cyclopean meals'

Theodore was amazed at all this and he asked about it, quoting the words of Scripture:

Deacon: Since it is written: *Neglect not the recital of elders for they also have learned from their fathers,*[428] please tell me now without restraint what was the reason for his eating alone, and if it is true as they say that he ate by himself.

Bishop: Yes,[429] he ate alone.—I should prefer that you, well bred as you are, Theodore, would not keep putting questions to me like a pack of greedy children. For you are grown to man's estate and it is more fitting for you to ask about the virtues which pertain to man, how was he disposed to courage, wealth, moderation. Now as regards his own person, tell us of his gentleness and sense of justice, almsgiving, sagacity in practical matters, manliness, his memory or his forgetfulness. *But meat does not commend us to God,*[430] whether we should eat or should not eat, but it is knowledge in cooperation with activity.[431]

Chrysostom did eat alone

He certainly did eat alone. This I know in part at least for these reasons.[432] To begin with, he drank no wine because of the heat which it brought to his head. But in hot weather he took some rose water. In the second place, his stomach did not function properly due to some ailment or another, so that he often found the food prepared for him unappetizing and asked for something else. Then, too, it happened that at times he simply forgot to eat and put it off until evening, either because he was embroiled in ecclesiastical matters or because he was engrossed in meditation on spiritual subjects, for he struggled to miss nothing of the meaning of Holy Scripture. It is fitting that those engaged in such studies partake of no food at all or very little at the most. It is the custom for your elegant spongers to bring a friend to make sure there is someone with whom he may gorge and tipple and cackle in unseemly mirth. He takes the warm cup with the tips of his fingers and turns good table companionship into an occasion for slanderous gossip.

Chrysostom considered himself as steward of the Church

But I think the whole and more truthful explanation was this: he was excessively thrifty in dealing with men of dainty life and he considered it a sacrilege to expend money on such. At the same time, he removed the incentive for stealth among the stewards so they could not multiply by ten the expenses of the food, thereby getting for themselves what belonged to the poor. In addition to these reasons, he considered the multitude in the city with due deliberation and thought that as a steward of Christ he should look upon everyone, no matter what his rank, as worthy to eat along with him or else he should grant that honor to no one.

He had observed the bad behavior at table and the amount of the outlay on the poor, and he shuddered at the whole business, bidding great farewell to such abuses, repeating to himself the words of Acts: "Men and brothers, it is not right that we should serve at table; but let us appoint men to this task who are worthy; let us give over our time to the Word and to prayer."[433]

The table a source for sin

Just as the champion horse no longer able to race about the stadium is relegated to the mill where he trudges round and round in an endless circle, so it is with a teacher when too weary to impart lessons of virtue. He then casts out the net of the dining table; would that it were among the hungry and the needy from whom he might win the blessing of the Lord: *For I was hungry and you gave me to eat.*[434] But if it is only to hear good things spoken about himself by those in power, or glory that fades all too soon, or a return invitation, or simply in order to avoid being called a skinflint, that man is not mindful of the woeful curse of the Lord: *Woe to you when men shall bless you.*[435] He did not say "the poor" but "men"—*for according to these things did their fathers to the false prophets.*[435]

My dear Theodore, let us not seek for the fame of a false prophet as do the lovers of vainglory. *For John came neither eating nor drinking, in the way of righteousness and they say: "He has a devil." The Son of man came eating and drinking and they say: "Behold a man that is a wine-drinker, a friend of publicans and sinners."*[436]

Hospitality to be practiced with discretion

Deacon: Dear father, it was not at all to blame or run down such austerity that I pursued the inquiry for your precise definition. For I knew the character of the man from reports on him and also from writings which have come down to us, both homilies and letters.[437] It was in order to learn what he stood for so that I could imitate his many actions. Now who could be so utterly insensate as not to realize that one loses more at table than one gains, unless one happens to play the host to saints in their need?

Bishop: And I made all this perfectly clear to you, most zealous friend of the truth, Theodore, not to underrate the virtue of the fathers and especially that of their good hospitality. For it is one of the remaining virtues conducive to piety which the lord of patriarchs practiced. One trapped by his table the Savior God;[438] another was host to the angels.[439] The former was given a son-in-law in his old age;[440] the latter obtained deliverance from Sodom along with his daughter as a reward.[441] The Apostle also speaks of them, encouraging us to imitate them:[442] *Do not neglect to show hospitality to strangers, for thereby some have entertained angels unawares.*[442]

Now the host must have the cunning of a serpent, but the guilelessness of a dove,[443] and he must pay attention to both precepts: *Give to every one who begs from you*[444] and *Do not bring every man into your home,*[445] lest he receive a wolf instead of a sheep, or a bear instead of an ox, selling off his gain for a loss. First of all, it would be helpful for him to examine the place where a man has been placed, whether it be a deserted place or a populous one. Then he should consider how he is situated to act as host; is he the sort who can put up with strange customs? And he should use judgment in regard to the one who claims his service—be he rich or poor, well or sick, in need of food or clothing. It is in these very things that effective charity operates.

A priest must be moderate in hospitality

Now the blessed Abraham did not give hospitality to governors or generals or men of power in the world about him, those who boasted of horses glittering with their halters and bits, or of Persian trousers[446] with bronze bells attached to noise far and wide the clamor of high conceit. And Abraham inhabited a desert place and he received those who came there.[447] They came to their patriarch across the desert, drawn there by the fame of his virtue or by their own poverty. [Now poverty is the mean between excess and deficiency; the excess of riches and the deficiency of begging.][448]

Now Lot lived in a city worse than a desert and he befriended strangers passing through because of the inhospitable inhabitants.[449] But if one lives in a well-regulated city, as, for example, Constantinople, in which all are in a sense guest-masters, it is quite possible that some priests *neglect the ministry of the Word*[450] and busy themselves with food-accounts. Such persons forget themselves and become hotel-keepers instead of teachers by watering down their doctrine, and pure knowledge vanishes. So the reproach of the prophet is earned: *Your inn-keepers mingle the wine with water.*[451]

Just as there is all the difference in the world between wine and water for the weary, so much does teaching surpass inn-keeping. In the one case a man benefits his fellow citizens, in the other he helps posterity; the one does good to those who are now here, the other benefits those who are to come. One helps those present by conversation, those who are to come can be reached by writing. Of such was our Savior in the flesh. He fed five thousand men, not in the city but in the desert;[452] He taught those who were there with His own lips,[453] but He saved the world through the Gospel writings.[454] This is to be said especially for the words of men who carry the Spirit.

There are foods for the body and foods for the soul

Do not be astonished, Theodore, if a man should fill the hungry with food, but rather when he frees the soul from ignorance. The former fills the belly with bread and vegetables either for money or freely, and such are easily found when the need arises. But rarely is one found who nourishes with the Word, and when he is found, he is either not believed at all or believed with difficulty. Evil spirits work hard against the salvation of souls. It was the famine of the teaching of the Word that the Lord God threatened to send in punishment, and He spoke to his prophet: *I shall send forth a famine upon them, not a famine of bread and of water but a famine of hearing the Word of the Lord.*[455] And in regard to a famine which is perceived by the senses, one must leave the city or country which lacks food and go to another place to be saved as the holy patriarchs did when they went down to Egypt from Palestine.[456] And in regard to famine of mental food, which happens to churches only when teachers are lacking, as the Prophet says again: *They will run from the east to the west, seeking the Word of God, and they will not find it.*[457]

The Old Testament against high living

For what good is there that does not naturally come from teaching? What evil is not to be found as a result of excessive eating and drinking? There are diseases, quarrels, upset stomach,[458] and the rest of ills. When was Eve dispelled from Paradise? Was it not when she partook of the fruit of the tree at the advice of the serpent, not being satisfied with the available food?[459] When did Cain commit the terrible sin of fratricide? Was it not when he was the first to partake of the firstfruits, keeping them for himself in his greediness?[460] When did the children of Job suddenly find their table a grave? Was it not when they were eating and drinking?[461] When did Esau lose the blessing? Was it not when he became a slave to his belly, outwitted by a trick?[462] When was Saul deprived of his kingdom? Was it not when he consumed the finest of his sheep, going against the law?[463] When did the people of Israel provoke their God to anger? Was it not when they yearned after the tables of Egypt and begged the teacher for meat and caldrons?[464] Now as regards Hophni and Phineas, the sons of Eli, why were they killed in one hour in war? Was it not because they used to take meat intended for the sacrifice out of the caldron with flesh-hooks?[465] What of Jacob the blameable, why did he "kick"? Was it not after he had grown *fat and thick and gross?*[466] When did the Sodomites run riot against nature? Was it not when they had beclouded their judgment by continual drinking,[467] and are so referred to by Ezechiel saying in anger: *In abundance of wine and fullness of bread they lusted themselves* (that is, the city) *and her daughters* [468] (that is, the villages, which always imitate the city)? When did the ancients lose the principle of moderation anyhow? Was it not about the time when they had grown old on their couches?[469] The prophet bitterly complains: *Those who eat the lambs out of the flock and sucking calves out of the stalls, who drink strained wine, and anoint themselves with the finest ointments, and they are not grieved over the affliction of Joseph.*[470]

To whom did Isaias apply the curse of woe? Was it not for those who arise early to drink? He spoke as follows: *Woe to those who rise up early and follow strong drink, who tarry late into the night, for wine shall inflame them; for with the harp and the lute, they drink wine, but they do not regard the work of the Lord.*[471]

When were the priests of Bel put to shame by Daniel? Was it not when they were betrayed by the dust and proved guilty by their food and drinking?[472] But why should I say more about those who chose the broad highway and reviled the narrow path?[473] The word of the Savior is proof enough for me to indict the meat-hunters, as He did in the scriptural text where He shows the unnamed rich man who was such a good liver while he was alive, begging the poor man Lazarus for a crust of bread and a drop of water and getting nothing.[474] Let us look at the choir of the saints of old and learn what kind of teaching they practiced. Was it by a revered life and ordered speech, or was it by drinking bouts and sumptuous banquets? Enoch was the first to be translated; was it because of his faith or his drinking parties?[475] Then, too, Noah saved the whole human race by faith in the wooden ark[476] that time the world was purified. I ask you, was it through a program of drinking parties and impure actions that this was accomplished, or was it by fasting and prayers?[477] Then when he took a little liquid refreshment after that great flood, is it not true that

Holy Scripture records his nakedness and disgrace rather than his honor?[478] The blessed Abraham conquered the five kings at Sodom and preserved Lot; did this come about by faith and justice or was it by eating and drinking?[479]

And Theodore spoke up:

Deacon: If you are bringing in Abraham, will you not listen also to me? Someone is going to tell you that he won the war by faith, but actually he tricked God by the table, as you yourself took it in your explanation.

Bishop: Dear me! Since Abraham trapped God by means of the table should we not all abandon faith and the other virtues and organize drinking bouts? In that case we would differ not one bit from inn-keepers and hotel managers who put up shop along the way for the sake of profit. And take virgins now, striving to be holy in body and spirit for the glory of God, they should bear children as Mary bore Christ.[480] If they did that, then they would differ in no way from common harlots. If teachers must accommodate themselves to the pleasures of the table because Abraham did so for the Lord, then virgins should bear offspring since Mary did so. Away with that notion, most highly honored friend! Let us not despise what was done at a proper time and place previously, or is still being done, for each one is well aware of the proper course of action, if only he is willing to do it.

More examples drawn from the Old Testament

To resume our argument, did Jacob the wrestler[481] take away the goods of Laban by his austerity, or was it rather by indulging in drinking bouts?[482] He said: *I was consumed by the heat and by the frost at night and sleep departed from me,*[483] and except for bread and clothes he asked for nothing more while in prayer: *If you will give me bread to eat and clothing to put on, of everything that you give me I will give to you the tenth part.*[484] He did not say: "I will spend it on tables."

Take Moses now, that spokesman and faithful servant of God,

what sort of table did he spread the time he gathered the people together on the mountain?[485] What kind of drinking goblets did he
have? He melted the rock with his staff because the people did not
believe.[486] He was the guide for six hundred thousand men from
Egypt;[487] he erected the Tables of the Law to guide the people in the
way of truth.[488] Now, I ask you, was it sky-blue goblets and sowbelly
and Phasian fowl[489] or was it fish from the deep sea, well-seasoned
Tyrian wine, and white loaves[490] that he placed before those he
would teach? Or was it merely words?

Deacon: But, father, somebody will give you this answer: "Give me
manna[491] also and the same water, and I will seek nothing more."

Bishop: And who would be so blunt of wit as to prefer material manna
and water from the spring to spiritual instruction?[492] Then take Samuel. He was a teacher of the people, and after twenty-five years in se-
clusion at Armathem, did he ever turn anyone away from the
worship of idols at table and not by the word?[493] When did the king
who was likewise prophet and psalmist[494] ever set a sumptuous table,
he who said: *For I did eat ashes like bread, and mingled my drink with
weeping.*[495]

Elias the Thesbite caused a fast to be made over the whole world
and he made the greedy go short of food against their will for three
years and six months; what kind of table did he use to win them from
their faults?[496] What kind of cooks did he have? Did he not receive his
daily bread from crows?[497]

That wise Daniel who foresaw the future, what kind of table did
he prepare for the Assyrians? Was it not by fasting and prayer that
he killed the dragon and vanquished Bel, muzzled the lions, and persuaded the king to renounce the gods of his fathers[498] by confession of
the God who really is?[499]

What tables and what kind of dainty food did the choir of the
rest of the prophets or apostles use? Were they not teachers? Was not
everything under the heavens entrusted to them? Are we not their
successors? Does not the Word desire us to imitate them and observe
their ways as Paul teaches when he says: *Imitate their faith, considering
the end of these conversations.*[500] What kind of honey cakes had John the
Baptist, the herald of repentance[501] in the desert? Not only did he not

prepare meals for those who visited him, but he gave them a bitter reception with his reproaches. His piercing looks not only shook up[502] their befouled consciences, but his very appearance and his words cut away the abscesses of their souls like a great knife.[503]

You brood of vipers! Who warned you to flee from the wrath to come? Bear therefore fruits worthy of penance.[504] And do not depend on baptism alone or on the fact that you are children of Abraham.[505]

The teaching of Paul considered

Then we come to the Apostle to the Gentiles,[506] who abolished circumcision[507] so that he might establish the circumcision of faith,[508] Paul, *the vessel of election.*[509] Is he to be found giving up all his time together to the table? Debtor he was to be sure, but this was the last of those debts.[510] Does he owe it to the unbelieving Gentiles to share at table with them as soon as possible?[511] Now what does he write to Timothy, bishop of Ephesus? *Attend* to the luxury of your table, or: *to reading, to exhortation, and to teaching.*[512]

(The blessed John was especially untiring and vigorous in these very things.) He kept saying: *Be urgent in season and out of season, convince, rebuke, and exhort.*[513] (No one could object that two of these modes of address are bitter and the third is pleasant enough, nor could anyone claim that the third is brought in with a certain amount of leniency. The very bitter *convince, rebuke* are connected with *exhort* and not *flatter.* Now exhortation which is made with understanding is more bitter to your pleasure-seekers and to the down-and-out should they find them more burdensome. For there the soul may be opposed to conviction under the stress of some emotion and may be indifferent to what is said. Then exhortation, provided only that it be easily and gradually offered in a kind and trusting fashion, is as it were refined in a slow fire and so cut into pieces.)[514]

What does Paul mean speaking thus to Timothy? Is it of drinking-bouts and festivities or does he speak of the revered accounts[515] of his tribulations? He said: *You have fully known my manner of life.*[516] In that manner I managed in my presentation with heartful purpose to work for the glory of God.[517] In all his convincing of error, is there ever a mention of the table?

Now let us see what message he sends to Titus, bishop of Crete,[518] whether the matter under discussion is in regard to food and drink or to conviction and teaching. He says: *For this reason I left you in Crete, that you should set in order the things that are wanting . . . that you might charge some not to teach otherwise, not to give heed to fables and endless genealogies.*[519] And he said in addition the manner of reproof: *Cretans are always liars, evil beasts, lazy gluttons.*[520]

Now let them tell us, those belly-worshippers and master trenchermen and lecherous women-hunters[521] who rail against John's ascetic way of life, where does one find drinking commended anywhere in the Old and New Testament? Granted it is mentioned when dealing with an alien people as a sign of peace, for like beasts they live by the law of the table.

Moderation its own reward

When did drinking bouts lead to anything but sin? Why should I say "sin" rather than "greater idolatry and murder of brothers," as it has been written: *. . . the people sat down to eat and drink and they rose up to play.*[522] Play, then, was the offspring of drunkenness: *Come, we shall make gods who will go before us.*[523] They were so uprooted by the wine that they sought gods who could be moved about, and they abandoned God who is Himself unmoved and performs all things without making a step. What does the prophet say: *The priest's lips shall guard law, and they shall seek the word from his mouth, for he is a messenger of the Lord*[524] —and not a cook.

And what about the tower in Chalanne,[525] when was it built? Was it before or after the wine-drinking? Was it not after wine when Noah had set out the vine-cuttings and was the first to reap the fruit of shame?[526] If this is so it was not from drinking or from vine cultivation, but from immoderation. When was Joseph sold off by his brothers? Was it while they were busily shepherding their flocks, or was it when they were butchering and eating the best of the sheep in luxurious idleness and meditating mischief against their brother in their drinking bout?[527] When did they bring in the head of John the Baptist on a platter for the young harlot? Was it at a convocation of wise men or at a drunken brawl of the lawless?[528] Take the blessed

Paul now. Did he keep up his speaking while eating and drinking until midnight, or was it not in fasting and teaching and leading to the faith those who did not know God?[529]

Now we come to the Chief Shepherd, the chief Teacher, the chief Wise Man, Jesus the Christ, He who is Corrector of error common to all mankind—where is He to be found eating in a city except at the passion?[530] But this was the fulfillment of the mysteries.[531] And what is He found saying to His own overanxious disciples? Is it about food or reading? *Labor not*, he says, *for the meat that perishes, but for that which endures.*[532]

Chrysostom not interested in food

Then the good John may well say with the Lord: "My drinking bout is the instruction and spreading of the Word; for this I was called for the salvation of the people."

Meat does not commend us to God, neither if we eat it, nor if we do not eat it.[533] For this is the custom among the Gentiles: to entice by means of the table those whom they wish to entrap; since they cannot persuade them by speech, they say: *Let us eat and drink, for tomorrow we shall die.*[534]

The Apostle directs a more offensive correction on them as he says: *Be not seduced. Evil communications corrupt good manners.*[535] When he says "evil communications," he means the talking that revolves about these things.

CHAPTER 13
CHRYSOSTOM'S ACTIONS DEFENDED

Bishops are no exception

Deacon: What you said was done sincerely and with much learning as well as it should be. *Woe unto him who calls sweet bitter and bitter sweet. Woe unto him who puts darkness for light and light for darkness.*[536] Still someone will say: "We do not maintain this at all, that John was given over to tables such as these." For unbridled ambition is the root of the love of pleasure,[537] but stinginess carried to extreme is proof of a small mind. True, he could have invited only bishops, and the more devout of them especially, or if not these, he might have invited his own clergy in imitation of our Lord when He ate with the twelve apostles.[538]

Bishop: You have raised the most convincing arguments, most truth-loving man, if the clergy had been satisfied to partake of a meal with John, even if it were an hour or even a day late.[539] They wished to have a great feast with all the trimmings served up at once. It would have been unthinkable to spend lavishly the food of the sick or poor in providing the healthy with a banquet. What kind of a law would this be that the learners would lay down the law for the teacher, the sick would prescribe for the physician, or those aboard ship would tell off the pilot? Is it not always the other way, the doctor cures the sick, the teacher sets the students on the proper path, the pilot woos[540] the safety of the passengers? Now those who are anxious to enjoy life are fully confident in the doctor or the pilot, and they willingly undergo every pain and hardship even though the outcome is uncertain. To the teacher of better things is entrusted the business of expelling sicknesses and disease, and he has been trained to overcome a whole flood of overpowering passion. Yet some oppose him with uncontrolled tongues and stir up everything with unwashed feet.[541]

If John had given himself over to the tables, how many worthwhile people could he have satisfied, living as he did in such a great city with everyone expecting to dine with him, either to get his blessing or because they were poor or even because he was greedy? When would he have had leisure for meditation on God? What of his ministry to his people, his study of the Holy Scriptures, the looking after widows? Who would have given time to young virgins, or cared for the sick, or helped those in distress, or turned back those who were wandering astray, or shown sympathy for the down-and-out, or looked after those in prison? How could he have escaped Ezekiel's most awful curse of God: *Woe unto the shepherds who feed themselves and do not feed the flock! You did not bring back that which had strayed; that which was lost you did not seek, the weak you did not visit, that which was broken you did not bind up; the fatlings you killed and ate.*[542]

Paul writes of these: *You bear with a man, if he brings you into bondage, if he devours you, if he takes you captive.*[543] *And you clothe yourselves with the wool, but you do not feed the flock.*[544] Jeremiah speaks of shepherds too lazy to pasture their flocks: *Many shepherds have destroyed my vineyard.*[545]

A priest's good reputation

The deacon speaks:

Deacon: After a while he could have also served those people and still attended to his ecclesiastical duties. In this way he would not have appeared to have a bad reputation, seeing he was so great in other respects.

Bishop: This is what the priest should seek for, so as not to have a bad reputation: to have full range for his speech, his earnestness and zeal, and the other priestly prerequisites. Now do you not realize, my most honored Theodore, that one of the beatitudes among those set down by our Lord has to do with unjust statements? *Blessed are you when they shall revile you and persecute you and speak all that is evil against you.*[546] *Woe to you when men shall bless you, for so their fathers did to the false prophets.*[547]

How could the mouth trained in divine precepts and the ear accustomed to hear divine oracles participate in idle table-talk when the Lord says: *No man can serve two masters*, and He continues: *You cannot serve God and mammon.*[548]

But first let us make a search into the meaning of mammon, lest we find ourselves not even serving those two masters, but mammon only. Now mammon does not mean the devil, but rather the vain things of this world, which the Word would remove from His disciples.

The true priest works for eternity

Deacon: Come back, most reverend father, to the rest of your narrative. Your demonstration about the matter of the tables has been quite adequate. Please do not get irritated at my objections. I have only wanted to learn more so I kept asking you in greater detail of your abundant learning.

Bishop: That may be very nicely said of you, too, Theodore, most eager lover of learning.[549] (I was myself once one of those most eager to please the mob at the table.) Now a bishop, especially if he is in a large city, *having abandoned the ministry of the Word,*[550] who does not have in his hands day and night the tablets of the Law and should delegate another to look after the poor, is far different from those who said: *Behold we have left all things and followed You. What then shall we have?*[551] Such a one must be numbered among those who said: "Lord, did we not do so-and-so in Your name?"[552] Then he will hear along with them: *Depart from me, you cursed;*[553] *I do not know where you come from.*[554] For the Word does not recognize wordless workers.[555] His eye is too pure to look upon evil things.[556]

Now many of your so-called bishops are desirous to rid themselves of the well-deserved hate which they had earned, and they simply exchange one evil for another: covetousness for vainglory? This is because of their own character and their lack of zeal in spiritual matters. With one hand they do wrong in lavish fashion for the sake of shameful gain, and with the other they deck out sumptuous tables and rear pillars for lofty buildings.[557] In this way they gain a reputation for being good and industrious workers and reap honor instead of dishonor, forgetful of the Ecclesiast who built great edifices and hated them and was really opposed to them when he wrote: *I built myself houses and gardens* —and so on—*and behold, all was vanity. And I hated all my labor, wherein I labor under the sun.*[558]

Note that he did not say over the sun, for by that he would have been downgrading spiritual toil. I say this not in condemnation of those who build a necessary edifice in good taste or improve church property. I refer to those who squander money that rightly belongs to the poor in hanging walls and water cisterns three stories high and disgraceful baths for effeminate men all hidden away, or those who expend their money on buildings uselessly. Sometimes it is a pretext to obtain more money or make a good impression upon their favorite pets—in other words, all is sacrificed to please sinners. Far be it from me, O famous Theodore, that I should ever strive to please such evil people, for I should in no way please them except by not being pleasing to Christ.

John accused of deposing sixteen bishops

The deacon was greatly astonished at this and spoke up:

Deacon: What you have said makes perfect sense and I have no objection. But if you know anything at all of the doings of the holy John while in Asia, please share it with me. After all, this whole *Dialogue* concerns John.

Bishop: Yes, I surely do.

Deacon: Were you there yourself or have you learned it from another?

Bishop: No one told me; I was not absent from a single session of the trial.

Deacon: Please tell me exactly what happened; how it began and how it ended. Especially since Theophilus claimed in his indictment that the blessed John was so power-drunk that he deposed sixteen bishops[559] in one day and then proceeded to ordain men of his own choice to take their places. Actually Theophilus was anxious to dignify his own thoughtless conduct and so glorify himself.

Bishop: This wonderful Theophilus did nothing unexpected when you only consider his character. He not only wrote against John, but what he wrote was all lies. He thought by those means to conceal his own shame but actually he made it into an example and so unwittingly proved that John was innocent as was the case of Balaam.[560] For if he deposed him, it was not necessary to indict or exile him, since the disgrace of deposition is sufficient punishment for the deposed person. But since the virtuous man stood steadfast and unsubdued he obtained victory by that very defeat, but the envy of that victory remains the carrying off of the defeat of a senseless victory. But Theophilus blew himself up like a great bubble boiling over inside himself, writing tracts and detractions.[561] This is what Isaiah meant when he cried woe to those who take every opportunity of making, telling, and writing lies: *Woe to those who write*, says he, *for they write iniquity.*[562]

Eusebius accuses Antoninus

Now in regard to the number of bishops in Asia deposed by John, it was not sixteen, but rather six. This I assert as though at God's seat of judgment. I shall not subtract from the quantity of the number nor add to the quality of his actions; as the case is, so shall I tell it. In the thirteenth year of the indiction[563] some bishops arrived in Constantinople from Asia on business, and they had some other bishops with them also, Theotimus[564] of Scythia, one from Thrace, Ammon[565] the Egyptian, and one from Galatia, Arabianus.[566] They were all metropolitans, advanced in years; the total number of bishops was twenty-two. When they were all gathered together in communion[567] a certain Eusebius[568] from a town called Kilbia, bishop of Valentinopolis,[569] took advantage of the occasion and presented memoranda before the synod on the first day of the week. These were directed against Antoninus,[570] bishop of Ephesus, and of course he had prefixed the name of John to follow the precedent.[571] The charges were listed under seven headings:

First, that Antoninus had melted down church plate of silver and deposited the proceeds to the account of his own son.

Second, that he had taken away marble from the entrance to the baptistry and installed it in his own private bath.

Third, that he set up pillars which had belonged to the church for many years in his own dining hall.

Fourth, that a servant of his had committed murder and was kept in his service and never brought to trial.

Fifth, that he had sold lands left to the church by Basilina,[572] the mother of Emperor Julian,[573] and appropriated the money for his own use.

Sixth, that after parting from his wife he had again had relations with her and they had children afterward.[574]

Seventh, that he considered it law and dogma to sell episcopal consecration at prices proportionate to the position.—And there are here present persons who have paid such money and been consecrated, as well as the person who accepted the money, and I have proofs of all these transactions.

CHAPTER 14
ANTONINUS IS TRIED AT EPHESUS

Bishop John presides

Deacon: I beg you, father, please finish off your narrative for the company[575] here present is hurt to hear such talk about bishops, let alone that bishops actually do such things.

Bishop: Woe is me that I should see these days the priesthood being bought with money, if indeed it is a sacred office under these circumstances. *I have been a fool,*[576] prattling on about John's accusers who have brought us to this state of affairs.

But just be patient with me, so that you may admire John's reasonableness which he showed in these circumstances in overcoming his feelings for the time being. He said to Eusebius: "Brother Eusebius, since accusations made under stress do not easily admit of proof, please refrain from entering written charges against brother Antoninus, as we shall correct the cause of your grievance."

Eusebius persists in his charges

He became excited at these remarks and used rough language; he went into a tantrum against Antoninus and persisted in making accusations against him. John then called upon Paul of Heracleia[577] (for he seemed to be in favor of Antoninus) so that he might reconcile them. He arose and entered the church (for it was time for the sacrifice) along with the other bishops, and he gave the people the usual salutation of peace[578] and seated himself with the other bishops. But

Eusebius the accuser had entered the church unnoticed and presented another memorandum before the bishops and the people.
This contained the same charges and he swore at John with fearful
oaths, including even "by the salvation of Their Majesties." He
raised such a commotion that the laity was thrown into panic at his
brashness and thought he was urging John to beg the emperor for remission of the death penalty. Now John observing the intensity of
the man strove to keep the people quiet and did accept the document,
and after the reading of the heavenly oracle he called on Bishop Pansophius of Pisidia to bring forth the gifts. John then withdrew with
the other bishops, for he had an objection to offering the Holy Sacrifice with an uneasy mind according to the Gospel precept: *When you
bring your gifts,*[579] and so forth.

John addresses Eusebius

Once the people had been dismissed, John carefully considered
the matter and sat down in the baptistery with the other bishops. He
called up the accuser and addressed him before the whole assembly:
"I am repeating to you once more that people when vexed or angry
often say and even write down something when their proofs are actually quite ineffective. If, then, you are perfectly certain of the accusations which you are going to bring up (for neither will we reject
them if you are able to prove them, nor will we accept them if proof
is lacking), before reading the memoranda, choose the proper course.
Once the charges are read and heard by the people, and so become a
matter of record, you as bishop will hardly be able to request a with-
drawal of the charges."[580]

After this Eusebius still persisted in his frenzy, and they urged
that the memoranda made under the seven headings mentioned
above should be read again.

A charge of simony

When they had heard the purport of the memoranda, the older
bishops said to John: "At the very least, each one of the headings is to
be regarded as impious, and however you consider it as against the

sacred canons. But we are of no mind to spend all our time on the less important items; let the investigation begin with the more serious charges. Should they be true, the other items can be easily accounted for. The greatest single item should prove to be at the root of the others. As Scripture said: *The love of money is the root of all evil.*[581] For one who has *taken bribes against the innocent*[582] and considered exchanging for money the distribution of the Holy Spirit, how could he stop at taking plate or stones or any property of the church?"

Then John began the investigation by asking Antoninus: "What do you say about these charges, brother Antoninus?" He was forced to deny them (for how could he admit his disgrace at the very beginning?).

Those who had paid the money were questioned, and they likewise denied it. The carefully planned investigation into these charges lasted until the eighth hour,[583] when a judgment seemed to take shape because of certain points of evidence.

Witnesses are lacking

Finally it came to an end. As it was fitting, it came down to a question of witnesses in regard to who had given bribes and who had received them. But no witnesses were present, though they were badly needed. John perceived the difficulty of arriving at a conclusion; because he wanted to see the Church cleansed and to spare the witnesses, he decided to go to Asia himself. Antoninus perceived that John was untiring and was not to be tempted by bribes, and being aware of his own guilt in the matter he went secretly to those in power and asked them to prevent John's going to Asia. It so happened that this man had been managing some properties for the official.[584] He at once prepared a statement to be sent to Bishop John from the palace as follows: "This business is unthinkable, that you, the bishop and leader of our spiritual welfare, should leave the city at the very time when a great tumult is expected. Imagine, marching off for a long stay in Asia when witnesses could easily be brought here."

It was Gainas,[585] the barbarian, who was about to cause the disturbance.

John does not go to Asia

So what, then? Not to make the story any longer, John was persuaded to remain when he thought over the claims of justice as well
as the friction of the witnesses.[586] This was suitable for the accused,
that is the postponement for the witnesses, as it was possible to drive
them off by bribes or by mere force. John considered with some of
those present at the synod whether to send some of the bishops to
Asia to examine the witnesses.

More delayed action

At once three bishops were chosen to go: Syncletius,[587] metropolitan of Trajanopolis,[588] Hesychius[589] of Parius,[590] and Palladius,
bishop of Helenopolis. After the synod had passed a resolution and entered it into the minutes, that if either of the two litigants did not appear within two months and support his own pleas in Hypoepi, a city
in Asia, he should be excommunicated. (Now that place had been chosen because it was between those to be examined and was easy for the
bishops in company with Syncletius and his companions in the trial.)
Syncletius and Palladius were two of the bishops nominated, and they
went down to Smyrna for Hesychius, a great friend of Antoninus,
who feigned illness as a pretense. They at once wrote to both sides to
notify them of their arrival so that they might meet together without
delay in the city designated and so keep their promises. But they compromised each other,[591] the one side with bribes, the other with oaths,
and they had become friends even before the judges arrived. But they
put on the appearance of having rushed together to Hypoepi and they
thought that they would delude the judges by putting on the appearance of witnesses again, as though they were away from home on various kinds of business. So the judges asked the accuser: "Within how
many days will you bring the accusers? And we expect them." He
thought that they would be vexed at the sultry weather and leave (for
it was the worst of the summer heat).[592]

He promised in writing that he would within forty days either
produce the witnesses or submit to the penalties of canon law. Then

he was released to look for his witnesses; this he failed to do but went to Constantinople and hid there.

Antoninus dies

The judges waited for forty days as agreed, and as he did not appear they sent out letters all over Asia to the bishops proclaiming him excommunicate,[593] either as a deserter or as a false accuser. They kept expecting him for another thirty days and since he did not appear they left the country and went to Constantinople. There they met up with him and reproached him for his brashness. But he again made the excuse of ill health and promised to bring forth the witnesses.

And as they tarried awhile,[594] Antoninus, the defender for Eusebius, died.

Chrysostom invited to Ephesus

Then there came a resolution from Asia from the clergy of Ephesus and from the bishops directed to John. They made a request of him sealed with a solemn oath:

"Since in times past both the laws and we ourselves have been greatly confused, we thereby beg Your Honor to come, please, and lay down an order from God on high to the church of Ephesus.[595] It has been suppressed for a long time, both by those who are sympathetic to the ideas of Arius and by those who declare our own views with greed and love of self. This is especially so as there are many lying in wait like ravenous wolves, only too eager to seize the throne by bribery."

Chrysostom visits Ephesus

Now John was in bad health and it was the stormy time of winter, but he refused to consider the hardships, being mindful only to settle the problems with which the diocese of Asia was burdened because of the lack of experience or absence of shepherds. His zeal bore him up, and he boarded a ship and left the city.[596] A violent storm from the north came upon them and the sailors feared they might be wrecked on the Proconnesus.[597] They set the prow into the oncoming storm and ran under Mount Trito, where they cast anchors and stayed there while waiting for a south wind to reach Apameia. For two days they remained there, rolling about in the ship without food. On the third day they disembarked at Apameia,[598] where Bishops Paul,[599] Cyrinus,[600] and Palladius[601] were waiting for them. (John took them as fellow companions.) They finished the journey to Ephesus on foot and gathered together the bishops of Lydia, Asia, and Caria, amounting to seventy men. Ordination was celebrated[602] and all the bishops met in a very friendly atmosphere, especially those from Phrygia, and they derived great benefit from the words coming from John, as is written: *Wisdom is praised in the streets* (that is, in the speakers) *in the broad places she utters her voice with outspokenness*[603] (that is, in the hearts that have been enlarged through different kinds of hardships, as it is said: *In distress you did enlarge me*).[604] For wisdom is diminished in those who sow cockles and choke up the Word.[605]

Chapter 15
Six Bishops Deposed

Eusebius asks for action

This was the state of affairs when Eusebius, the cause of this long account and accuser of six other bishops, believed himself worthy to be admitted to communion with all the other bishops. Some of the bishops objected[606] on the grounds that a false accuser ought not be so admitted. In addition to this he came as a suppliant, saying: "Since the larger part of the case has been under consideration for two years,[607] and it was adjourned to allow witnesses to be questioned, I implore Your Reverence to God to allow me to produce the witnesses today. For even though Antoninus who received the bribes and proceeded with the ordinations is now dead, still there are those who gave money and were ordained."

The accused bishops confess

The assembled synod ruled that the inquiry be held. It began then with the reading of the minutes of the earlier action. The witnesses came in as well as the six bishops who had paid bribes to be consecrated. At first they denied the accusation, but the witnesses, some of them laity, some priests whom they had trusted, and even some women, all held to their statements. They told of the form of the pledges exchanged, the places, the times, and the amounts.

Finally those bishops with their consciences awakened confessed willingly enough: "Granted we gave bribes and we became bishops in hope that we would become free of civil obligations.[608] Now we beg to be allowed to continue in the ministry of the Church, if it be a holy thing to ask. If that is impossible, may we get back the money we gave? Some of us gave away furniture that belonged to our wives."

The synod passes sentence

John answered the synod in regard to those things: "With the help of God I shall set them free from the duties of the council chamber, asking the emperor for that favor. But you must order them to recover from the heirs of Antoninus the money they paid."

The synod ordered that they recover the money from the heirs of Antoninus, and that they must communicate within the sanctuary and were no longer to function as priests. There was fear that should they be compromised, a custom might come into fashion of selling and buying the priesthood—something worthy of Jews or Egyptians. Now they say that the destructive and falsely named patriarch[609] of the Jews changed the office of head of the synagogue every year, or at least every other year, for the purpose of collecting money. Likewise the patriarch of Egypt (Theophilus) is a worthy imitator of that man, so the prophecy might be fulfilled: *Her priests have taught for hire, and her prophets divined for money.*[610]

Fate of the condemned bishops

There are minutes of all these proceedings and also the names of the judges. The investigation did not take place in a single day, as Theophilus had lied about it, but it was drawn out over two years. Those who had been deposed surrendered and were so freed from the judgement that was to come. One of them was appointed to become legal defender of public affairs. In their places were substituted others who were unmarried men presentable in both life and speech. And so those men, so noble and quarrelsome after John's exile, got what they had coming to them (for this evil has no name[611] just as it has no existence).[612] They let into the Church again those who had been cast out four years earlier, but they thrust out those who had been canonically enthroned, thus scattering the sheep of Christ.

Ephesus receives a new bishop

Now, my dear learned Theodore, there followed the most laughable thing of all, but it is a matter for weeping rather than joy. The prophet says: *Both your ears shall tingle*[613] should you hear it. But since you are a lover of God,[614] you will weep at the sight of bishops carrying on as madmen and disgracing the gifts of Christ with darkened hands.[615] Now Peter and John[616] administered ordinations with fastings, prayer, much deliberation, and even with fear, but they on the other hand did so with debauchery, drunkeness, miserable bribes. Look at the men they ordained, miscarriages of men,[617] not fit to be placed with senseless pigs or dogs, as was foretold by Job from the mouth of the Savior . . . *whom I thought not worthy of the dogs of our flocks, who lived beneath the briars*[618] Then these companions of mummers and of Jews are entrusted with the ineffable mysteries[619] of the priesthood as though they were friends of the Savior.[620]

Hence the laity of orthodox persuasion stays clear of the houses of prayer. For this new and despicable form of derring-do has really spread from the church of Ephesus even to our shores. Why not? Ephesus is located on the sea and rumors spread very easily. For in the place of—rather, I should say, in the place of John who wrote the Gospel, that loyal disciple who leaned upon the bosom of Wisdom, whom Scripture calls *the one whom Jesus loved*,[621] he was succeeded by Timothy, the disciple of Paul to whom are addressed two epistles of Paul, to this succeeds the *abomination of desolation*.[622]

For they had consecrated and enthroned Victor,[623] the tribune who was a eunuch,[624] and they cast into prison the bishop[625] who had been installed by seventy bishops and who still languishes there. He had been well educated in the liberal arts[626] as well as Holy Scripture and had served three years as a deacon. If only the eunuch whom they had consecrated had spent some time in practicing the ascetic life, the evil would have been but half-bad! But look now at the worm of the earth, slave to his belly, full of lust, fierce, a drunkard, a fornicator, greedy for money, bigoted, covetous, condemned to mutilation[627] from birth, a man without sex, being neither male nor female, a raging maniac. He is one who (as I have been informed) carried theatre girls upon his shoulders at drinking bouts which were really quite satyric, his head decked out with ivy, a drinking bowl in his hand, playing the part of the mythical Dionysus[628] as arbiter of libations.

Now he did this, not before his initiation into the mysteries of Christ, but actually after his baptism, and it is clear enough from this that he does not believe in the resurrection. For how can one believe in the after life if he has defiled the very foundations of rising again?[629] As has been said: *How shall they preach unless they believe?*[630] This one is at least chaste in his conduct, fruitless because of the knife, but he is made upon *unfruitful works*,[631] because of his own disgraceful conduct.

These are the things that happened in Asia. That is what you wished to find out when Theophilus wrote about sixteen bishops being deposed by John. Now rest assured then that it is true, there were only six. We have kept the records safe with the signatures of the twenty-two bishops who were present from the beginning and heard the case, and the signatures of the seventy who brought about the deposition and finished the business of the trial.

CHAPTER 16
PORPHYRIUS

The deacon has his say

Deacon: Excuse me, father, but deeds such as these surpass even drunkenness and madness and any sort of tomfoolery. For maniacs, drunkards, and playboys, after some have sobered up and others have settled their stomachs, or when the boys become men, whatever you will, they then become ashamed of their earlier shameful deeds and whatever they may have said, and abandon their evil ways. But these people have done these things in their full maturity, fully sober to all appearances. Yet they do not repent of their deeds, but they pray (if pray they do) to persist in their wickedness without charge and without penalty. For they did not refrain from placing the Holy Gospels on a befouled head[632] on which chorus girls have sported. Shall we not number such among those who placed a crown of thorns on the head of the Son of God?[633]

But if you yourself know the circumstances of the consecration of Porphyrius[634] as bishop of Antioch, or of those who performed the ceremony, what kind of life he had lived before, whether he was obscure or famous, please tell me what you know. Tell us about his teaching; was it true or false, especially since he had sent off a letter[635] to the Church of Rome and it was not deemed worth an answer?

The bishop speaks only the truth

Bishop: My speech shall be accurate, for I will not forget the Master's voice which says: *Men shall give an account on the Day of Judgment for every idle word.*[636] I may make bold and even say: "And for every idle hearing."

Now stay on the safe side. If you find me not speaking the truth, do not spare me bacause I am a grey-beard, but the account must accord with actual fact. For what profit would there be for me for what I said today or yesterday if I have been lying when I am put to eternal shame before the judgment which knows no error? How will I bear the millstone[637] of backbiting around the neck of my mind when I am cast down to the bottom of hell because of those who were led into sin by my lies?

An account of Porphyrius

This Porphyrius had spent quite a long time in the service of the Church as deacon and as priest in the presbytery, but all the same the character he bore was altogether not in keeping with those long years, as he was of no benefit to the Church. He was ever antagonistic to the devoted bishops in his area, and he used his position as bishop of this most important city along with the magistrates in his power to make business deals. He contrived to prevent honorable ordinations and insinuated himself into the friendship of bishops in high office with his clever know-how (as one should say), and he dragged them down to his own level against their will and even held ordinations which were "against the wind."[638] A terrible thing is flattery, as the comic poet Menander[639] has it, the more so when it has been combined with an evil disposition:

> O Pamphila, 'tis hard
> for high-born wife to battle with a courtesan.
> She works more mischief; knows of more, she knows no shame;
> at flattery she's better.[640]

Porphyrius' character delineated

As the wise Solomon said: *The words of flatterers are soft; they smite upon the innermost chambers of the belly.*[641]

Not only is he a stranger, or actually an enemy, to temperance in carnal pleasure, as the vulture is to sweet myrrh, but, as they say, he is even given over to Sodomitic practices.[642] Now nature dictates laws, limits, and barriers upon our pleasures; according to what many say, he has trampled down the barriers, broken the limit, and put himself above the law. Thus he has produced the impression that he exhibits himself and entertains along with jugglers and jockeys and actors who play the parts of olden days, showing off their legs

with distorted motions. He even had the gall to compete with jugglers, nor did he disdain friendly intercourse with them. As a matter
of fact, charges of such a nature are to be found in the records of several of the magistrates. He had not read the proverb: *What you ought
not to do, do not even think of doing.*[643]

[Through him the mediator was slain with blows,[644] and the
finder was exiled, and the juggler made to flee.][645]

They say that in addition to all these wicked deeds he, after his
ordination, was found guilty of melting down Church plate and shar-
ing it with the magistrates. This was to make it seem that he had
power not in word only but in his tyranny over any who were so unfortunate as to fall under his power.

Constantius preferred as bishop

At the same time of John's exile to Armenia occurred the death
of Flavianus, bishop of Antioch. Porphyrius noted that the whole
populace, men as well as women, hung around the neck of the priest
Constantius. He had served the Church from his earliest years and
was a man whom judges[645a] call ambidextrous (for what is commonly
called the left hand was in his case more skillful than the right hand
of others). Now at first he served by writing letters,[645b] and he was
altogether innocent of dishonest gain and bribery. Then he was promoted to lector and deacon. He easily conquered that desire for
women which is so prevalent among men, as the writer of Proverbs
says: *The hand of the elect shall easily prevail.*[646] For even the most evil[647]
of men may conquer the concupiscence of the body, either through
fear or through shame hindering it by necessity, but it is only those
who truly love God who rise above the lower passions because of
love for higher things. These the Holy Scriptures call the elect in the
phrase: *The hand of the elect shall easily prevail.*[648]

He certainly was meek if ever a man was, ascetic in his habits,
had discernment of vision and sharpness of intellect, was reluctant to
chastize, conscientious, ever able to draw inferences by reflection.[649]
He was merciful, not a lover of money, just in his judgements, long-
suffering under stress, vigorous in persuasion. He often fasted until
evening, so that he might free those who were oppressed with suffer-

ing. He was of august appearance, keen of countenance, swift in his gait, unblemished as was fitting, and he kept a flower of a smile on his face even in periods of sickness.

Porphyrius ordained in a private ceremony

Porphyrius brought it about to banish Constantius by bribery in this manner. He sent a message to those in power over the bishops at the capital, and he managed to have him exiled to Oasis by imperial rescript[650] as destructive of the people's morale. Now Constantius got wind of this and fled to Cyprus saved by his friends. But Porphyrius put the priests Cyriacus and Diophantus[651] and other clergy under arrest. He kept Acacius, Severianus, and Antiochus under close observation for a suitable time when the whole city should go out to the suburbs to observe Olympia, a festival held every four years in honor of the labors of Hercules.[652] During this feast whole flocks of women, so to say, fling themselves out with the crowds to Daphne[653] for a look at the contestants.

He burst into the Church with the aforementioned bishops and a few clerics and privately ordained him behind locked doors and in such great haste that they did not even finish the closing prayers for fear they might be discovered. (Such is adultery, its offspring and deeds are spurious.)

Porphyrius threatened by the populace

Severianus and his clique *having taken sufficient*[654] fled through the pathless mountains to escape the terror of men; however, they were very close to God whom they despised. Once the public theatre was empty the people returned to the city and it was announced to them what Porphyrius had done as well as the little drama[655] of Acacius. The people endured that throughout the night until the morrow like men punished for adultery; they arose then and flowed through the city with fire and kindling with full intent to destroy Porphyrius along with his household effects. But he was well aware of the very deep hatred he had inspired, and he abandoned his God and fled to the military commander.[656] He filled his hands with

money and that diverted him from the war against the Isaurians, but
he opened war against the disciples of the Savior instead. The plun-
dering Isaurian bandits laid waste Thosus and Seleucia while Porphyrius and Valentinian,[657] the governor, plundered the church of
the orthodox with armed soldiers. They stamped with their feet on
the awe-inspiring image of the Cross which the orthodox carried on
their shoulders instead of the Teacher while they offered litanies on
the devastated land.

The people are aroused to action

A few days went by and Porphyrius hastily sent to the capital a
message in which he pressed upon the rulers who were in the same
class as he was a certain old man who was still youthful to be appointed as night prefect.[658] He was of an evil disposition and a
warped mind. This was in order to make himself ruler of the city by
bringing false charges against worthy citizens in complete security
on his own part. This was actually mimicking the wiles of Nero,[659]
the man who fought against God. It was not his way to persuade men
by logic, but rather to worry them with brutishness and hostility. He
did not aim to please God by bringing in the wandering souls, but
rather to gorge his serpent-like body crawling along on its chest.

Some of the laity gathered unwillingly in the church on the pretext of fear, but actually they were cursing the life-style of those in-
truders and stayed there awaiting help from God.

There are worse things than cruelty

To these things Theodore in amazement spoke up:

Deacon: Dear father, I see something which rubs against nature in
these actions. For the most part, the vainglorious seek to please
men[660] and are found to be flatterers, and they provide a good table
for the sake of being loved and hearing nice things. I have heard of
some who allow themselves to be spit upon. I cannot for the world
imagine Porphyrius or any one else for that matter who could have
wielded threats and punishments and even exile.

Bishop: That is a wonderful thing, Theodore, that they attained to such a measure of evil that not only were they not anxious to please men, but they did not consider the shameful nature of what they did. For evil surpasses evil in evil. For then evil surpasses vainglory when it hopes to get the upper hand of the unwary by flattery. But when they are found to be above flattery and the blandishments of the table, it resorts to intimidation and torture. Then it employs extreme cruelty and fear to entice those unaffected by either safe living or flattery, as is the case with the martyrs. For there both ruses are tried: the snare first of all of the bribes and honors so cleverly manipulated for those panting for empty glory. Failing that, the prospect of punishment made way for the frying pans and instruments of torture and wild beasts and every sort of outrage, but at least it brought out in bright colors the brave and the God-fearing.

At any rate the people of Antioch met in secret, not even going near the walls of the church, and even the revered women over whom the money-loving prelates lost their senses. As for what happened at Constantinople, what more can one say? What great numbers left the Church and met in the open air as said above. Why not even the ecclesiastical dignitaries ever had so great an audience, an audience of silent listeners, but they had no voice for speech.

Olympias and Theophilus

Deacon: You have freed my mind which had been enslaved by all those doubts by presenting the facts to me openly, father. Your consistent narrative and sincere explanation have convinced me that these things really happened, since a fabricated story has no consistency in itself. If you can do so without too much trouble, please tell us something about Olympias, if you know anything about her.

Bishop: Which one do you mean? You know there are several of them.

Deacon: I am referring to the deaconess of Constantinople who was the wife of Nebridius,[661] the ex-prefect.

Bishop: I knew her well indeed.

Deacon: What kind of a woman is she?

Bishop: Do not say "woman" but rather "manly creature."[662] She is a man in everything but body.

Deacon: In what way?

Bishop: In her way of life, her works, in knowledge and courage in misfortunes.

Deacon: Then why should Theophilus abuse her?

Bishop: Which Theophilus do you mean?

Deacon: The lord bishop of Alexandria.

Bishop: It appears to me, Theodore, that you have covered up those great floods of words in forgetfulness.

Deacon: How is that?

Bishop: The one who did not spare truth but trod it underfoot, as my own account has proved, and he did not respect the Church on earth for which the sole-begotten One, as we preach, was made to die that all may be one;[663] but this man has not honored Church nor Savior— do you think now he would take into consideration a widow who devoted her life to prayer? Look into this matter diligently and see if he ever reviled a man of evil deeds, he who always hated piety. Why can you not conjecture from his letters how he contradicts himself in each one? Epiphanius,[664] bishop of Constantia in Cyprus, who served the Church there for thirty-six years—well, Theophilus made him out as a heretic or a schismatic at the time of Damasus[665] and Siricius.[666] But later on, writing to Pope Innocent and reviling the blessed John, he is to be found calling Epiphanius a most holy saint! How often do you suppose he kissed the knees of Olympias in hopes of getting money from her whom he now reviles. She threw herself on the ground[667] at this and shed tears at a bishop doing such things. But what were his grounds for reviling her?

Olympias befriended monks

Deacon: Simply because she took in monks whom he had expelled.

Bishop: Now is that the proper thing to do, for a bishop to expel a disciple, to say nothing of a monk?

Deacon: Only if they provoked him or spoke evil of him.

Bishop: But would it be proper for him to vent his own personal anger, supposing there were some accusation? How then should Theophilus consider the insults[668] which Christ received, this man who thinks only of his own good reputation? Why could he not have imitated the Teacher who said: *Being reviled we bless.*[669]

Deacon: What then of the monks who happened to be heterodox?

Bishop: By all means he should have corrected them and persuaded them. He should not have exiled them.

Deacon: And supposing he did this and they were still not convinced, since they are an obstinate lot?

Bishop: He should have carried out the Apostle's teaching: *A man that is a heretic, after the first and second admonition, avoid, knowing that such a one is perverted.*[670] He does not mean exile him, plunder him, and drive him out of his home by royal decree.

Deacon: You are telling me the standards of a perfect man, one who loves God and who has suffered much.

Bishop: And still it is not great praise that is given if one puts up with an inferior. Unless one is as perfect as possible, how can such a one be a bishop?[671] He who is imperfect will never be considerate of those who are imperfect. How can he bear the name of Theophilus if he does not love God? If he lives up to his name he should bear insults readily. But if he does not love God, it is only too evident he does not love himself either. How could he who is his own enemy love others? And this is not at all surprising that he found fault with Olympias for befriending monks.

Deacon: We grant that Theophilus performed a rash action in exiling them whether they really were orthodox or heretical. At any rate the deaconess[672] should not have taken them in.

Olympias' actions justified

Bishop: How does it appear to you? Did she do right or wrong?

Deacon: I maintain that she did wrong.

Bishop: And doing good is sometimes judged otherwise?

Deacon: Certainly so; whenever good is bestowed on evil people who should not be treated well.

Bishop: What about the five thousand whom the Savior fed with five barley loaves?[673] Would you say they were good or bad?

Deacon: Apparently they were good, seeing that they were fed by the Savior.

Bishop: But why were they fed with barley loaves if they were good?[674]

Deacon: Because of the scarcity of white bread, and also because of their hunger.

Bishop: Why were they reproved for their lack of faith?[675] As good men or as bad?

Deacon: If they were reproved, they were evidently bad.

Bishop: But how can good men be bad at the same time?

Deacon: By all means.

Bishop: In what way?

Deacon: They could be good as compared to the worst, and bad in comparison with the better.

Bishop: Well said! By the same token monks were both good and bad. And that most trustworthy woman befriended them as good men, but the wonderful bishop expelled them as bad, something which he should not have done.

Deacon: But he will tell you: "You took in my enemies to my grief."

Bishop: But that is entirely his own fault, for he called them enemies, he who ought to have suffered insults in imitation of Christ.[676]

Deacon: What about the five thousand who were reproached by the Savior as you said. Are they not referred to in Scripture?

Bishop: When they were gathered together a second time they came to Jesus[677] and heard the words: *You seek Me, not because you saw signs and wonders, but because you did eat of the bread and were filled.*[678]

Deacon: That is most clear.

Bishop: If a man is blamed, he is bad to that extent.

Deacon: True enough.

Bishop: Were they bad or good whom the Savior fed?

Deacon: Granted that they were bad; for *They that are whole need not the physician, but they that are sick.*[679]

Bishop: So then did Olympias do an evil deed when she imitated her Lord who *makes His sun to rise upon the good and bad and rain upon the just and the unjust*[680] and the Pharisees revile Him and say to the disciples: *Your Master eats and drinks with publicans and sinners.*[681]

Deacon: It would seem that, contrary to the general opinion, praiseworthy actions are condemned and disgraceful deeds are approved.

Bishop: Theodore, why would you ever say something like that, truth-loving man that you are.

Deacon: It is this: if you had not clarified everything for me in your exposition, I too should have been led astray to hold the same senseless notions as others, not attracted by the aspect of freedom but by the ranting of Theophilus.

Bishop: Is not the opposite true if it is proved that these same holy men are not only not bad men, but men who led others from evil to doing good?[682] Then surely the one who reviles them is more to be pitied than protected as one who always opposes the good and supports the bad.

Deacon: So be it as you said. For even if they can not be proved to be wise and holy men (as many assert), then let Olympias be judged free from blame from these same logical arguments, since she had imitated the Savior in her actions.

Bishop: Which of the two seems to you to give greater witness to good works, the Gospel or Theophilus?

Deacon: Please restrain yourself. Granted that he drove out men because of his anger and his love of power, and that he reviled Olympias because of superstition[683] and hate, using the monks as a pretext. Once he failed to get anything from her by his cringing flatteries except food and lodging, he turned against her and reviled her. This is his way with everyone.

CHAPTER 17
THE MONKS AND OLYMPIAS

Hierax and Ammonius

Bishop: Now listen, best of deacons, for I perceive that you are good for all the people. Your zeal now in your youth augurs well for an honorable old age. These men from their tenderest years, reared as they were by Christian parents, submitted to God and, while still young, refused to enslave themselves to vanity and to follow the mob. Instead they went to an uninhabited place in the south far removed from the world. There they built huts for themselves to protect them from the fierce heat of the sun and the dew of the air. They lived there and spent the time in prayer and reading and they gained a livelihood by the work of their hands for the support of their bodies. They thought it better to herd with gazelles and sparrows and buffaloes than to banquet with men who were ignorant of God. The eldest of these monks was Hierax,[684] who still goes by that name and who has reached the age of ninety. He had once been well acquainted with the blessed Antony.[685] Another was Ammonius,[686] who was close to sixty, and there were also two of the monastic brotherhood and one bishop. They were fitted with a prisoner's collar and banished under Valens[687] (as everyone in Alexandria knows). They were so far advanced in learning that no moot point in Scripture escaped them. Two of them fell asleep, ending their lives in Constantinople. Now Ammonius had foretold his own death, as Aurelius[688] and Sisinnius[689] affirm; he said that there would be a great persecution and a schism among the churches, but that those who caused it would meet a shameful end and the Church would become united. This shall come to pass and part of it has already happened.

The persecutors are punished

(Soon afterwards disease seized the bodies of some of the bishops and laity. It rent them with various and sundry afflictions: it burst through their innards with slow fever; the whole surface of the body was affected by an unbearable itching, scratched by fingernails and accompanied by continual visceral agony. One had his feet swollen and livid with hydropsy; another who had subscribed to the letter of condemnation[690] found those very fingers shaking with discharges alternating cold and hot from his four extremities. The belly was distended and mortification of a certain member exuded an unpleasant odor to a great distance, breeding worms in addition. To these symptoms were added asthma and difficulty of breathing, plus dilation of the limbs. Then came nightmares[691] of charging dogs, which changed into barbarians carrying swords and yelling in a strange language in a voice like the breaking of the wave upon the beach.[692] This made their attempt at sleep into a restless night. Another fell from his horse and his leg snapped off like a stalk and he died at once. Another lost his voice for a period of eight months;[693] he wasted away on his couch unable even to raise his hand to his mouth. Still another's legs were being consumed little by little as far as the knees in a kind of erysipelas for a space of two years. Another's tongue was swollen, so they say, with a burning fever and pressed against his teeth, and so closed the entrance to the body. Since he could not make use of his tongue, he made a written confession of his sins on a tablet.

(One could perceive the divine anger working against them in various forms of revenge.[694] For they were irritating the Physician and Charmer of souls[695] and had expelled His interpreter from the workshop of salvation. For this they were turned over to the physicians of the body to be tortured by drugs which are generally considered beneficial but which do not accomplish salvation. For who will cure the one who is undergoing punishment from God?[696] As the prophet says: *Shall physicians rise and praise Thee?*[697] So did they all die who worked against the peace of Your Church, O Lord.)[698]

The Desert Fathers[699]

Now it is said that the tomb of the monk Ammonius drives out the shivering fevers.[700] He is buried in the tomb of the apostles beyond the sea. They say that Bishop Dioscorus prayed especially that he might see either peace in the Church or his own death. He was deemed worthy of death since the world was not deemed worthy of

peace; he was in the martyr's shrine facing the gate of the city.[701]
Now most of the women have given up making oaths by the martyr
and swear by the prayers of Dioscorus instead. As regards the other
anchorites, the whole story would be too long and perhaps, famous
man, time is running out.

Deacon: Who would be so thrice unhappy that he would not give time
to hearing tales of heroism? Please speak on, I beg you, and take my
mind from earthly thoughts with your fair manner of speech.

Bishop: There is another Hierax and despite his Greek name[702] he has
a beautiful character adorned with spiritual qualities. When he first
took to the ascetic life he went to Mount Porphyrites,[703] far beyond
the boundaries of Egypt and the Thebaid, far from the breath of anyone.[704] Here he lived for four years practicing alone those virtues
which would be his salvation. Then he spent twenty-five years at Nitria with the above-named fathers. He was confronted by "demons,"
as he used to tell us himself.[705] These "demons" held out to him the
prospect of a long life, *transforming themselves into angels of light.*[706]
They were anxious to shake him from *the hope set before him.*[707] They
said: "You have years to live; how will you persevere here in the desert?"[708] But he, in full consciousness of faith, made reply: "You cause
me great distress in allotting me a period shorter than I had planned;
for I made up my mind and prepared to stay two hundred years in
the desert."

They heard this and went off howling.[709] Such was the man
whom demons could not budge even when they invented a long period of time to breed accidie.[710] He was the man whom Pope Theophilus exiled and forced to leave by decree, that he come to the
capital of necessity. Now that Ammonius has fallen asleep, he has returned to the desert mindful of the parable of the plow.[711]

The two Isaacs described

Then there was a priest Isaac,[712] a disciple of Macarius,[713] who
had been a disciple of Antony himself. He was very much attached
to the desert, fifty years of age, and he had all the Scriptures by

heart. He used to take up horned serpents in his hands[714] without being hurt. He was a virgin from the womb and, when seven years old, had taken to the desert and after being there for forty years he was winnowed out[715] by Pope Theophilus along with the monks mentioned above.

There was another Isaac,[716] likewise a priest, who was both pupil and successor of Cronius, the priest who had been a pupil of Antony. He was also very learned in the Scriptures like the other Isaac. He was most hospitable and full of love for his fellow men, and had set up a guest house in the heart of the desert for the care of monks and of those who came there to see the blessed fathers. They say that he was an utter stranger to anger and had spent thirty years in solitude; he too was cruelly treated along with the others.

Now the first mentioned of those named Isaac had one hundred and fifty ascetics under his direction. When Theophilus was still a true lover of God he had appointed seven or eight of Isaac's disciples as bishops. The second Isaac had two hundred and ten disciples, many of whom are also numbered among the bishops. These then are the men I spoke of about two days ago,[717] and because of Isidore the priest they were driven from the desert. Both priests and Levites[718] disregarded them and it is to the shame of men that a manly woman should take them in and it is to the accusation of bishops that a deaconess[719] should befriend them. Her fame is enrolled in all the churches for many reasons. She imitated that Samaritan[720] whoever he was who discovered the man beaten up by robbers and half dead on his way to Jericho. He settled him on his own beast of burden and brought him to the inn; he combined the oil of love of a fellow man with the astringent wine to heal his swollen wounds.

Olympias' life-style described

Now let this be said of her. I am not the one to speak of the wealth of money or goods[721] that she divided among the needy, but rather they should do so who were her beneficiaries[722] (for I was out of the country quite secure from want). Only listen now to her greater virtue. She was an orphan, taken in marriage, but it was not allowed by the all-knowing God who foresees[723] the outcome of men's lives that she should not serve bodily pleasures which rule over men even for the space of twenty months, for the man joined to her was soon made to pay the debt of nature. They all say she is still a virgin. While it is possible that she may have obeyed the apostolic injunction: *I will that the younger women marry, keep house,*[724] she was not able to, although well situated by birth, wealth, and liberal education. Besides she had great personal beauty, as well as the grace of blossoming womanhood. She leaped freely like a gazelle over the snare of a second marriage, *for the law is not laid down for lawless persons, profane,*[725] insatiate for destruction.

Now it happened that through some kind of satanic malice her untimely widowhood was reported[726] to the ears of Emperor Theodosius,[727] who at once desired to marry her off to a relative of his, Elpidius,[728] a Spaniard. Again and again he kept pressing this person[729] to give in to his demands, but she refused, saying: "If my King had desired me to live with a male He would not have taken away my first husband.[730] But He knew that I cannot make a husband happy,[731] so He liberated him from the bond and me likewise from the most bothersome yoke, and He freed me from subjection to a man while He laid on me the *gentle yoke*[732] of chastity."

When he received this reply, he gave orders to the prefect to hold her property under trust until she would be thirty years old. That officer was egged on by Elpidius and he carried out the emperor's order at once and with a vengeance. She was to have no privilege with even the most celebrated bishop, and she was not to attend church, so that out of absolute boredom she would prefer marriage. But she was pleased at this and, giving thanks to God, she made reply to the emperor: "You demonstrated towards my lowly person a kindness most becoming an emperor and commendable in a bishop when you entrusted this great burden, which has been my worry, to proper administration. You will do much better should you order it to be distributed to the poor and the churches. I have been praying for quite a while that I be set free from the embarrassment of vainglory which would be mine if I distributed it in charity. Let me not be so seduced by earthly things[733] so as to lose the soul's true riches."

When the emperor heard of her ascetic life on his return from the war against Maximus,[734] he ordered that her property be under her own management.

Deacon: Quite rightly then did John pay her such honor, she who led such an ascetic life.

Bishop: I agree, for she does abstain from flesh food and likewise refrains from washing most of the time. But if her health requires it (for she has a delicate stomach condition) she bathes wearing a light chemise, since she is ashamed to regard her own naked body—at least so I have been informed.

Olympias practices great charity

Deacon: She is said to have contributed everything to the holy John's expenses.

Bishop: But what could she really show worthy of his virtue? Certainly she provided him with an assurance of his daily barley-cake;[735] and surely this is no small thing for those who work for Christ, meditating as they do by day and by night on the things that are of Christ. As Paul says when greeting Persis, who had probably toiled as has Olympias: *Salute Persis the beloved who labored much in the Lord;*[736] . . . *for all seek their own, and not the things of Christ.*[737]

I know that she did even more to keep the blessed Nectarius to the extent that he took her advice on ecclesiastical policy as well. But why should I speak of Amphilochius,[738] Optimus,[739] Gregory,[740] Peter[741] the brother of Basil,[742] and Epiphanius, bishop of Cyprus; all these she presented with lands and money. As Optimus was dying at Constantinople, Olympias closed his eyes with her own hands. In addition to this she graciously supplied whatever they needed for the miserable Antiochus, Acacius, and Severianus, as well as for priests who came to the city, and numerous ascetics and virgins also.[743]

Chrysostom accepted charity reluctantly

Now John had judged that he was sent to serve as a model as it were for bishops to follow in regard to his manner of life. He was to preach repentance, as Paul[744] said, at his own expense, not touching

on what belongs to the Church. So he accepted food for each day as
it came, always avoiding anxiety. They say he was like a man who
was ashamed even to be partaking of food.[745]

As is the nature of apples, when they become fully ripened,
they cannot endure to stay on the branch, but they await the hand of
their master.[746] Thus it is with the saints. When they transcend the
natural order, they long for the beauty of heavenly things even before their appointed time to die—they are eager to see the promise
fulfilled. This we perceive, too, in children brought up in high estate. Knowing that something sweet will follow the regular meal,
they turn down necessary food so as to save their appetites with
which they will eat their fill.

These words are for those who set forth on the same path in the
spiritual ascent; for *if the wise man hear a prudent man, he will commend
him, and add unto it.*[747]

CHAPTER 18
CHRYSOSTOM'S WAY OF LIFE

St. Paul was his example

Deacon: You have been a comfort to me, reverend father, in your
thorough and careful explanation. What you said agrees with and
even adds some grace to what we have heard. Still I must say the up-
keep of John would have been no burden on the Church had John
taken his rightful share from the Church, according to Scripture: *The
laborer is worthy of his hire.*[748] And again: *Who feeds a flock and does not eat
of the milk of the flock? Who plants a vineyard and does not partake of its
fruit?*[749] Are not these things and many more in Scriptures?

Bishop: You have spoken correctly and sensibly, Theodore.
Only add to what you have quoted the following which deals
with the holy law which allows those engaged in holy acts to eat of
the sacrifice. Paul, ever intent upon good, puts it: *I did not use the
power,*[750] referring to the body, *that I may become a partaker of the Gos-*

pel,[751] referring to the spirit. He would not become *a hindrance to the weak*,[752] as is said: *If anyone see you, who has knowledge, sitting at meat in weakness, will not his conscience, as he is weak, be purified?*[753] Would he not be tempted to imitate those very weaknesses? For if the whole business rested with us alone and no one followed us to be supported by the laity, then it would not be amiss for an offender to say: "Let us enjoy life as we will, plucking all the good one can."

But those who come after us regard us as the teachers and keep our law and customs before them. We live, then, *not for ourselves alone, but for Him who died for us and rose again.*[754] And we are to bolster up the weakness of the people and lead their ranks to a higher degree of temperance and to greater simplicity, reminding ourselves of what has been said: *Who is the man that fears the Lord? He has appointed for him a law in the way that he has chosen.*[755]

John set a good example

Now the Master lays down the law for the rash and the miserable who commit sin thoughtlessly, welcoming the "*spirit of bondage*"[756] according to the Psalmist David: *The Lord shall give a law for sinners in the way*,[757] but He shall punish the transgressors. But the just man transgresses the law of bondage out of love for the Master and insists on his share of son by adoption, and he becomes a lawgiver to himself.[758] Of such was Job in work and in word: *I made a covenant with my eyes, that I would not so much as think upon a virgin.*[759] What then was this covenant? That they who fight against temperance should be deprived of their eyesight.[760] Likewise David says: *I have sworn and am determined to keep the judgments of thy justice.*[761] He bound with an oath the wavering and doubtful nature of his judgment.

Now John was one to imitate the fathers like a true son, not as a bastard,[762] and make easy the way for the common people. He made himself a lawgiver and judge over those who were torn by various desires, leading them to a stricter mode of life.[763] John girded himself with unflinching resolution and kept away from drinking bouts and parties of gossips and men who joked and wasted their time and talents. He armed the eye of his soul[764] with the panoply[765] of the spirit, lest folly effect an entry through drinking or indecent talk and so wreak havoc on moderation, according to what is said: *Evil communications corrupt good manners.*[766]

Chrysostom follows scriptural precepts

Therefore plots were formed against John; brightly as he shone he was as troublesome to them as a lamp is harmful to the bleary-eyed. Such was his fellow in suffering, Jeremias, who wept at the perfidious rulers and priests, calling out: *Who will give water for my head and fountains of tears to my eyes? And I shall weep for my people day and night.*[767] And again: *Who will give me a lodging place, the farthest in the desert?*[768] *And I will leave my people and go from them, for they all commit adultery.*[769]

He calls the gathering of the false prophets and priests *an assembly of transgressors.*[769] So, too, he elsewhere calls upon God, not that God does not know, but because we are to imitate him. *Lord, I did not sit in the assembly of jesters, nor did I make a boast of the presence of Thy hand; I sat alone, because Thou hast filled me with threats.*[770]

David sings in like manner: *I have not sat with the assembly of vanity and with the transgressors I shall not enter.* And he adds to this to make it clear: *I have hated the congregation of the evil doers, and with the ungodly I will not sit; I will wash my hands in innocence* (that is, the active powers), *and I will go around Thy altar, O Lord.*[771]

But these men had less concern for the altar and turned their backs to it,[772] both in purpose and in manner of life. Not only did they do this with unwashed and blood-stained hands, but by giving and receiving bribes and by false statements in writing, and by trampling on it with muddy feet.[773] It is of them that Ezechiel, the prophet, speaks metaphorically:

And he brought me to the door of the court, and I saw, and behold, a hole in the door. And he said unto me: "Dig through, son of man!" And I dug through, and behold, a door. And he said unto me: "Go in and see the wicked lawlessness, which they do here." And I went in, and behold, every likeness of creeping thing, and beast, and vain idols, abominations. And he said unto me: "Thou hast seen, son of man, what the elders of the house of Israel do in the dark, in the chamber (referring to their unclean mind) *for they said: "The Lord does not see us, the Lord has forsaken the earth." And he said unto me: "You shall see yet greater lawlessness, which those do." And he brought me to another place, and showed me, and behold, there sat women weeping for Tammuz.* And again: *He brought me into the inner house of the Lord; and behold, there, twenty-four men, and their faces turned away, and their backs to the altar. And he said unto me: "Are these small things, that the house of Israel does?"*[774]

We were forced to remember the passage of the prophet because of these rather thoughtless persons *who think they are somebody and deceive themselves.*[775] They are the ones who disturb the peace of the Church since they have turned their backs to the table of the Lord, they *whose judgment does not cease, and their destruction does not slumber,*[776] *who mind earthly things.*[777]

Judas, the brother of James, says this of them: *These are they who are hidden rocks in your love feasts, feasting with you without fear, shepherds that feed themselves; clouds without water, carried along by winds, wild waves of the sea foaming out their own shame, wandering stars, for whom the blackness of darkness has been reserved for ever.*[778]

Now when he called them *clouds without water*, he meant the evil hail which is so destructive of the vine. By *wandering stars* he was alluding to the enemy of the ship. Now the ship and the vine are the Church. What must necessarily follow from this? Listen once more to that same prophet Ezechiel expounding:

And he showed me, and behold men came from the upper gate which looks toward the north, every man with his slaughter weapon in his hand. And one man in the midst of them, clothed down to the feet, and a girdle of sapphire upon his loins. And they went in, and stood beside the brazen altar, and the glory of the God of Israel which was upon them went up from the Cherubim to the threshold of the house. And he called the man who was clothed down to the feet, who had the girdle upon his loins. And the Lord said unto him: "Go through the midst of the city, even Jerusalem, and set the sign upon the foreheads of the men that sigh and that cry for all the lawlessness that is done in the midst of them." And to them he said (evidently to the six who had the slaughter weapons): *"In my hearing go into the city after him* (clearly, after the man who put the signs upon their foreheads) *and smite; let not your eye spare, neither have pity; slay utterly the old men, the young men, and maidens, and little children and women. But do not come near any man upon whom is the sign, and begin at my sanctuary." Then they began at the elders which were in the house of the Lord.*[779]

An explanation of the preceding

Should anyone think this prophecy has to do only with what happened in Judea, such a one must surely be unaware of the sojourn of the Savior on earth (for Ezechiel was not functioning as a priest before the Captivity). He was a mere stripling of a child when taken into captivity under the dispensation of God along with the tribe of Eli. When he was in his thirtieth year, while functioning as a priest there in captivity, he was deemed worthy of the sight of things to come, as he himself tells us: *Now it came to pass in the thirtieth year, in the fourth month, on the fifth day of the month, when I was in the midst of the captives by the river Chebar.*[780] And a little after this: *The word of the Lord came to Ezechiel, the priest the son of Buzi the priest, in the land of the Chaldaeans by the river Chebar.*[781]

Then, if some one should feel constrained and say to us: "It was the Savior who went on ahead and placed the sign of the cross upon the men's foreheads, but when they did not have faith in the Savior, the Roman empire followed in the days of Vespasian,[782] who forty years later[783] destroyed the synagogue which was the cause of evil." Now we readily accept[784] a person who thinks in this manner and we invite him as a son of the Covenant[785] to be persuaded by Paul, an initiate in these matters, who has this to say regarding all such books: *Now all these things happened to them in figures, and they are written for our correction, upon whom the ends of the world are come.*[786]

But I do not say these things because I pray that an iron sword[787] should come upon the enemies of God—away with that thought! But the prophet does not mean a sword of iron, but rather of some other form of punishment of which the same Ezechiel speaks: *The land upon which I bring a sword* (I *bring* for *I will allow*) *and the people of the Lord take a man and set him for their watchman, and the watchman sees the sword coming, and blows into the trumpet and warns the people, and he that hears hears, and does not keep guard; and the sword comes and takes any one, his blood will I require of him, because he did not hear the sound of the trumpet.*

And again: *But if the watchman sees the sword coming, and does not blow the trumpet, and does not give warning to the people, and the sword comes and takes anyone, his blood will I require at the watchman's hand, because he saw the sword and yet did not blow.*[788]

Now the blessed John did not sleep the sleep of unbelief, nor was he careless with the carelessness of pleasure, but he beheld ever before his eyes the danger that was to come and he cried out more loudly than a trumpet, making no uncertain sound.[789] He bestowed on all men certain knowledge of the sword of the devil and he called on all to flee from it. And those who had a pure conscience, a sign as it were upon the forehead of their souls, were saved along with you, the faithful of Rome,[790] by the grace of God. Now those with a corrupt conscience inflamed the people and the priests with arguing amongst themselves, so they hid their own conscience in the general wickedness.

Proper use of the opportunity

Deacon: Well said! Granted that it is impossible for a man to be entirely blameless and perfect in this present life, as Scripture says time and again: *Who shall boast that he has his heart pure? Or who shall be confident that he is clean from sin?*[791]

Be that as it may, the blessed John did not know how to make the most of an opportunity, for one ought not to assault those in power.

Bishop: My dear Theodore, you appear to me a veritable Panurge.[792] You showed us sympathy as became you, and with a certain amount of compassion, too. However, I find you little by little rather fond of scoffing; as a matter of fact, even his avowed enemies never berated his mannerisms so severely.[793]

Deacon: Why should you be angry, dear father, you who are considered a lover of the truth, simply because I said John did not make use of opportunity? Holy Scripture says: *Do not stand in the way of rulers.*[794] And again: *Buying up the opportunity*[795]—this especially for those who do not heed advice or help.

Bishop: Blessed are you who so explain the Scriptures; for the phrase: *Do not stand in the place of riches*[796] of Ecclesiastes is meant for those who are not worthy of the priesthood and unable to undertake it, and it is a timely warning.

When he speaks of rulers, he means the apostles in the first place, those who taught righteousness; for they are the rulers clothed with the *spirit of power*,[797] and after them their imitators. Now the phrase, to buy up the opportunity, is used not that we should become hypocrites, but that when an occasion of sin should occur, "we shall buy up the opportunity" with virtue and not sell ourselves to sin. He who is this way "buys up the opportunity" discovers that he has little by little bought his whole life. He passed up the so-called pleasures of life to find something above life.[798] So it was with the martyrs, surrendering their physical bodies to inherit immortality. In a very true sense they "bought up the opportunity."

More examples from Scripture

If these things are not considered to be so, then surely Moses, Elias, Daniel, John the Baptist, Isaias, Peter and Paul, to mention only these, all failed to recognize their opportunities. Moses did, since he fled for his own safety after reprimanding someone and then keeping the sheep of a Gentile in the mountains.[799] Elias, downcast in his sorrow and overcome by weariness, found no shade under wall or rock, but lay under a juniper tree, which afforded him but little shelter.[800] Isaias was sawn into pieces.[801] Because of his piety Daniel was cast into the lion's den.[802] Michaias[803] was kept in prison (some say it was an innermost chamber) and forced to down the *bread of affliction*[804] and hardly enough water, and he dragged out his days with the hope that his life might be shortened through bad treatment, all because of his outspokenness to some king. Now what will you tell me about John, who was peerless *among them born of women?*[805] Did he not know how to grasp at an opportunity? His head was cut off because of his clearly expressed reproach of the adultery of Herod.[806] Actually he showed the same concern as a physician who cauterizes or cuts away an incurable ailment of a patient.

Chrysostom did not fear to reproach evil

For the same reason, too, our John reproached all, either from pity or affection. If the Baptist did not recognize the opportunity how did he acknowledge the Architect and Creator[807] of all ages when he said: *Behold the Lamb of God who takes away the sin of the world?*[808]

How is it that Paul and Peter did not recognize an opportunity, they who were staunch pillars of the Church? Even after their death an opportunity is given; the way is either closed or open[809] for those who are repentant and have but to knock at the door. For Peter was crucified with his feet in the air to signify his going to heaven, and Paul was beheaded because he was outspoken about Christ; it was better that he lose his head so he would not lose the head of Christ, who is Head of all. Do not accept those who say evil and criticize the outspokenness of the saints. That is the custom of the pagans and the conceited ones who find their pleasure in making merry at the expense of the saints' courage.

A personal grudge must be avoided

Neither must the sword be dull nor the bold speech be undone. Kindness and bold speech are as closely related as scent and perfume. But if reproaches are offered individually[810] to make one's own family or friends or relatives, in an embarrassing situation, the outspoken person could be said to have been unaware of the right opportunity. Should the Church be like a shambles where truth must out, praise to the well-doers and blame on the worthless? Why should we take it so hard when reproaches are made and no names mentioned and it is really for our own benefit? In that way we are actually feeding our faults, unmindful of Him who said: *Whatsoever is sold in the shambles, eat asking no questions.*[811] If this is not done the saints will again be the occasion for stumbling to some cities and lands because of their reproaches, and others again they led astray[812] by their praises.

Was John's boldness of speech justified?

Take the holy John, first of all. He reproached the country of Phoenicia[813] for inviting his enemy Satan, for he says: *Shall the tribes of the Phoenicians cut him (the leviathan) into pieces?*[814] Then Moses and the prophets censure Egypt and call it an *iron furnace*[815] and *darkness*,[816] and they praise Palestine, calling it the *land of promise*.[817] But Egypt is found to be the *land of promise* for the good, and Palestine is not only an *iron furnace* but *outer darkness* as well to the sluggards who do not believe. It is not the places in themselves, but the inhabitants thereof who make them good or evil.

But why should I stretch out my discourse unless it is an introduction to what follows? Now when Paul calls the Cretans *liars*,[818] the Galatians *senseless*,[819] and the Corinthians *puffed up*,[820] and so forth and so on, was he thinking only of the faults of each particular group and reproaching them separately or was he referring to all mankind in general? Or once more, when he calls the Romans[821] *faithful*, the Ephesians *enlightened*,[822] and speaking in more exalted rhetoric, he called the Thessalonians *lovers of the brethren*,[823] was his praise intended for only these people? Surely not. Guided by the Spirit, he imposed praise and blame. Thus the praiseworthy man will recognize it and be spurred on in his zeal; the evil man will recognize the rebuke and renounce the cause of his blame. Now the Galatians are not the only foolish people, nor the Cretans the only liars, nor the Corinthians the only proud ones. These are qualities that appear everywhere. The human nature which commits sin and does good is one,[824] and in one and the same circumstance it turns to evil or to good, all depending on the person's conscious choice. This then was John's way when he boldly spoke out in church, or rather he cut into pieces the meat of virtue for the hungry and removed the seeds of sin by open reproaches, persuaded by Him who said: *Them that sin reprove before all, that the rest also may have fear.*[825]

But should there be any so ill with pride or foolishness that they desire to be praised for the pleasures, God's own servants had no such custom.[826] For those who grow angry at censure for greed and fornication and other foul pleasures of the same sort, claim that these things ought to be acceptable, harmful though they be.

Chapter 19
Chrysostom was neither Proud nor Overbearing

Pride is shown by isolating oneself

Deacon: Many thanks, father, for the hospitality of your brotherly love. We found this most helpful and it will be remembered as long as we live.

(After these high compliments Theodore was quiet, and one of those present spoke up: "But how could you consider him haughty[827] as he was a being endowed with all those graces?"

(*Bishop:* Did you yourself know him for a haughty man or do you have it from someone else?

(He answered: "I did not know the man, but I heard from a tanner that he was rarely to be seen in a group of people except in church. He was irked by long conversations with those who wished to communicate with him. This is positive proof of disdain and pride, to flee from communication from those who desire it.")

John the Baptist also withdrew from crowds

Bishop: But what sort of a man is he to find fault with John's philosophy, a tanner who takes the stench of his workshop everywhere with him? If fleeing the crowd is proof of disdain, then John the Baptist must have really been a conceited man, going off as he did to the desert.[828] And the same could be said of the Savior, for it is written: *Jesus seeing the multitudes went up into a mountain, and when He was set down, His disciples—not the multitudes—came unto Him.*[829] And again: . . . *seeing the multitudes He withdrew apart.*[830]

Now the good John imitated Him as far as he was able, and he withdrew from the crowds. He took his delight in being with those who desired to learn.

Deacon: Your arguments from Scripture are well chosen. But what have you to say about his being insolent,[831] not only to a great crowd but also to one or two persons?

A single person can be a crowd

Bishop: One single person can be a harmful and especially misleading crowd, such as the man who said to Jesus: *Master, I will follow You whithersoever You go.*[832] And the Savior, was He not fleeing the crowd when He said: *Foxes (have holes)* [833] and so forth?

But you are not able to persuade me that John ever swore from the time he was baptized, or made an oath, or slandered, or lied, or caused or took part in frivolous talk.[834]

Deacon: I did not say anything like that at all, except that he was insolent.

Bishop: Oh best of friends, how is it that he who did none of these things would be insolent and unable to guard his tongue? A small sin is a defilement as well as a great one.

Deacon: I beg you, what do men say and when will they cease speaking?

Bishop: Listen to me and pay no heed to nonsensical talk. You will never defend yourself on that score. Those who do not live right have no upright reputation. They always reason from probabilities and they waste all their time at this, especially if no one dares to contradict them. They speak the strangest things about the Savior, even God Himself, who in life and word and deed was above man[835] and above prophet.[836] They heap up arguments like a herd of swine or a swarm of flies (for so they wished it at the time). For some said: *He seduces the people.*[837] But others said: *He casts out devils in Beelzeboul chief of the devils.*[838] Others say: *Behold a gluttonous man and a wine-bibber.*[839] Still others: *He is a Samaritan and has a devil.*[840]

What profit would it be for me to bring together all their idle talk? The Savior Himself was fully aware of what was going on when He spoke to His apostles: *Whom do men say that I, the Son of Man, am?*[841] His disciples gave answers, speaking the most complimentary attributes about Him: *Some say Elias, some Jeremias, others John the Baptist.*[842] They were quiet regarding the words of the vilest of men.

Once more He asked them, separating them from the men he had mentioned before (for in his opinion they were not truly men, but the sons of God, for to us the Word *gave power to become children of God*).[843] *But whom do you say that I am?*[844] They did not all answer, but only Peter, expressing the mind of all of them: *You are the Christ, the Son of the living God.*[845] The Savior accepted the correctness of this reply and spoke out: *You are Peter, and upon this rock* (that is, the "confession")[846] *I will build My Church and the gates of Hades shall not prevail against it.*[847]

John will be honored as a martyr

Even now you should discover the same characteristics in the blame or honor given not only to John but to all. Just as at the very time that Christ and the apostles were being reviled the Ephesians were shouting: *These are they that have turned the world upside down.*[848] All that has ceased now and they are in their glory.

In the same way you shall find it after this generation; they will be honoring John as a martyr,[849] and those who were opposed to his good name will have rotted away. And those of a swinish or canine character will go about saying: *He deceives the world . . .* [850] and so on, but the disciples will look into the matter carefully, as though saying: *You are the Christ, the Son of the living God.*[851]

Now if in the case of Christ the Savior, only twelve of the many thousands of persons really did recognize Jesus at first,[852] and most people even now speak foolishly about Him, why should we be concerned as to what is said about John, who could scarcely be compared to Christ's spittle? Now why do I say 'to the spittle,' not to the hem of His garment? For *all nations*, says Isaias, *shall be counted as a drop from a bottle, and as spittle.*[853]

John's humor considered

Concerning what you said about his insolence, this is the situation, the facts are this way. First of all, John found it well nigh impossible to grant favors, not to mention being insolent, to anyone. When it came to his own colleagues, disciples, clerics, or bishops, should be perceive any of them bragging of their abstinence from anything, or the achievement of bodily discipline, he would joke with them and give them an opposite name. As, for example, he would call your proud peer who primps at the pump an "Old Soak." The man who claimed to be living in holy poverty he called a "Give-me Guy." The "Charitable Charlie" was referred to as "Gangster."[854] (This is a gracious way of teaching one's close acquaintances by stressing such qualities which they do not possess.) One thing is certain: He honored a well-tempered youth over a licentious old man and a learned oldster above an ambitious young prig; a lay person who practiced asceticism much more than a scholar who was greedy, and a pious man living in the world over and above a lazybones monk.

Scriptural reproof more severe than John

Now those who are seeking honors may consider John insolent, but he addressed himself to those who came to be enlightened, using a reproof contained in Holy Scripture: *O generation of vipers, who has warned you to flee from the wrath that is to come?*[855] So too in Acts Paul speaks to the high priest: *God shall strike you, you whited wall.*[856] And in some place the Savior speaks to the Jews: *An evil and adulterous generation seeks for a sign.*[857] And in another he addresses all the Apostles: *O fools and slow of heart.*[858] In still another place he calls Peter Satan: *Get you behind me, Satan, for you are an offence unto me.*[859]

Really, there was no serious offence to bring about such strong reproaches.

Scriptural warrant for shunning the crowd

Let us welcome the love of learning in silence since we cannot judge spiritual persons.[860] They do not revile us out of hatred for us, nor do they love the desert because of pride, training themselves for service out of love. Therefore, whoever were described to us in the holy records as good men because they are found turning away and declining the company of the ignorant,[861] it is because they fear that after a while they might become accustomed to their ways and either become degraded or even take on their evil habits.

First of all, Sara[862] advised her husband Abraham to banish from the hearth the son of the handmaid while he was still a mere child on the grounds she thought him unworthy to play with her son Isaac. She feared that with the two of them enjoying themselves[863] together he might be corrupted by Ishmael's behavior and manners. Then Jacob[864] fled for his own safety into Mesopotamia to make his sojourn there. And Lot was enjoined by the angels to leave the irreligious people of Sodom.[865] And Moses, as I said before, *when he was grown up denied himself to be the son of Pharaoh's daughter*,[866] made up his mind to remove himself from the tyrant[867] and his retinue and he advised those who shared his opinion to come away with him and prepare for the exodus.[868]

The prophets also avoided the wretched crowd and stayed in the deserts for the most part. The apostles said of them: *They wandered in deserts, and mountains, and caves, and the holes of the earth.*[869] It was to avoid associating with the lawless and because they well knew that company with such tends to deceive and to degrade those who spend their days together. Not only that, but association with such company is blameable and poisonous and can only lead to shame. For it is not natural to put up with something unpleasant or even to tolerate it briefly, for "like always attracts like."[870] As it is said: *Every beast loveth his like.*[871]

But the unlike is hostile and foreign. Now who could ever persuade a seed-picking dove or a pigeon to be fed with martens or ravens? Or the grass-eating goose or heron to herd with the bone-picking vultures? *What fellowship has light with darkness,*[872] or for that matter virtue with vice or evil with the good?

Teacher and physician compared

Deacon: How is it, then, that the Apostle says: *I became all things to all men, to the Jews as a Jew, that I might gain Jews; to the weak as weak, that I might gain the weak; to them that are without law, as without law, that I might gain them that are without law?*[873]

Bishop: That Scriptural text, dear friend of mine, does not bear upon what you have said; for Paul did not say: "I became careless to the careless, or frivolous to the frivolous, or covetous to the covetous," or anything like that. But he did say: "I became as this or that," not "I became this."

(Now I became this or that does not mean the same thing as I became this.) "As," then, is both the words and the action of the Apostle. Coming down to their level possibly accomplished no great gain, but it certainly did no harm. *I became to the Jews as a Jew in order to gain Jews.*[874] Still, he was of the Jews, being circumcised;[875] how then does he say *as a Jew* and not *Jewish?*

He was often found observing the Sabbath and fasting along with them in no contradiction to the teachings of the Savior,[876] with the intention of bringing the Jews to a more perfect way of life by this association with them.[877] So it is with physicians. They do not always stay with their patients or have the benefits of the same sickness,[878] and they do not rage with the same delirious cravings. The same manner of life behooves the teacher. He does not waste time among crowds but leads a quiet life, making investigations and seeking out the difference of characters of many different kinds.[879]

So it is too with skilled physicians. They spend a good deal of time at their books and read up on the causes of sicknesses, and so prescribe the proper remedies. They approach the ill only to find out their symptoms and to administer the medicine; they do not play games with them or dine with them. It is not the part of the medical craft to eat with one's patients or to play with them, but to restore the ailing to health.

Therefore, I beg you, stop at once and do not keep up the torture on these points. Virtue is never conquered by the censure of every chatterbox. But rather accept my opinion and put a guard at the portals to your ears to protect them from everything they hear, lest they should sound off with every report stored up in their memory to the disturbance of your mind. Please, let me finish the rest of my account for I must be on my way.

And Theodore spoke up:

Deacon: What of those bishops who were sent along with our delegation? I am referring to Eulysius and Palladius and Cyriacus and Demetrius. We have heard by the grapevine that they were banished.

Bishop: If what I previously told you about the blessed John is perfectly clear to you and is not a patchwork of lies, I will try to explain anything you desire provided you remember those things.

Chapter 20
The Saints Find Their Reward in God

Saintly example and results

Deacon: I am as fully acquainted with what you said as though I were at the places in my own person. Proof is sufficient that I believe your account when you consider my close attention. While my memory of it is still fresh I shall write it down upon prime parchment as a memorial to our generation and as a help for those who are ambitious for the episcopate.[880] Such men should be like the holy John, or like yourself, who have imitated the way of the martyrs for the sake of truth; either that or simply abandon even attempting a burden beyond their strength and be satisfied with the humdrum life of the layman.[881] For it is better to give passage money to experienced pilots to make a safe journey than to usurp the pilot's place and thereby lose both vessel and cargo by shipwreck. You have described everything concerning the blessed John: how he lived a strict life and likewise how he managed in the churches, both in Antioch and in Constantinople, and how he was arrested and packed off into exile and all these bitter trials which he reaped from evil disposed persons. You told us too of Porphyrius and the Eunuch[882] of Ephesus. Now please, tell us the rest. Who of them died in prison? Who of John's communion were banished? It is only right that we should honor their memory to encourage the faithful. Here in the earthly realm servants who suffer on behalf of their master either by imprisonment or blows or torture are in turn richly rewarded with acts of kindness and even granted their freedom. How much more so do those who suffer for the sake of Christ merit honor and goodwill from the Church. The Apostle says of them: *As prisoners with the prisoners, evil entreated with those that are evil entreated, as being themselves in the body.*[883] For *precious in the sight of the Lord is the death of His saints.*[884]

Chrysostom's followers also suffered

Bishop: You have spoken very well. Now listen. As for the bishops, a first rumor had it that they had been drowned in the sea. However, the true story is that they were banished beyond the borders of their own territory into barbarian zones,[885] where they are even now still kept prisoners under police guard. A deacon who had travelled along with them said that Cyriacus was at Palmyra, a frontier post of Persia some eighty miles farther inland from Emesa.[886] He said that Eulysius of Bostra[887] in Arabia was some three days away at a fort called Misphas, close by the Saracens. Palladius was kept under guard near the Blemmyans[888] or the Ethiopians at a place called Syene.[889] Demetrius was in the oasis in the neighborhood of the Mazici (there are other oases). Serapion had been accused of numerous unfounded charges and he underwent bodily tortures at the savage treatment from his judges, even to the extraction of his teeth, and report has it that he was finally banished to his own country.[890] Hilarius,[891] an aged holy man, was transported to innermost Pontus after he was beaten up, not by the judge mind you, but by the clergy. He had spent eighteen years not eating bread but partaking only of herbs or boiled wheat. Antonius[892] exiled himself to live in the caves of Palestine. Timotheus[893] of Maroneia[894] and John of Lydia[895] are both supposed to be in Macedonia. Rhodon[896] of Asia went on to Mitylene. Gregory[897] of Lydia is said to be in Phrygia. Brisson,[898] brother of Palladius, left his church on his own initiative and lives on his own little farm, cultivating the land with his own hands. Rumor has it that Lampetius[899] is being cared for somewhere in Lydia by a certain Eleutherus[900] and spends his time reading. Eugenius is in his own country. Elpidius, the great bishop of Laodicea, and Pappus have spent three entire years never even coming downstairs,[901] devoting themselves to prayer. Heracleides of Ephesus has been shut up in the prison of Nicomedia for four years now.

As for the rest of the bishops in communion with John, some lost courage and communicated with Atticus, being transferred to other churches in Thrace, and some disappeared altogether. Report has it that Anatolius[902] is in Gall. As for the priests, some were exiled to Arabia and Palestine. Tigrius[903] went to Mesopotamia. Philip[904] fled to Pontus and died there. Theophilus[905] lives in Paphlagonia. John, son of Aethrius,[906] established a monastery in Caesarea, Stephanus[907] was exiled to Arabia but the Isaurians dragged him from the jailer and freed him to go to Taurus. They say that Sallustius[908] is in Crete. I have heard that Philip[909] the ascetic, the priest in charge of the schools,[910] is lying sick in Campania. Sophronius,[911] the deacon, is in prison in the Thebaid. Paul[912] the deacon, the assistant to the steward, is said to be in Africa. Another Paul,[913] deacon of the Church of the Resurrection, is in Jerusalem. Helladius,[914] presbyter of the palace, lives on his own little farm in Bithynia. Many of them are hiding out in Constantinople, others have gone off to their own countries. Silvanus,[915] the holy bishop, is in Troas, living as a fisherman. Stephanus,[916] the ascetic who had brought letters from Rome,[917] was flogged for that reason at Constantinople and thrown into prison for two months. Communion with Atticus was offered to him as a pretext for liberty but he refused and was flogged most unmercifully, the skin being torn from his ribs and his breast (I have seen it myself). However, his life was saved by the loving care of Christ, if only for further trials; for after ten months of medical care he was banished to Pelusium.

There was a certain soldier of the Imperial Guard,[918] Provincalius[919] by name. He was accused of being friendly to John and was exiled to Petra after many stripes and cruel torture. A household servant of Elpidius[920] the priest was hired, they say, with a bribe of fifty coins to slay the holy John by treachery. He was caught with three swords on his person and he wounded seven of his captors, one after the other. They buried four of them at once and the remaining three were saved only after a long period of medical care, but the murderer went scot-free.[921] The blessed Eutropius,[922] undefiled of women, a cantor,[923] was struck and flayed most unmercifully on his sides and forehead so that his eyebrows were pulled out. Finally oil lamps were lit close to his ribs which had been laid bare to the bone on both sides, and he expired on the rack. He was buried in the middle of the night by the clergy who had committed this crime. God himself joined in attesting to his death by a vision of singers as a sign of the similarity of his death to the passion of the Savior.[924]

The adventures of the eastern bishops

The deacon who returned to us from the bishops[925] told us that the prefect's officers in charge of them treated them so badly in carrying out their orders, which came from heaven knows where, that they prayed for death and a welcome release from life. The money which the bishops had for their own expenses on the journey was taken from them and divided among themselves by the guards. They forced them to ride bareback and made a two-day journey in one day by riding until late evening and starting out again before dawn. Their stomachs could scarcely keep down the little food that was given them; their guards did not spare insulting them with indecent and irreverent language. They took away Palladius' boy servant and forced him to give up his notebook. One of those in charge treated Demetrius very badly and he kept driving him on with a spear[926] until late evening. Soon afterwards that guard was stricken with pain and he died in terrible agony, and the inspired ones knew this was the punishment for his cruelty. Palladius had told him beforehand (so a fellow soldier[927] told us): "You shall not make another journey, but shall die a miserable death."

They did not permit them to visit a church; they put them up in inns where there were crowds of prostitutes or in the synagogues of Samaritans or Jews, mostly from Tarsus. And then a new thought inspired them in their distress, something not considered before. One of the bishops spoke up:[928]

"Why do we grieve over our lodgings? Is it our concern where we stay? Are we responsible as though we committed sin of our own volition? Do you not realize that everything that has happened and will happen that God is glorified in all things?[929] How many of these prostitutes who had forgotten God, or perhaps never had knowledge of Him to begin with, have been brought to the fear and knowledge of God? When they saw us so badly treated did they better their own way of life or at least did worsen it? It is no small matter for the reasonable soul to have a little relief even in a time of suffering; it is as it were a stimulus to self-control.[930] As Paul, the teacher of sacred things who submitted to the same evils, says: *We are a sweet savor of Christ among them that are being saved and and among them that are perishing,*[931] because *we have been made a spectacle to angels and to men.*"[932]

The local bishops in communion with Theophilus throughout the entire East (as an ascetic who came forward said)[933] came to such a pass in their cruelty that some of them not only failed to demonstrate consideration and moderation but also persuaded the officials to drive them out of the city more speedily by the use of bribes. They who were most guilty in this respect were the bishops of Tarsus[934] and Antioch,[935] Eulogius,[936] bishop of Caesarea in Palestine and above all the bishop of Ancyra[937] and Ammonius[938] bishop of Pelusium. This last-named forced the soldiers in charge, first by bribes, then by threats, to act still more savage to them so they would not allow members of the laity who wished to do so to offer them hospitality.

History repeats itself

Just so the blessed John, when writing to Gaius in his catholic[939] epistles, condemns a certain bishop but commends the hospitality of Gaius and calls on him not to imitate evil bishops. This is the reading:

Unto Gaius the beloved whom I love in truth. Beloved, I pray that in all things you may prosper and be in health, even as your soul prospers. For I rejoiced greatly when some came and declared to me, that you walk in truth, and wherein you did refresh the saints. I have no greater joy than this.[940] And afterwards he added: *I wrote unto the church, but Diotrephes, who loves to have the preeminence among them did not receive us, prating against us with wicked words; and not content therewith, neither does he himself receive the brethren, and them that do he forbids, and casts them out of the Church.* And a little later he adds advice: *Beloved, imitate not that which is evil; for he that does good is of God; he that does evil has not seen God.*[941]

I have quoted this entire passage regarding the wickedness of the olden time long ago to show up the mind of the kind of Diotrephes' we have today. But he praised and admired the bishops of the second Cappadocia,[942] because they displayed great grief with much weeping about the banished bishops. Especially was this true of the most gentle Theodore of Tyana and Bosporius[943] of Coloneia, who held the bishoprics for forty-eight years, and Sarapion[944] of Ostracina, who had held the office of bishop for forty-five years.

The wicked apparently prosper

Theodore was speechless for a long time and finally said:

Deacon: Father, what are we to say of these doings? Is it really *the last hour*[945] and the *falling away* which Paul mentions as prelude to those things and the rest: . . . *that the son of perdition who opposes may be revealed?*[946]

The very notion of the evil people being successful and even prospering in such deeds and getting along for so long a time and gaining more power, but the good people are persecuted and are slandered, and this drives me into great fear that He is very close at hand.

Bishop: By all means, my dear intelligent man, the end is close at hand, according to what is said: *Little children, it is the last hour.*[947] *The master of the house went out about the eleventh hour,*[948] *to hire laborers into his vineyard.*[949]

Now the last of the twelve hours is the end; and if the Apostle spoke of the last hour over four hundred years ago, so much more so it is now by all means the end.

The simile of the sieve

Now all these things from the very beginning came about by the Lord's permission. It was for the training of the saints; the devil is begging for them.[950] Such was the word of the Savior: *Simon, Simon, Satan asked to have you, that he might sift you as wheat; but I made supplication for you, that your faith may not fail.*[951]

Now Jesus did not make supplication for Peter alone, but for all who have the faith of Peter. For the sieve can only signify the circle of earth filled with pleasures and pains which form as we say various openings through which worldly people descend to hell. They are separated as it were from the good grain by those holes. Some pass through the hole of gluttony, *whose god is their belly;*[952] some through that of love of pleasure of which the prophet speaks: *lead astray by the spirit of fornication,*[953] (for *neither fornicators, nor adulterers, nor the effeminate shall inherit the kingdom of God*).[954] Others pass through the hole of covetousness,[955] such as have espoused the bride of idolatry; others through anger and pride—they are the ones who loved bestial darkness of whom John said: *He that hates his brother is in darkness until now,*[956] for *anger*, says the writer of Proverbs, *destroys even the prudent.*[957]

Some fall through accidie and forgetfulness, since they do not cherish wakefulness of memory and keep saying: *My heart slept through weariness*[958] (those whom the world calls wretched and says: *Woe unto you who have lost patience, and what will you do when the Lord shall visit you?*).[959]

Others again go through the whole gamut of irrational self-display of whom the psalmist declares: *For God hath scattered the bones of the men-pleasers.*"[960] Others fall through the hole of false pretense[961] or pride, which is disdain; the prophet rebukes them as deserters: *The proud have transgressed exceedingly, yet have I not swerved from the law.*[962]

Now each of these vices is followed by others much worse. Envy follows pride; hatred, stinginess,[963] and lying follow upon covetousness; passion is followed by anger or revengefulness, insolence and murder;[964] fornication is followed by forgetfulness, heedlessness, idleness, indifference, unprofitable loss of sleep. Vainglory is followed by inquisitiveness, acts of bribery, illusions, hypocrisy, snobbery, traits of partiality, quackery; pride is followed by overweening arrogance, heartlessness, impiety, distractions of the mind, and so forth and so on.[965] There is no call for me to speak further, giving more force to my argument; what has been said is well demonstrated.

Only pride has no contrary virtue

To each one of these vices God has assigned its contrary virtue. Thus self-control is opposed to lust, temperance to greediness, justice to covetousness, meekness to anger, joy to sorrow, memory to forgetfulness, patience to accidie, good sense to foolishness, courage to cowardice, humility to vainglory, and so on; and Holy Scripture is opposed to all of these.[966] Only to pride has He not given its contrary virtue, because it is so overwhelmingly bad; He has kept it for Himself as He said: *God resists the proud.*[967] So prays the prophet also, saying: *Lift up your hand against their pride, even to the end.*[968] And again: *Render to the proud their desert.*[969] And so as: *The tree is known by its fruit*[970] (as the Lord said: *By their fruits you shall know them;*[971] so is each man, whether he is a saint actually or only so-called).

More scriptural illustrations

This is why the good fortune of the wicked is always undisturbed, for God puts up with them for a long time.[972] This is indeed fitting for Him[973] to predict for us, what the saints have undergone earlier as a consolation for us who suffer.[974] First of all there is Job, the son of patience;[975] what did he say after much suffering?

As for me, is my reproof of men (referring to his shamelessness)? *Why should I not be impatient? Look unto me, and be admonished, and lay your hand upon your mouth. For if I remember, I am troubled, and pains take hold of my flesh. Wherefore do the wicked live and become old in riches? Their seed is according to their desire, and their children are before their eyes, their houses prosper, nowhere is fear; the rod of the Lord is not upon them. Their cow does not cast her calf; she is preserved from heat; she is with young and does not fail. They abide as sheep forever. Their children play, taking the psaltery and harp, and rejoice at the sound of the psalm, they fulfill their life in good things, and they sleep in the rest of hades. Yet he says unto God: "Depart from me, I do not desire to know Thy ways."*[976]

David the long-suffering, the singer of the divine judgments, intones something like that: *I will sing to you of mercy and judgment, O Lord.*[977] *How good is God to Israel, even unto them that are pure of heart. But my feet were almost shaken; my steps had well nigh slipped.*[978] And why? *For I was stirred at the lawless, when I saw the peace of sinners.*[979]

And in another passage again he reproaches them for their wealth, saying: *Their oxen are fat, their sheep bring forth abundantly, abounding in their streets, their garners are full affording store from this unto that. Their daughters are beautiful, adorned in the likeness of a temple.*[980] And he adds in admiration at their evil harmony and peace: *There is no outcry in their streets, nor falling of a fence in their houses.*[981] Then he inveighs against the debased opinions of the crowds, saying: *They counted as blessed the people who have these things;*[982] and he adds: *Blessed is the people whose helper is the Lord God of Israel.*[983]

But I must not stop at this point or I shall run the risk of falling short with my proofs.

Listen now to what Habakkuk has to say, striking his breast in his distress at the same time: *How long, O Lord, shall I cry, suffering wrongfully and you will not hear.*[984] He called the sons of his neighbors his own and being full of brotherly love he added: *I will cry unto you and you will not save. Why did you show me iniquity, and that I shall look upon labors that lead to hardships and impiety? Judgment is against me, and the judge takes reward. Therefore is the law perverted, and judgment does not go forth, unto the end; for the wicked does oppress the righteous.*[985]

In the same spirit does Jeremiah, the most sympathetic of the saints, cry out when in a quandary over all other men: *Righteous are you, O Lord, when I shall plead with You; yet will I speak judgments unto You, O Lord. Why does the way of the wicked prosper? All they that set at naught are at ease; You did plant them and they took root* (this is instead of saying: "they live riotously") *and they bore fruit* (certainly not of the Spirit). *You are near their mouth and far from their reins.*[986]

The wise prophet Sophonias[987] has a passage with the same force; he is reproaching men for slandering their neighbors and finding fault with divine providence,[988] and he is even declaring the saints were wretched. He speaks in the Lord's person: *Your words have been unsufferable to me, says the Lord. And you said, Wherein did we speak against You? You said, He is vain who serves God; and what profit, that we kept his charges, and that we walked as suppliants before the Lord Almighty? And now we call strangers happy, and all that work lawless things and built up, and they resisted God, and are delivered. These things spoke they that feared the Lord, each one to his neighbors.*[989]

Paul, the herald of piety,[990] adds this to what has been said: *But evil men and imposters shall wax worse and worse, deceiving and being deceived.*[991] Then he points out vile conditions in which saints are held, saying: *For I think that God has set forth us the apostles last of all, as men doomed to death; for we are made a spectacle unto the world and to angels, and to men. For even unto this present hour, and both hunger and thirst, and are naked, and have no certain dwelling place, and labor with our own hands* (cataloging his bodily sufferings) *being reviled we bless; being persecuted, we endure; being defamed, we entreat; we are made as the filth of the world, the offscouring of all things even unto now.*[992]

The good and just God spreads out the world before us for certain unspeakable reasons like a race track,[993] but we on our part must cooperate as we see fit, using the free will He has given us and paying the just penalty for our misdeeds, just as the law says: *I have set before your face, death and life, choose what you will.*[994]

Why He set it so, it is not for us to say at the present time except that He did so set it.[995] For it were not wise for us to come into the world without sin[996] and without struggles before us, and with our mind not firmly set in the right path, for to the Divine and Eternal alone can sinlessness be imputed.[997]

Deacon: You have confronted our difficulty very well and nicely, too, father. You have given eyes to the souls of those here present who were somewhat perplexed, some not having a good knowledge of Holy Scripture, others not understanding that the Church is designed through all ages as a training school.[998] She points out to her own crowned victors, men and women alike who had eaten the body of Christ, but not without paying the price. But the confusion you have suffered and the breakdown between the churches cause us great grief.

Truth shall conquer in the end

Bishop: I wonder at you, most honored of men, Theodore. First of all you grant that suffering has a certain benefit; then you turn about-face and say the very opposite. You bless us as crowned victors, then say that we are miserable exiled persons bereft of our church buildings.[999] To me you seem to be as affected as those rustic spectators at the Olympic games; they stand with open mouth at the sight of the prizes, but they behold with horror and tears the blows which the contestants exchange with each other.

I myself would much prefer to travel the valleys and glens and the deep seas with truth than to possess great honor which the present world thinks of as prosperity and to be burdened the whole while with falsehood. If I possess truth I shall possess all things, for all things serve truth.[1000] Should I possess falsehood I am not my own master, as I am not hers. Once I have truth I do not wish to have her simply as a mistress or a slave or even a neighbor, but rather as a sister.

If at all possible I would prefer to have her as a bride to profit in her pleasure and even to inherit it as my own wife. For she is the daughter of absolute truth and the good man is her son-in-law. For he who has this zeal is rejuvenated and does not grow old and fade away. He has a zeal hotter than fire;[1001] his language is sharper than a sword; his life is more free than that of an eagle. Relentlessly he runs as to a house-mother to meditate on Holy Scripture; he blossoms continually with gladness, he is not daunted by fear. He carries himself with courage; he is filled with religious enthusiasm; he hates no man. He has concern for those who live rightly. He calls those men blessed who contentedly mind their own business. He sorrows with the sorrow of the Spirit at priestly carelessness, against which the Apostle spoke: *Grieve not the Holy Spirit, whereby you are sealed unto the day of redemption.*[1002]

He who turns his back on the Spirit carelessly grieves with the Holy Spirit. Finally (but why should I rehash the whole thing?) he died, grieving no man but only the demons and their neighbors. His time was more than enough; he did not fritter away his days in evil acts. He doubled the money that had been entrusted to him,[1003] and he paid off ahead of time the interest of good works; in a short time he fulfilled many years.[1004] He did not make a will[1005] in regard to his property, since he had already disposed of all by his life and thinking. Did death knock at the door of his emaciated body? Before John beheld him outside, he shouted: *Let us go from here*,[1006] and he intoned the Psalm: *Woe is me that my sojourn has been so long*,[1007] and had it not been that his Master had sent him he should have begun legal action against Him because He came so tardily.

But he is happy now, freed at last from his frail body that suffered so much, as one goes from a delapidated guest-house that was about to come tumbling down. He pricked up his ears at the One who said: *Well done, good and faithful servant*,[1008] knowing that he would hear the rest. Now let this torrent of words be proof sufficient to you of my reasons, *for out of the abundance of the heart the mouth speaks*.[1009]

Falsehood carries its own punishment

Now he who lives with falsehood has a sorry life. At one time he rejoices exceedingly at the addition to his money bag, or at his miserable reputation, or at the love of some miserable whore, or even at the discomfiture of another. On the other hand, sometimes he sorrows on the point of death, spending his time in dreams of change and uncertainties. His nights are sleepless and troubled. He imagines plots against himself even by his associates. He has lost faith in himself and distrusts all men as liars.[1010] This is what he resembles: he is as cowardly as a rabbit, as bold as a swine, as deceitful as a chameleon, as roguish as a partridge,[1011] as pitiless as a wolf, and as untameable as a mouse. He is his own enemy, jealous without cease, punishing himself though he reckons it not. One who continually plots evil for others inevitably brings it on himself.

Did death sting him? He gave away everything to gain a little, so dear was it to him. What time was granted him he frittered away heedlessly; not only did he not double his penny,[1012] but he did not even save it.[1013] He trembles constantly like a leaf, not wishing for old age, and still he worries himself with foolish imaginings of senile men. He fears death as a god, for to him the material world is God. But what then? He turns pallid, he shivers, he is in agony; he anticipates the judgment of God and tortures himself with the thought. His conscience keeps badgering him without let or hindrance. He recalls his evil deeds one by one; at last his sufferings are far worse than those of evil-doers being whipped. He crawls down before those in power for the time being[1014] like an abject slave; he pays shameful flattery to the world. Instead of one Lord he has ten thousand masters, so he should save himself from being the servant of truth. He strives to be above fear, yet he fears everyone.

The Church of Rome decides

Let it be said that I have told you all I can. Should there perchance be someone who can give an account which is truer or in more graceful style, let him correct my worthless attempt. I should welcome him gladly as a corrector and friend of the brethren, and I would give thanks to the Savior for everything.

But now, please, do me the favor and give me an account of the synod in the West, and thus you will confirm my arguments, if they are agreeable to you and have been of any help.

After a pause in the narrative Theodore spoke up:

Deacon: May the Lord grant mercy on that day[1015] to you who have given me this wonderful narrative, because he held off from communion with such people and also for such a clear picture. May the Lord bear in mind every sacrifice of John, that he did not cease from being outspoken right up to his death. The decision of the church of Rome was that they should by no means be in communion with the bishops of the East, and especially not with Theophilus, until such time the Lord should grant an opportunity for an ecumenical synod,[1016] which would heal the rotted limbs of those men who had perpetrated these deeds. For even though the blessed John has gone to sleep, nevertheless truth is very much awake for which a search shall be made.

Chrysostom's enemies are the Church's enemies

I would gladly meet face to face with those who perpetrated such offenses in the Church and say to them: "Where is your priesthood? Where is your holiness? Where is your gentleness and common bond[1017] of your human nature? Where are the precepts of the Savior?"

I mean: *If you are offering your gift, and remember that your brother hath aught against you, go your way, first be reconciled to your brother, and so offer your gift.*[1018]

Where is this one: *If any man smite you on the right cheek, turn to him the other also?*[1019] Where is your meditation upon the Scripture—I mean: *Behold, what is beautiful and what is pleasant, but for brothers to dwell together in unity?*[1020] Or this one: *Let brothers be helpful in times of adversity?*[1021]

Why have you ever turned this one completely around: *A brother helped by a brother is a strong city?*[1022] Now a *brother* when falsely accused or plundered *by a brother* is *as a city* which has been distressed and without walls. How is it that you people, not once but three times wretched,[1023] could have tried to accomplish this very irreconcilable project? By what kind of reasoning did you not refrain from your murderous attack against John as though he was your enemy? And how has it come to this pass that you are so enraged against one another? How could you ever have shown so great a change as you did from mildness to ferocity and to change to savagery? I am amazed and exceedingly shocked at this complete about-face of yours. I see that everything is thrown into a complete state of confusion. Why have you become so overbearing in your boldness that you insult this suckling and nursing[1024] Church of God and hack this teeming womb to pieces? Thus the prophetic message is fulfilled in you: *Because they did pursue their brother with the sword, and brought to destruction the womb upon the earth.*[1025] By this womb the divine and saving Word concurred, sowing and planting you and also John for countless good and useful works.[1026]

Instead of being of mutual help to each other, what has ever happened that you determined not to hold your peace and live quietly for the time to come? You were created to help one another mutually; why would you abuse this grace? Not only did you not make others' burdens more bearable, but by pushing them aside you cut them off from their own relatives. Listen to the voice of the prophet crying out to you: *Have we not all one Father? Did not one God create us?*[1027]

Who really breaks the law?

But you tell me: "John sinned against the law." In what way? The same law which you have trampled on and brought to naught by your evil ways. Where then is the law of nature which bids us make corrections in a spirit of gentleness? Why then do you abuse even the law which enemies observe and persecute and act against them in a way only befitting an enemy? Would it not have been much better had you associated with them and shared with them in common, had you come to common agreement in counsels for the giving of thanks and being well pleasing to your Father?

Now complete harmony in their enjoyment of blessings is a virtue in children; their parents rejoice in it and look forward to nothing greater than this. Rest assured on this point that there is no other tie of friendship and good disposition than being sincere and doing everything as is pleasing to the Father, who is the source of our being, our support, and our very preservation.[1028]

God's punishment must surely follow

But you have despised God as a fool and brought on war within the Church, as the prophet said: *They established madness in the Lord's house,*[1029] instead of pressing and urging each other along. In addition you waged truceless battles among yourselves against the mind and purpose of the Father.

I can say in addition to this that it has exceedingly enraged even God Himself and moved Him to wrath as well as all who approach Him: His sons, your own brothers, and it ill behooves Him to remain silent (for He is not negligent or unmindful of the well-being of His children).[1030] For that reason is He angered at your folly and tyranny over those you have wronged. Therefore He does not judge it right that you should get off scot-free (for He has already begun your punishment). For it would not be becoming to Him or safe for you; your calamity is unbearable and there is no remedy at hand. He beholds you much the worse because of blows and bruises without number as a result of your chastisement.

A great senseless and most unbending cloud presses down upon you, your brethren, your kin, your associates, and also your allies and those who dine with you, those who share the same couch with you at the table,[1031] in a word, all those who happen to be closely bound to you in one and the same relationship. Now you have perverted all these relationships into the most bitter hatred since they were exiled from their own countries and from their family hearths, and they went far away deprived of city or home. Furthermore, you brought it about that they became fugitives as far as it was in your power to do so. Nor did you impose a time limit on their exile, but as far as you were concerned it would be forever, so savage-hearted you are and so completely led astray.

Chrysostom is glorified

This is the profit which you gained over them and over the blessed John. You stirred up your spiteful hate into fiery passion;[1032] it was like a sword that has been sharpened. Up to now you have loosened your tongue[1033] against John and nursed your wrath instead of welcoming profitable instruction, and you poured out accusations against the Church, defiling those who would listen. And these are the same ones whom *the Lord will reward according to his works*[1034] in mercy and in loving kindness.

O blessed John, with what kind of words shall I weave an *unfading crown*[1035] to bring you? I do not fear to praise you now you have finished your race[1036] (for you have breasted the highest wave). Or shall they be those words of the law spoken by Moses when he blessed the active Joseph and the contemplative Levi the priest[1037] (for I see them both in you)?[1038]

Blessed of the Lord be his land, and from the mountains of heaven, and dew, and abysses of springs beneath, and in the time of fruits, the turnings of

the sun and the comings together of the months, from the heads of the moun-
tains which are from the beginning, and from the heads of the everlasting
hills; they shall be on the head of Joseph (and every man shall be as Joseph)
and upon the head of the brethren whom he ruled, glorified among his brethren
as the first-born. The beauty of a bull are his horns, his horns are the horns of
a unicorn; with them he shall push the nation, even unto the end of the
earth.[1039]

And to Levi he said (and to whosoever imitates him): *Give to Levi*
his signs, and his truth to the holy man, whom they tried in trial, and reviled
at the water of contradiction. Who says to his father and mother, I have not
seen you, neither did he acknowledge his brethren, he observed your oracles,
and kept your covenant; he showed your judgments to Jacob, and your law to
Israel. He shall ever place incense upon your altar upon your feast day. Bless,
Lord, his strength, and accept the work of his hands; smite the eyebrows of the
enemies that rise up against him, and let them that hate him rise not up
again.[1040]

I should also add to this and say: "Jesus Christ, let not those who
love him be ashamed; for yours is the power forever. Amen."

Bishop: And this is the practice of your mind, O Theodore, you
seeker after noble truths,[1041] to produce (as the Savior said) *new things*
and old[1042] from the treasury of your mind. Now, by old things he
means the teaching of purely human wisdom; by new things are
meant the oracles of the Holy Spirit.

You have given an agreeable account to both sides of John's
character from these treasures.[1043] It augured well for your own common sense when you spoke of the offenses committed against him
and to weave for John the crown he so well merited from the blessings of Moses. As priest he served without self-interest; true it was,
that in his zealous judgment he did not know father or mother or any
blood kindred, but those who loved and labored for the Word.

At present we have men who claim to be bishops—a lowly
breed who have bogged down in acquiring money and military operations and striving for honorable positions. They transgress the
law which says: *The priests shall not give their sons to the rulers, and them*
that run beside the king.[1044] They squander the things of the Spirit in intrigue, in various miserable plots, in imprisonments, and in banish-

ments. They drink themselves into a state of debauchery, thinking that they can dishonor the friends of virtue of whom the Savior said: *The days shall come, in which they who kill you will think that they do God service.*[1045]

Ambition breeds jealousy

Now he certainly was not thinking of the Gentiles, for then he would have said "the gods," since by the word "god" they mean many gods. Now when He speaks of the one and only God He made it clear to those who were now ravaging the Church on the plea they were really helping it. Thus they cover up their own willfulness, jealousy pretending they are concerned for the good of the Church they have ravaged by their deeds. But even though they are so clever the outcome of events will make it quite clear they were really the underdogs of the one who boasted: *I shall never be shaken from generation to generation without evil.*[1046] For the serpent, the inventor of lawlessness and the cultivator of the worst form of envy, did not find a newer type of heresy. So he infuriated those in authority in the Church to mutual slaughter to satisfy their desire for the episcopal office and even the primacy in the episcopate. It was for this they tore the Church asunder.

Chrysostom's enemies inspired by satan

For if the harmony of the Spirit of God had its abode among the bishops and if John had been the source of doing evil, and was therefore unworthy of the priesthood, or because of his overweening pride (as Theophilus says),[1047] then the all-powerful wisdom of God[1048] would have prevented his exercising his priesthood by canon law. Or it could have found means by which he could have been removed without confusion and wailing, either by death or paralysis, or by loss of voice. We know that some of those who resisted him have suffered and will continue to suffer these very things. Now it is only too clear that the route they followed was the work of the devil and unworthy of the Savior—he was not simply deposed, he was exiled—John had been destroying the devil's own kingdom.

I realize that John deposed six bishops with every right to do so for they were guilty of buying the dignity of Holy Orders. I spoke of them earlier. Then who wept? Whose nose dripped blood? What cobweb was broken? Who left his house? Who was fined an obol? Who in all Asia, beggar or craftsman or farmer or shoemaker or fellow commoner, did not rejoice at what had been done for the vindication of the sacred canons? Each one cried out: *How are Your works magnified, O Lord? In wisdom did You do them all!*[1049]

For where God is at work everything is done in wisdom, but when that demon who hates good gets a chance, everything is likewise done in ignorance. Monstrous evils follow close upon ignorance: envy, murders, strife, false emulation, evil tempers, arguments, mutual discord, loud noises, plots by the ignorant, the ambitions of those in power, the gallows, torture by fire,[1050] blood lettings,[1051] intolerable fines, confiscations, breakdown of divine ordinances, contempt of law, rejection of moderation, universal schism, policing by land and by sea, instruments of torture used on ship, on horses, on foot, anything to impede those who travelled for the sake of truth.

God abides His time

How then could they say: "John was expelled by God's dispensation"? Let those who spread such nonsense say to me: "Was the all-powerful wisdom of God at a loss (so I said) to stop John by some unseen power if he was unworthy? Or to persuade those who disagreed with him to bear patiently with his actions without the use of force by the magistrates? For if God is the same God who cooperated with Moses for the freedom and obedience of Israel while Pharoah cried out openly: *I know not God and I will not let the people go,*[1052] how did He need the help of earthly magistrates to help where John was concerned?"

Was it because He had grown old, or was too weak, or without any help? And He who had revealed the adulteries of some and the pederasties of others and the witchcraft and magic of still others, now would He have been powerless to correct John?

Or again, He caused a man's tongue to swell up with a constriction so that he was forced to make his confession in writing.[1053] Another met his death in a sudden crisis. And a third was tormented by worms so that he lay for about a year speechless upon his couch. Still another was attacked by a most painful case of gout. Another's legs were badly burned. And there is also one who all know died of a most disagreeable death.

Now I ask you: was He who allowed all those things to happen too weak to prevent John from committing sacrilegious acts (as you say)? Was it that He needed the help of so-and-so before He could exile John and so add to His own glory?

God punishes and rewards

They deceived themselves, not knowing[1054] the command of the Word. Now one can hardly call a man sacrilegious who distributed gold or silver or silken fabrics, the food of moths,[1055] to the poor. But he is sacrilegious who sells the teachings and ordinances of the Savior for money and good reputation and pleasures of the table. Next is the one who treats outrageously a holy man adorned by his life and words, the man through whom the Savior gave to drink of the Word from a chalice or a plate as it were, the viaticum for their salvation to those who love Him. Let them be called sacrilegious who robbed the Apostolic Church in sacrilegious manner, they who deprived her of such illustrious teachers and who sell ordinations for money.

The divine justice will hunt them down to correct their evil actions. For if those who corrupted[1056] the law of Moses[1057] were driven out of the temple by the Savior with a whip made of cords because they were selling doves there,[1058] what kind of punishment do they receive who barter the priesthood of the new covenant, except to be cut into shreds by the *iron rod*[1059] of the Chief Shepherd?

As the Apostle says: *A man that has set at naught Moses' law dies without compassion on the word of two or three witnesses. Of how much sorer punishment, do you think shall he be judged worthy, who has trodden under foot the Son of God, and has counted the blood of the covenant, wherewith he was sanctified, an unholy thing, and has done despite to the spirit of grace? For we know Him who says, Vengeance belongeth unto me, I will recomp-*

ence, says the Lord. It is a fearful thing to fcll into the hands of the living God.[1060]

May God who made this holy man glorious, this saintly shepherd, this lamp of justice, may He grant to us part of the inheritance with him in the awful day of righteous judgment. To Him be glory, honor, majesty, and magnificence, to the Father, Son, and Holy Spirit, now and evermore to all ages. Amen.

Here ends the historical dialogue of
Palladius, bishop of Helenopolis,
with Theodore, deacon of Rome,
on the life and deeds
of our father and
archbishop of Constantinople,
John the Golden-Mouthed.[1061]

NOTES

LIST OF ABBREVIATIONS

AB	Analecta Bollandiana (Brussels 1882–)
ACW	Ancient Christian Writers (Westminster, Md.-London-New York-Paramus, N.J. 1946–)
Arndt-Gingrich	W.F. Arndt and F.W. Gingrich, trans. and edd., *A Greek-English Lexicon of the New Testament and Other Early Christian Literature* (Chicago 1957)
Baur	Dom Chrysostom Baur, O.S.B., *John Chrysostom and His Times* (2 vols., Westminster, Md. 1959–1960)
Bigot	E. Bigot, editio princeps of *Dial.* (Paris 1680)
BZ	Byzantinische Zeitschrift (Leipzig 1892–1943)
Coleman-Norton	P. R. Coleman-Norton, ed., *Palladii Dialogus de vita sancti Johannis Chrysostomi*
DACL	*Dictionnaire d'archéologie chrétienne et de liturgie* (Paris 1907–1953)
DCB	W. Smith and H. Wace, edd., *Dictionary of Christian Biography, Literature, Sects and Doctrines* (4 vols., London 1877–1887)
Dial.	Palladius, *Dialogus de vita sancti Johannis Chrysostomi*
HE	*Ecclesiastical History*
HL	Palladius, *The Lausiac History* (trans. by R. T. Meyer in ACW 34)
LCL	Loeb Classical Library (London 1912–)
LSJ	H. G. Liddell-R. Scott-H. S. Jones *et al.*, *A Greek-English Lexicon* (Oxford 1940)
LTK	Lexikon für Theologie and Kirche (2nd ed., Freiburg 1957–1967)
MG	J. P. Migne, ed., Patrologia graeca (Paris 1857–1866)

Moore	H. Moore, trans., *The Dialogue of Palladius concerning the Life of John Chrysostom* (New York 1921)
NCE	The New Catholic Encyclopedia (New York 1967)
ODC	F. L. Cross and E. A. Livingstone, edd., *The Oxford Dictionary of the Christian Church* (Oxford 1974, *repr.* 1978)
PGL	G. W. H. Lampe, ed., *Patristic Greek Lexicon* (Oxford 1970)
Pring	J. T. Pring, *The Oxford Dictionary of Modern Greek* (Oxford 1965)
Quasten	J. Quasten, *Patrology* 3: *The Golden Age of Greek Patristic Literature from the Council of Nicaea to the Council of Chalcedon* (Utrecht/Antwerp 1960)
RE	A. Pauly-G. Wissowa-W. Kroll, *Realenzyklopädie der klassischen Altertumswissenschaft* (Stuttgart 1891–)
SCA	Studies in Christian Antiquity (Washington, D.C. 1941–)
Schläpfer	L. Schläpfer, O.F.M.Cap., trans., *Das Leben des heiligen Johannes Chrysostomus* (Düsseldorf 1966)
Sophocles	E. A. Sophocles, *Greek Lexicon of the Roman and Byzantine Periods from B.C. 146 to A.D. 1100* (New York 1957)
Tillemont	L. Tillemont, *Mémoires pour servir à l'histoire ecclésiastique de six premiers siècles* (16 vols., Paris 1693–1712)
VA	St. Athanasius, *The Life of St. Antony* (Trans. by R. T. Meyer in ACW 10)

Introduction

1. Sozomen, *HE* 8.2.
2. Socrates, *HE* 3.1, makes Libanius responsible for the

apostasy of Julian, who later on became emperor and persecuted the Christians, hoping thereby to reestablish paganism.

3. The surname of Chrysostom, "the golden-mouthed," was given to him because of his eloquence, but certainly not in his lifetime. It occurs in its earliest recorded form in 553 and was so used by Pope Vigilius. Cassian and Cassiodorus soon introduced the term to the West.—Here may be mentioned a few books on Chrysostom, first of which would be the monumental work of Dom Chrysostom Baur, O.S.B., *John Chrysostom and His Time* (Westminster, Md. 1959–1960). This is in 2 vols., one dealing with his education and priesthood, the other with his episcopate, banishment, and death; it is a translation of the second German edition. D. Attwater, *St. John Chrysostom–Pastor and Preacher* (Milwaukee 1939). Cf. also Quasten 424–482; NCE 7.1041–44; LTK 5.i.1018–21.

4. Socrates, *HE* 6.3.

5. Baur 1.4.

6. *Dial.* 5.

7. Theodoretus, *HE* 5.36. Coleman-Norton xi–xiv gives a list of the sources for the life of St. John Chrysostom. He mentions the *Vita s. Porphyrii episcopi gazensis* by Mark, the deacon of Gaza, who accompanied Porphyry on a visit to Constantinople and a meeting with Chrysostom there. It throws great light on Chrysostom's last days in Constantinople. The text was edited by the members of the Philological Seminar at Bonn (Leipzig 1895) and was the basis of a translation into German by R. Rohde (Berlin 1927) in the series *Hortus Deliciarum* and of an English translation by H. F. F. Hill (Oxford 1913). There is also a critical edition with French translation by H. Grégoire and M. A. Kugener, *Marc le Diacre, Vie de Porphyre évêque de Gaza; texte établi, traduit commente* (Paris 1930).

8. *HL* 38.

9. *HL* 35.8–9.

10. *Dial.* 20 contains a list of bishops, largely exiled, who had supported Chrysostom. Brisson's name is there. He was addressed by St. John in *Epp.* 190 and 204.

11. According to Marcus Diaconus, *Vita Porph.* 4, the air in Palestine was drier, with a greater difference in temperature between day and night, but not between seasons.

12. For the whole discussion, see ACW 34.6–7, 162–63. To

what is presented there may now be added B. Berg, "The letter of Palladius on India," *Byzantion* 44 (1974) 5–16. This article, however, is in no way convincing.

13. For a close study of identical phraseology and vocabulary as well as the use of biblical quotations in both *HL* and *Dial.*, see Coleman-Norton lii–lix. For parallel phrases and expressions, cf. Moore 201–203.

14. Cf. *HL* 35.2: "From Palestine I went to Bithynia and there . . . I was thought worthy of ordination since I had taken part in the state of affairs connected with the blessed John."

15. Cf. *HL* 61.7 where Palladius tells of Pinianus, the ex-husband of Melania the Younger, living with thirty monks reading and engaged in gardening and solemn conferences: "They honored us not a little when we were on our way to Rome because of Saint John the Bishop."

16. Cf. *Dial.* 20.

17. Cf. H. Delehaye, *The Legends of the Saints*, with a Memoir of the author by Paul Peeters, translated by D. Attwater (New York 1962) 35–40; 123–24. The original *Les Légendes Hagiographiques* first appeared in 1905 and a second edition in 1906. Mrs. V. M. Crawford translated this into English, *The Legends of the Saints* (London 1907). This was reprinted in 1961 with a new preface and selected bibliography by R. J. Schoeck and compared with the third French edition (1927), new material being added in square brackets. A revised edition of the French third edition was published by Paul Peeters in 1955 in the *Subsidia Hagiographica* 18a. This is the basis of Attwater's translation and also includes a complete bibliography of the scientific writings of H. Delehaye.

18. Cf. the stimulating article by F. van Ommeslaeghe, "Que vaut le témoignage de Pallade sur le proces de Saint Jean Chrysostome?" AB 95 (1977) 389–414. Cf. also his article "Jean Chrysostome en conflit avec l'impératrice Eudoxie: le dossier et les origines d'une légende," AB 97 (1979) 131–159.

19. *Palladii Episcopi Helenopolitani De Vita S. Johannis Chrysostomi Dialogus. Accedunt Homilia S. Johan. Chrysost. in laudem Diodori, Tarsensis Episcopi. Acta Tarachi, Probi & Andronici. Passio Bonifatii Romani. Evagrius de octo Cogitationibus. Nilus de octo Vitiis. Omnia nunc primum Graeco-Latina cura & studio Emerici Bigotii, Rotomagensis. Luteciae*

Parisiorum. Apud Viduam Edmundi Martini, via Jacobaea, sub aureo Sole, & Abelis Sacrificio. M.DC.LXXX. Cura Privilegio Regis Christianissimi. The *Epistola nuncupatoria* is dated *Luteciae Parisiorum prima die mensis Decembris anno M.DC.LXXIX.* The *Summa Privilegii* was granted 31 October 1679 and entered in the *Acta Typographorum Parisiensium* 18 January 1680. The colophon reads: *Prima Editio absoluta fuit die 31 Januarii 1680.*

20. *Palladii Episcopi Helenopolitani De Vita D. Ioannis Chrysostomi, Archiepiscopi Constantinopolitani, Dialogus, Ambrosio Monacho Camaldulense Interprete. Nunc primum ex impressione representatus MDXXXIII. Cum privilegio ad decennium.* The colophon reads: *Venetiis, apud Bernardinum Vitalem Venetum, MDXXXII, Mense Februario.*

21. H. Moore, *The Dialogue of Palladius concerning the Life of Chrysostum* (London, S.P.C.K. 1921).

22. L. Schläpfer, O.F.M.Cap., trans., *Das Leben des heiligen Johannes Chrysostomus* (Düsseldorf 1966).

TEXT NOTES
CHAPTER I

1. Some manuscripts of the *Dial.* have "Bishop of Aspuna." Cf. Tillemont 11.523.

2. The beginning of the *Dial.* recalls the opening lines of Plato's *Republic*, in which a conversation introduces the speakers in an offhand manner but gradually leads to the subject under discussion. This reflects the rhetorical training which was received in the Greek and Roman schools. Cf. H. I. Marrou, *A History of Education in Antiquity* (New York 1956).

3. Chrysostom, *De bapt.* 11, says: "There is no need to cross the sea, nor traverse mountain ranges; sitting at home with reverence and compunction you may find Him."

4. A reminiscence of Homer, *Iliad* 1.6: ἐξ οὑδὴ τὰ πρῶτα . . . .

5. Cf. Ovid, *Fasti* 1.211: *opum furiosa cupido.*

6. This certainly shows the thinking of St. John who said (*Hom. in 1 Tim.* 12): "He made some things to be common as the air,

the sun, the sky . . . distributing all things equally, as to brothers. He made other things to be common, as baths, markets, cities . . . but strife comes in when men use that cold word: 'Thine, mine.' . . . Necessary things are common, but we do not observe their community even in the least things. How then can a possessor of wealth be a good man?"

7. The deacon wishes the bishop to come to the point with an oratorical flourish as a university lecturer waiting for applause. This again must be a literary tour de force.

8. Cf. *HL* 61.1, where Palladius refers to an earlier passage where he promised to say more about Melania later.

9. A reminiscence of 1 Cor. 9.24.

10. Matt. 19.10–14, freely quoted.

11. Heb. 5.1–6, freely quoted.

12. Cf. Num. 1.45–46.

13. Cf. Num. 17.23 and Heb. 9.4.

14. "Vainglory" may not be the word to translate this. Palladius would have used κενοδοξία as in *HL* 58.5. εὐδοξία must mean the reputation, good opinion, which others had of them.

15. Cf. Num. 17.1.35.

16. Cf. 2 Sam. 6.3, 6, 7; 1 Chron. 13.7, 9, 10.

17. This was a Samaritan town, also called Gitta. Cf. Justin Martyr, *Apol.* 1.26, and Eusebius, *HE* 2.13. It was not far from Flavia Neapolis, Justin's own birthplace. Justin is quoted by Eusebius who informs us that Simon had a great following at Rome, where he was honored as a god, although it is doubtful he ever went to Rome. Cf. Justin Martyr, *Apologia*, ed. A. W. F. Blount (Cambridge 1911) 41 f.

18. The translation is that of Moore, who points out that σοφίζω is so used in 2 Peter 1.16; cf. also Acts 7.19. Cf. *HL* 6.5: σοφίζεται πρᾶγμα τοιοῦτον.

19. In the New Testament there are mentions of the wolf, always in contrast to sheep. For similes and proverbs concerning the wolf, see LSJ *s.v.* λύκος; T. Gaisford, ed., *Paroemiographi Graeci* (Oxford 1966); R. T. Meyer, "Proverbs and Puns in Palladius' *Historia Lausiaca*," *Studia Patristica* 8 (Berlin 1966) 420–23.

20. He is anxious to procure an intangible gift of grace with tangible money.

21. 1 Cor. 3.19.

22. Acts 8.20.

23. Acts 8.22–23.

24. Cf. Ezek. 15.12, 32; 33.11; 2 Peter 3.9.

25. The time is the summer of 408, a year after Chrysostom's death. Cf. ODC 285–86.

26. It becomes increasingly clear how closely this is modelled on some of the introductory dialogues, e.g., *Euthyphro* or *Crito*.

27. John 14.27.

28. Palladius is here referring to the condition of the church in Constantinople torn by rival factions.

29. Cf. Matt. 10.23.

30. This is of course St. John Chrysostom, always referred to as John in the *Dial*. The appellation Chrysostom, the golden-mouthed, was added later.

31. ἀναγνώστης, "reader," was an order recognized as such by the early Church as early as the third century. In the Jewish synagogue there were lay readers and this was taken over by the early Christian Church, as witness the *Apostolic Constitutions* 8.10.10.

32. This was a special title reserved for the patriarch of Alexandria. It was derived from the Aramaic, *abba*, "father." Theophilus was bishop of Alexandria from 385 to 412. For his life, cf. DCB *s.v.* Theophilus (3).

33. This is the first deposition of Chrysostom, which occurred in late July 403. The second deposition was in Lent 404. Here Palladius refers to the first.

34. Pope St. Innocent I reigned from 402 to 417. Cf. DCB *s.v.* Innocentius (12); LTK 5.685–86.

35. We know nothing more of this Eusebius.

36. λίβελλος, from the Latin *libellus*, "memorandum, petition." It occurs often in this text in the sense of "complaint."

37. Pansophius is mentioned only here and we know nothing more about him.

38. Pappus is likewise unknown outside the *Dial*.

39. Demetrius, bishop of Pessinus, is addressed by Chrysostom in *Ep*. 148. For his life, cf. DCB *s.v.* Demetrius (10).

40. Eugenius is unknown outside the *Dial*.

CHAPTER 2

41. This letter is included in Chrysostom's own correspondence, but it can hardly be his own. Palladius says that he gives only the gist of it and it is in Palladius' own style, but a number of phrases from Chrysostom do occur in it. Pope Innocent's own answer, in Latin, was translated into Greek by Sozomen, *HE* 8.26.

42. εὐλάβεια a is a term of respect addressed to the clergy and to bishops in particular. Cf. L. Dineen, *Titles of Address in Christian Greek Epistolography to 527 A.D.* (Patristic Studies 18, Washington 1929) 20–24.

43. Deacons frequently accompanied bishops to councils and served as ambassadors. Letters written by bishops were frequently entrusted to deacons for safe delivery.

44. Paulus is mentioned by Chrysostom in *Ep.* 148. For his life, see DCB *s.v.* Paulus (64)

45. For the life of Cyriacus, cf. DCB *s.v.* Cyriacus (10).

46. This was Arcadius, who became emperor at eighteen. See NCE 1.741–42.

47. These were the Fathers of the Council of Nicaea. Canons 5 and 6 of that council had been violated.

48. So also the Council of Constaninople in 381, Canon 2.

49. A diocese without a bishop was said to be widowed.

50. ἀπαγόμενοι is used here as in 1 Cor. 12.2.

51. The metaphor is from the Greek games of contest. The wrestlers were well anointed with oil before the contests. So here it means that some of the clergy were carefully trained beforehand to bear witness against John.

52. Eulysius is addressed by Chrysostom in *Ep.* 148. For his life, see DCB *s.v.* Eulysius.

53. Lupicinius is mentioned only in the *Dial.* The manuscripts show various spellings of the name.

54. The life of Germanus is to be found in DCB *s.v.* Germanus (32).

55. It is possible that this is the Severus addressed by Chrysostom in *Ep.* 101. For his life, see DCB *s.v.* Severus (13).

56. κατηγόρους ἀλείφων, literally "anointing the accusers,"

which occurs often in this text. Here it is used in a pejorative sense; compare "greasing the palm" with money for a bribe.

57. Constantinople was a diocese in the Province of Thrace, which extended as far as the Danube. Its ancient metropolitan see was at Heracleia, which had been the ancient civil capital.

58. κυριῶσος was an official informer to the emperor, from the Latin *curiosus*, "spy scout." See Sophocles 686.

59. Is this some of the "naughty rhetoric" to which Tillemont referred? I can make no sense of this sentence, which Moore translated: "For there is none yet." Bigot: " . . . neque enim hic iniquitas stetit, sed ad priora adjecerunt & alia."

60. νοτάριος (Latin *notarius*), a secretary and member of the emperor's staff. See Sophocles 786; PGL *s.v.*; RE 17[1].1058.

61. The same locution occurs in *HL* 21.5.

62. This was the Saturday of Holy Week, Easter eve. Eusebius, *Vita Constantini* 4.22, speaks of the vigil of Easter and the multitude of candles. It was a pious belief that Christ would appear in glory on Easter eve.

63. The βῆμα was the raised portion of the church where the altar and bishop's throne were located. It was restricted to the clergy.

64. κολυμβήθρα, originally a pool to dive into. It occurs in St. John's Gospel 5.2 for the Pool of Bethzatha. Later it came to mean a baptismal font as here.

65. They were ἀμύμητοι, "uninitiated, profane." The term applied to the non-Christian as well as to the catechumens. The Liturgy of St. John Chrysostom bade all the unbelievers and catechumens to leave the church before the Mystery.

66. κολοφών, "top, finishing, end." A colophon was added to the end of a manuscript giving the scribe's name, the patron who had hired him, the date. This practice was carried over into early printed books. Chrysostom, *Hom. in Ps. 124*, says: "Death is the colophon of ills."

67. πόλεμος ἀκηρυκτος. Chrysostom, *De compunctione 1.5*, says: τὸν γὰρ πόλεμον . . . καὶ τὴν ἔχραν τὴν ἀκήρυκτον.

68. Here some manuscripts have γραμμάτων, "letters," instead of πραγμάτων.

69. Coleman-Norton has likewise enclosed this passage in parentheses.

70. Not only did their actions break the *ius gentium*, but every church law as well in going into a distant diocese.

71. The separate edition of St. John's letters contains this sentence but it occurs in none of the manuscripts of Palladius.

72. Cf. Eph. 5.25–30.

73. Chrysostom addressed *Ep*. 192 to Venerius. For his life, cf. DCB *s.v.* Venerius (1).

74. Chromatius (ob. 407) is addressed by Chrysostom in *Ep*. 144. For his life, cf. DCB *s.v.* Chromatius.

CHAPTER 3

75. Literally "the equal thing of the communion." In ancient Christian times the bishops used to send each other portions of the consecrated elements as a sign of unity and good will. Irenaeus, quoted by Eusebius, *HE* 5.24, tells of this practice. Canon 14 of the Council of Laodicea expressly forbids this practice at Eastertide. Later on this was replaced by letters of recommendation, carried by travellers to another area to show that they were Christians in good standing, something already seen in apostolic times; cf. 2 Cor. 3.1; Rom. 16.1.

76. Sozomen, *HE* 8.26, quotes a letter from Pope Innocent to the clergy of Constantinople telling them that he is calling a synod, but he did not list those conditions.

77. This Peter could have been either DCB *s.v.* Petrus (45) or (48).

78. Martyrius had been archdeacon of Constantinople before Sarapion. He is supposed to have delivered a panegyric of Chrysostom while he was bishop of Antioch. For his life, see DCB *s.v.* Martyrius (4).

79. . . . τὸν Θεὸν ἱκετεύων. Cf. *HL* 17.12, where the same phrase occurs.

80. This letter is only to be found here. It is numbered as *Ep*. 15 in the collected correspondence of Pope Innocent.

81. . . . παιγνιωδῶς, "in a childish manner, playfully." The word appears to be hapax. Cf. PGL *s.v.*

82. Cf. Matt. 18.17; 1 Cor. 5.9.

83. Sozomen, *HE* 8.26: "We write that we must be lead by the canons laid down at Nicaea, which alone the Catholic Church ought to follow." The fifth canon of Nicea prescribed that persons excommunicated by the bishop of a province could not be admitted to communion by other bishops; but to prevent undeserved excommunication, two synods should be held in each province every year to inquire into doubtful cases. What Pope Innocent proposed would be legislation dealing with the whole Church rather than a single province. Here Theophilus, having excommunicated Chrysostom, would have to justify his action. Cf. Moore 22–23.

84. This is in a figurative sense, as though time rode by galloping on horseback: παριππάζω. It occurs in the same locution in *HL* 6.7, and it occurs in chapter 17 *infra*. According to PGL it is monocetic, that is, is used only by Palladius. This again is silent proof that Palladius wrote both the *Dial.* and *HL*.

85. Nothing more is known of this man.

86. This was the Church of St. Sophia and it was during the second expulsion of St. John. This occurred on June 20, 404. Cf. Baur 2.305 ff. Sozomen, *HE* 8.22, and Socrates, *HE* 6.18, give contradictory accounts of the alleged guilty parties.

87. This is the only place where Paternus is mentioned.

88. Acacius was bishop of Berea. His dates: 326–426. Cf. DCB *s.v.* Acacius (4).

89. For the life of Paul, cf. DCB *s.v.* Paulus (34).

90. Antiochus (*ob.c.* 408) was bishop of Ptolemais. Sozomen, *HE* 8.10, says his eloquence was so great that he was called Chrysostomus. For his life, cf. DCB *s.v.* Antiochus (1).

91. Cyrinus (*ob.* 405). For his life, cf. DCB *s.v.* Cyrinus (1).

92. Severianus (*ob. ante* 430) was bishop of Gabala. St. John preached a *Homilia de recipiendo Severiano*. For his life, see DCB *s.v.* Severianus (2); LTK 9.698–99.

93. We know nothing of a synod after St. John's second expulsion, let alone a distinguished one. There is a "lack of logical sequence in the sentence which may point to a corruption in the text" (Moore 24 n. 1). We must accept this, as does Coleman-Norton 155. At the beginning of chapter 11 *infra* there is a hint of a third trial at which St. John, "outspoken as ever," claimed that he was never even

given opportunity to clear himself of the charges of setting St. Sophia on fire. Apparently by that time the whole incident of the charge had been forgotten?

94. Job 32.18, where text reads συνέχει for LXX ὀλέκει.

95. Cyriacus is addressed by Chrysostom in *Epp*. 125 and 148. For his life, see DCB *s.v.* Cyriacus (8).

96. Theodosius, father of Arcadius, had issued such edicts against Arians. Chrysostom was now treated as a heretic.

97. Arsacius (325–405) is denounced by Chrysostom in *Epp*. 125. For his life, see DCB *s.v.* Arsacius.

98. Porphyrius was bishop of Antioch from 404 to 413. For his life, cf. DCB *s.v.* Porphyrius (4).

99. καλόγερος. Cf. *HL* 18.26; 35.5; 44.4; ACW 10.183. In later Greek this developed the meaning of monk. Cf. French *caloyer*. Cf. R. T. Meyer, "Lexical Problems in Palladius' *Historia Lausiaca*," *Studia Patristica* 1 (Berlin 1957) 44–52.

100. Anysius is addressed by Chrysostom in *Epp*. 162 and 163. For his life, see DCB *s.v.* Alysius; LTK 1.679–80.

101. Palladius thus refers to himself in the third person. This should make clear to all that he was not the bishop of the *Dialogus*.

102. *Codex Theodosianus* 15.2.37 contains this edict, but John's name does not appear there. It was dated August 29, 404.

103. This is the famous monastic legislator of the West (c. 355–c. 445). For a complete account of the man and his work, see O. Chadwick, *John Cassian* (2nd ed., Cambridge 1932). For a brief biography, cf. DCB Cassianus (11); NCE 3.181–83.

104. Studius was addressed by Chrysostom in *Ep*. 197. For his life, see DCB *s.v.* Studius (2).

105. Eutychianus. For his life, see DCB *s.v.* Eutychianus (8).

106. This John died in 423. Cf. DCB *s.v.* Joannes (557) (561).

107. Eustathius is unknown outside the *Dial*.

108. The third charge of the Synod of the Oak was that John had sold a great quantity of the treasures of the Church.

109. He is mentioned above in chapter 1.

110. Domitian is addressed by Chrysostom in *Ep*. 217. For his life, see DCB *s.v.* Domitianus (5)

111. Originally the revenues of the Church were entrusted to the bishop to be distributed among the clergy and the poor. This was

done through the deacons and archdeacons. Finally regular stewards were appointed, always chosen from among the clergy. Canons 25 and 26 of the Council of Chalcedon required that in the vacancy of the see the revenues should be managed by the steward "that the administration of the Church may not be without witnesses and the property of the Church be wasted and the clergy exposed to cavil." Cf. also Moore 26.

112. Vallagas is unknown outside the *Dial.*

113. Optatus succeeded Studius as prefect of Constantinople. He was a pagan and a bitter opponent to the faith. He tortured those who had been accused of the burning of St. Sophia, one of his most prominent victims being Eutropius, who died under torture. For his life, see DCB *s.v.* Optatus (8).

114. . . . ἐπὶ ξύλον, literally "on the rack." This may have been a rack for torture. GPL however quotes this passage and others under the meaning "of a wooden (horse?) to which victims were fastened."

115. . . . καὶ αἰκισμὸν νώτων. Some MSS read ὤτων, "ears," and Bigot so prints it, but he translates, *in tergo verberum notas*, "marks of blows on the back." However, he prints a reading from G, νώτων in the margin. Moore 26 translates "mutilated ears." G adds: καὶ πληγὰς διαφόρων βασάνων, "and blows of various beatings."

116. This letter is no longer extant.

117. Theodosius the Great (c. 346–395) divided the Roman Empire between his two sons, Arcadius (377–408) receiving the eastern half and Honorius (384–423), the western part.

118. We have no information on this synod.

119. Honorius is so anxious for peace that he asks his brother to help maintain it, for peace in the spiritual realm must also mean peace in the material realm, which both brothers now share since their father's death.

Chapter 4

120. This whole passage is briefly summarized in Sozomen, *HE* 8.28.

121. Aemilius, Cythegius, Gaudentius, Valentianus, and Bonifacius are all unknown outside the *Dial.*

122. The letters of Chromatius and Venerius are not extant.

123. It was from these four bishops from the East that Pope Innocent had learned about the doings in Constantinople. Sozomen, *HE* 8.28, reported the gist of Innocent's letter, mentioning the four bishops "who were with us in Rome." This makes Palladius an eye-witness to what had happened.

124. Cf. Jer. 20.4; Apoc. 17.1–6; 18.2, 4, 5, 24.

125. The confusion of the first person and the third person is in the original. In vivid situations Palladius falls into the first person as narrator; this can be considered further proof of his authorship of the *Dial.*

126. This suburb of Constantinople is unknown to us.

127. Both Patricius and Valerianus are unknown outside the *Dial.*

128. For the life of Marianus, see DCB *s.v.*

129. Actually Arsacius, brother of Nectarius, was appointed and occupied the throne for but a year and Atticus succeeded him when he died November 11, 405.

130. The coins, νομίσματα, were each equivalent to Latin *nummus*, the standard coin.

131. This Paul is unknown outside the *Dial.*

132. Inexactly quoted from Eph. 5.15–16.

133. Lampsacus is on the east coast of the Dardanelles. Cf. RE 12¹.590–92.

134. This is Otranto in southern Italy.

135. Cf. Exod. 1.8–22; 5.4–19.

136. . . . ἀνδρόπλουτοι , . . . ἀνασείστριαι. The words are both hapax, coined apparently by Palladius himself. Cf. PGL; Sophocles.

137. These women were friends of the Empress Eudoxia. Their names are unknown outside the *Dial.* as also the husband Promotus, but Saturninus was mentioned by Chrysostom in his *Homilia cum Saturninus et Aurelianus acti essent in exsilium*. For his life, see DCB *s.v.* Saturninus (24).

138. The *Dial.* was composed in 407 or 408, a year or so after

Chrysostom's death. Cf. also Quasten 179 f. The phrase "fall to sleep, to sleep in the Lord," comes from early Christian times, implying that death is but a sleep before the final Resurrection. Cf. A. Rush, *Death and Burial in Christian Antiquity* (SCA 1, Washington 1941) 1–22: "Death as a Sleep."

139. Ps. 5.7. Cf. *HL* 17.1.

140. This is merely an inference from John 8.44–47.

141. Ps. 63.12.

142. Palladius is the reputed author of a treatise *Epistola de Indicis Gentibus et de Bragmannibus*. This was first edited by Bysshe (London 1665) with a Latin translation. A passage there parallels this one in the Greek very closely and I here add from Bysshe's Latin: . . . *mentiens enim, illum cur persuadet injuria afficit; injuriam etiam facit cui credidit mentienti, fidem adhibens, priusquam vera edidicerit.*

143. This is one of the *agrapha*, "non-Scriptural sayings" attributed to our Lord. It is frequently quoted by the Fathers.

144. κομπήσαντες. I have followed Coleman-Norton, who adopted it from Moore's brilliant conjecture, by a change of only one letter, where the manuscripts read κομπάσαντες, "with boasting," which makes no sense. As Moore 34 n. 5 said: "It is not enough for a statement to be plausible, and couched in pleasant language, it must be tested by facts."

145. . . . ὀδόντων ἔρυμα, a reminiscence of Homer, Odyssey 23.70: ἕρκος ὀδόντων.

146. Ps. 141.4; 39.2.

147. Jer. 9.20.

148. The story of Susanna and the Elders in Dan. 13.1–64. It does not occur in the Hebrew or the King James versions but is in the Vulgate and the LXX.

149. Jer. 7.16.

150. Hos. 7.9, 11.

151. Hos. 7.8 f.

152. See also Sozomen, *HE* 8.3, for this embassy to Rome.

153. χειροτονία, literally "stretching forth of hands." The term ordination was applied to episcopal consecration as well as to priestly ordination.

154. Palladius knew the Egyptian temples well, having spent

time in Egypt with the Desert Fathers, and a large part of his *Lausiac History* contains biographies of the monks living there. Cf. Quasten 177 f.

155. 1 Sam. 16.7.

156. Eph. 5.1.

157. Dan. 13.1–64.

158. "If I see you seizing the property of others, and otherwise transgressing, how shall I believe you when you say that there is a resurrection?" Chrysostom, *Hom. in 1 Cor.* 3.

159. The text is corrupt here and so Bigot made an emendation and translated: *Infamiae in sene iudicium est, juvenilis formae corruptio.* I have followed Moore's translation.

CHAPTER 5

160. Socrates, *HE* 6.3, tells us that the father was named Secundus and the mother Anthusa. The father died shortly after John's birth, leaving Anthusa a widow at twenty.

161. Sozomen, *HE* 8.2, tells us that when Libanius was on his deathbed he was asked who should follow him in his teaching. "It would have been John," said he, "had not the Christians taken him from me."

162. He was taught rhetoric by the famous Libanius, a sophist and bitter enemy of the faith. Andragathius taught him philosophy.

163. Cf. Rom. 3.2; 1 Peter 4.11.

164. The training of a professional rhetorician in these times can be properly appreciated by a careful perusal of Libanius' own autobiography (*Sermo* I), the Greek text, edited with introduction, translation and notes by H. F. Horman (Oxford 1965).

165. "Were I to demand the smoothness of Isocrates, the weight of Demosthenes, the dignity of Thucydides, and the sublimity of Plato, the testimony of Paul might be brought against me." So Chrysostom wrote in the *De sacerdotio* 4.6.424 while still a deacon. (Trans. by W. A. Jurgens [New York 1955] 76.)

166. Meletius was bishop of Antioch from 361 to 381. For his life, see DCB *s.v.* Meletius (3).

167. . . . λουτροῦ παλιγγενεσίαν, Cf. Titus 3.5. Baptism was withheld until the last possible moment. Sometimes it was the fear of falling into grave sin, but more likely it was the fear here that the sacrament might be administered by a heretic. Later on it was ruled that baptism by a heretic was valid.

168. Those who followed the bishops were the acolytes, which in the Western Church until 1971 was the last of the Minor Orders before the subdiaconate, the first of the Major Orders.

169. His teachers were Carterius and Diodorus who conducted a sort of Scripture study school called the *Asceterion*. Chrysostom induced two other students of Libanius to renounce the world, Theodore, later bishop of Mopsuestia, and Maximus, who became bishop of Seleucia.

170. Cf. *HL* 1.5; 38.8.

171. Cf. *HL* 38.3; 58.5.

172. Chrysostom refers to his early ascetic life in *De sacerdotio* 6.12 and *De compunctione* 1.6.

173. But George's *Vita* says, "Hesychius a Syrian," which is possibly more correct. Syrus is unknown outside this *Dial*.

174. . . . ἀπομιμεῖται τὴν σκληραγωγίαν. Cf. *HL* 2.1: μεγάλα σκληραγωγίᾳ and also *De sacerdotio* 2.12: τοῦ σώματος σκληραγωγίαν.

175. . . . ἀπομαχόμενος ταῖς τῆς ἡδυπαθείας σπιλάσιν. It is characteristic of the σπιλάδες that they cannot be seen under the water and one can be wrecked on them before any danger is suspected. Cf. Suidas, *Lexicon* ed. I. Bekker (Berlin 1854) 971. *HL* 2 tells of Palladius' stay with Dorotheus in the desert and how they wrestled with rocks bringing them up from the seaside in hot weather to build huts for other anchorites. Thus he conquered his bodily passions by hard toil.

176. Cf. *HL* 1.5: " . . . I was in my full prime, needing not so much precept as hard bodily toil."

177. This would have been in 374–76 and here the Old and the New Testaments are meant. Mabillon, *Traité des études monastiques* (Paris 1691) 116, says that he learned the New Testament by heart. It is strange that the farther away we get from the actual events, the more vivid the affairs of his life appear to his audience.

178. Cf. chapter 12 below for his frugal eating habits in later

life, what Seneca called the behavior of a queasy stomach (*fastidientis stomachi*). Like the great St. Bernard he suffered from continual stomach trouble, and in *Ep.* 5 he said he had a "cobweb body."

179. Chrysostom always had a great admiration for the monastic life. *De sacerdotio* 6.8 says that the hermit makes progress in virtue more easily than he who is charged with the care of souls.

180. This would have been in 381 when he was thirty-six years old. He wrote the treatises *De sacerdotio* and *De virginitate* while still a deacon.

181. Flavian succeeded as bishop of Antioch when Meletius died in 381. For his life, cf. DCB *s.v.* Flavianus (4).

182. . . . ἀλίζων . . . φωτίζων . . . ποτίζων. The figure of speech called *homoioteleuton*, "ending alike," is end-rhyme in clauses or verses. This again is evidence of Palladius' training in the Greek rhetorical tradition. The time was 386–388.

183. This figure of speech originated in classical antiquity as the ship of state motif in both Greek and Latin literature, the earliest example in Theognis. The scholion on Aristophanes' *Vespae* reads: ἀεὶοί ποιηταὶ τὰς πόλεις πλοίοις παραβάλλοθσι. From the poets it was taken over by the orators, historians, and philosophers, e.g. Plato, *Republic* 488, *Philebus* 6.44.3ff.; Cicero, *Att.* 2.3.4. Later it was adapted by the Church Fathers. Cf. H. Rahner, *Griechische Mythen in christlicher Deutung* . . . *(Zürich 1945) 435–44*, or in its English translation, *Greek Myths and Christian Mystery* (New York 1963) 345–53.

184. Nectarius was bishop of Constantinople 381–397. He was of senatorial rank and chosen for bishop by the emperor; according to Sozomen, *HE* 7.8, he was of advanced age but not yet baptized and was consecrated bishop of Constantinople while still wearing the white robes of a catechumen. As bishop he associated mainly with members of the court, thereby setting a precedent as it were. No wonder the people were later shocked at the severe criticism of his successor, John Chrysostom. For his life, cf. DCB *s.v.* Nectarius (4); LTK 7.874.

185. μαστεύοντες τὴν προεδρίαν. Moore translates; "to secure the supreme position." I believe that Palladius really meant μαστεύω in its etymological sense, connecting it with μαστός, "breast." Just as the infant eagerly seeks the breast, so did these men pant and struggle for the office.

186. πρεσβύτεροι μὲν ἀξίαν, ἀανάξιοι δὲ της ἱεροσύνης, a figure of antithesis.

187. πραιτωριοκτυποῦντες . . . δωροδοκοῦντες . . . γονυπετοῦντες. . . ; another figure of homoioteleuton. Of these the first is hapax, according to PGL, but the meaning is perfectly clear. The modern expression, "to canvass the palace," could be used. Sophocles 915 has, "to knock at the gate of the praetorium, to frequent the praetorium."

188. Eutropius was executed in 399. Chrysostom had delivered two homilies, *Pro Eutropio* and *Homilia de capto Eutropia*. For his life, cf. DCB *s.v.* Eutropius (20).

189. For this office, see J. E. Dunlap, *The Office of the Grand Chamberlain in the Later Roman and Byzantine Empires* (New York 1927).

190. Eutropius may have become acquainted with Chrysostom when he went to Antioch in 388 on a mission from Theodosius the Great to John of Lycopolis in Egypt. Cf. Claudian, *In Eutropium* 1.311–13; Sozomen, *HE* 7.72; *HL* 35.2.

191. E. Gibbon, *History of the Decline and Fall of the Roman Empire*, chap. II, n. 96, says that the distance from Antioch to Constantinople by the old Roman post road in the time of Theodosius (387) was 725 Roman or 665 English miles, and that a magistrate of high rank took six days.

192. Sozomen, *HE* 6.2, says the consecration took place February 26, 398.

193. . . . ἠντισκότει, for the impossible ἠντικότει, following the correction of Coleman-Norton. There is another reading, ἠψυχώθει, "he fainted away," which hardly makes sense here. That Theophilus was opposed to the consecration is clear from the subsequent events.

194. The text must be corrupt here. I have followed the translation of Moore 43, but he suggests: "He is very clever at reaching the invisible will and mind of a man from his visible countenance." Bigot translated it: *Vafer enim est, ex ipso adspectu occultum cujusque hominis consilium & mentem dignoscere.*

195. Cf. Mark 1.24 and Matt. 8.29.

196. ἡλίοϑ αἴγλην, a reminiscence of Homer, *Odyssey* 4.45.

197. Eccle. 1.25.

198. Sozomen, *HE* 8.3, says that Chrysostom was "naturally disposed to reprehend the misconduct of others."

199. These were the so-called *virgines introductae*, "women brought in" to do housework for the clergy, who were not allowed to marry. Some of these were women of the Church vowed to perpetual virginity. This situation led to scandal and the third canon of the Council of Nicaea forbade it except in the case of a mother, aunt, or older sister. Later councils were to reinforce this rule.

200. Cf. H. Achelis, *Virgines subintroductae: Ein Beitrag zum VI. Kapitel des I. Koreintherbriefe* (Leipzig 1902).

201. Palladius may be speaking figuratively here, but there is evidence from *HL* of monks leaving the desert for a visit to the lupanaria of Alexandria and returning with disease of the genitalia. Cf. *HL* 26.4.

202. Cf. Claudian, *De Consulatu Stilichonis* 2.111–13: *scelerum matrem . . . avaritiam*. According to Diogenes Laertius, *De vitis philosophorum* 6.50, Diogenes the Cynic is supposed to have said: τὴν φιλαργυρίαν . . . μητρόπολιν πάντων τῶν κακῶν. On Diogenes the Cynic, cf. *The Oxford Classical Dictionary* (Oxford 1970²) 348 *s.v.* Diogenes (2).

203. Cf. 1 Cor. 3.10.

204. Jer. 1.10.

205. βαλαντιόσκοπος, "bag-watcher; covetous, avaricious," Cf. Sophocles 295. The word is hapax legomenon.

206. Cf. Luke 3.14. The hangers-on and sycophants were attracted to the rich man's table by the torchbearers and they betrayed themselves by becoming flatterers and parasites in aping the rich.

207. St. Basil is supposed to have been the first in the East to found a hospital from episcopal revenues. Cf. ODC. 139 f.

208. ἡ ἱερὰ νόσος, "the sacred, or mysterious disease," often applied to epilepsy, which was thought to be caused by demons. Lexicographers differ, however, and it could be leprosy or elephantiasis. Elephantiasis is called by its true name in *HL* 17.4 and 18.4. The editor bracketed these words as they are not in all the manuscripts. It may have been a marginal gloss which was later incorporated in the text.

209. From the very first the early Church had grave concern for widowed women (1 Tim. 5.3; Acts 6.1). Elderly widows were

put in charge of the younger ones and later on this became the order of deaconesses of which Chrysostom's aunt Sabiniana is mentioned in *HL* 41.4. Cf. the article "Deaconess" in ODC 380f.; NCE 4:668 f. Cf. also E. A. Clark, "Sexual politics in the writings of John Chrysostom," *Anglican Theological Review* 59 (1977) 3–20.

210. This is often misunderstood. Chrysostom is by no means urging personal uncleanness. The public baths in the larger cities of antiquity were beautiful edifices and furnished the conveniences of a modern country club. Much gossiping went on there and there were many chances for immoral conduct. Even pagans such as Seneca avoided the public baths. Cf. *HL* 38.12; 55.2; VA 47. On ancient asceticism and bathing, see J. Zellinger, *Bad und Bäder in der altchristlichen Kirche* (Munich 1928) 47–92.

211. Cf. 1 Cor 7.8–9; 1 Tim 5.3–6, 9–16.

212. The *Apostolic Constitutions* 8.6 relate how the deacon led in the "bidding prayers," making the petition to which the people replied, "Lord, have mercy." Apparently it originated at Antioch in the 4th century and spread from there to Constantinople, and then to the entire East.

213. 1 Tim. 6.17.

214. Chrysostom was opposed on moral grounds to the public circuses as witness his *Oratio de circo; Contra circum et theatra; Homila adversus eos qui ad ludos circenses profiscuntur; Homilia contra ludos et theatra.*

215. Cf. John 10.14–17, 27.

CHAPTER 6

216. Cf. John 10.12–13.

217. Originally Eudoxia had shown respect and good will to John, but his homilies were directed against her luxurious way of life. For her life, see DCB *s.v.* Eudoxia (2).

218. διανοίας, but George's *Vita* says παροινίας here, "of his great drunkenness."

219. Isaacius Syriscus is mentioned only here and in Sozo-

men, *HE* 8.9. Sozomen, *HE* 8.9, says that while Chrysostom had high esteem for monks and helped them, he abused those who left the monasteries to trade upon the charity of Christian women.

220. Ps. 64.7.

221. Ἀμφαλλάξ, used for a tragic actor's high-heeled buskins which fitted either foot. Moore 49 n.2 suggested Bunyan's "Mr. Facing-both-ways." Sophocles 130 refers to this passage and translates it, "Both-sides, a nickname for Theophilus, bishop of Alexandria, because he was a time-server." Cf. also, Athenaeus, *Deipnosophistae* 3.116C.44.

222. Eph. 4.26.

223. Rom. 12.21.

224. Ps. 7.5. Palladius apparently made a slip in his citation here.

225. Isidore of Alexandria is mentioned in *HL* 1.1; 3.1; 46.2–3. For his life (c. 318–403), cf. DCB *s.v.* Isidorus (28); AA.SS. Jan. 1 (1643) 1015 ff. His feast is celebrated on January 15 in the Roman Martyrology.

226. For the life of St. Athanasius (c. 296–373), cf. DCB *s.v.* Athanasius (St.); ODC 101 f.: F. L. Cross, *The Study of St. Athanasius* (Oxford 1945); LTK 1.976–81; ACW 10.1–15.

227. The *xenodochium* was the guest house where travellers could stay if provided with letters from other Christian communities. Most large cities and monasteries had such a hospice.

228. The churches of Rome and Alexandria refused to recognize Flavian as bishop of Antioch. Chrysostom negotiated with him and Theophilus to restore harmony. Acacius and Isidore went to Rome to see Pope Damasus and the matter was settled. This was in 388.

229. . . . ἀγῦνασ ϛἀγωνασαμέηου, a *figura etymologica* or cognated accusative, a figure of speech. Evagrius (388–392) was the rival bishop of Flavian of Antioch. For his life, see DCB *s.v.* Evagrius (3).

230. χρυσίνος. This was the Roman *aureus*, worth about 28 *denarii*.

231. . . . τραπέζης τοῦ Σωτῆρος, that is, to "swear by the altar," a practice which Chrysostom censured in *Hom. in stat.* 15.14.

232. Cf. Exod. 11.11, 14.

233. λιθομανία, a hapax legomenon. Isidore said that it was

better to restore the bodies of the sick which are more properly temples of God than to build walls. Sozomen, *HE* 8.12.

234. λιπαρήσας . . . πολλοῖς. Cf. *HL* 3.1: ἦν πολλαῖς λιπαρήσας ὑποσχέσεσιν.

235. τοῦ ἀκλινοῦς ὀφθαλμοῦ. Cf. 2 Paral. 16.9; Ps. 32.18; Prov. 5.21; 15.3; Ecclus. 11.13; 23.19.

236. Cf. Ps. 15.5.

237. Mount Nitria is about 60 miles south of Alexandria. Sozomen, *HE* 6.31, says that the name is derived from the fact that they collect nitre there. Palladius, *HL* 7.2, tells us that there were fifty monasteries there containing some five thousand monks, some living in communities, others led the eremitic life.

238. Cf. Jer. 15.15; Exod. 34.6; Num. 14.18; Ps. 86.15; Rom. 2.4; 9.11; 1. Peter 3.20; 2 Peter 3, 9, 15.

239. ταυρηδὸν ὑπεβλέπετο, a reminiscence of Plato, *Phaedo* 117B: ταυρηδὸν ὑποβλέψας.

240. ὠμοφόριον, a long band of white woolen stuff draped over the shoulders. All bishops of the East wore it over the left shoulder to represent the shepherd bringing in a lost sheep on his shoulder. In the West this is the *pallium* worn by archbishops. Cf. ODC 1024 f.; DACL 13.1. (1937) 931–40; NCE 10:929 f., with illustrations.

241. Ammonius (ob. 403) is one of the famous "Tall Brothers." Cf. Palladius, *HL* 11.1. For his life, cf. DCB s.v. Ammonius (1); LTK 1.441.

242. For the life of Origen (c. 185-c. 264), cf. DCB *s.v.* Origenes (1), ODC 1008–10.

243. This would be the study of Holy Scripture and *lectio divina*. Cf. my "Palladius and the Study of Scripture," *Studia Patristica* 13 (1975) 487–490. Cf. also my *"Lectio divina* in Palladius," in *KYRIAKON: Festschrift Johannes Quasten* (Münster 1970) 480–84.

CHAPTER 7

244. Cf. Exod. 2.11–15; 11.3; 18.25–26; 31.18; 32.26–28; Ecclus. 45.1–5.

245. πρὸς τὸν Αὐγουστάλιον. Cf. *HL* 46.3. The *praefectus Aegypti* was governor of the province of Egypt after the second half of the fourth century.

246. The sixth Canon of the Council of Nicaea says: "Let the ancient customs prevail in Egypt, Libya, and Pentapolis that the bishop of Alexandria shall have authority over all of those, since a similar custom holds in regard to the bishop of Rome." At the time of Chrysostom this was the largest archdiocese in the world, having over a hundred bishops, thirty more than in the Roman West.

247. Dioscorus (*ob.* 403) was one of the four "Tall Brothers." He is mentioned in *HL* 10.1 and 12.1 as being the bishop of the mountain. For his life, cf. DCB *s.v.* Dioscorus (4); LTK 3.410.11.

248. ἀφωτίστων, "uninstructed, unenlightened." In Hebr. 6.4 the reference is to baptism. See also PGL 379.

249. παροικία, orginally meant "stay" or "sojourn of one who is not a citizen in a strange place," e.g., the Israelites in Egypt. Then it took on a meaning of a congregation or parish. Cf. Arndt-Gimgrich 634. In the case of a Christian community under the pastoral care of a bishop, it meant diocese.

250. ψίαθον. The monks used to sleep on only a rush mat. Cf. VA 7.

251. These would have been commentaries on Scripture, etc. There is ample evidence from *HL* that some of the monks at least were deeply read in the pagan classics as well as patristic writings, and even at this time the copying of Scripture was accounted a meritorious act and one of the noteworthy labors of the monks who could read and write.

252. St. Basil, *Ep* 93, is witness that monks in solitude kept the Blessed Sacrament in their cells and partook of it when they so desired.

253. λαβόντες αὐτῶν τὰς μηλωτάς. Cf. *HL* 22.11: λαβὼν οὖν τὴν μηλωτὴν αὐτοῦ. All the monk had in his worldly possessions was his sheepskin habit and a rush mat on which to sleep.

254. That is, for Jerusalem. In 176 A.D. Hadrian renamed it "Aelia Capitolina." Cf. Eusebius, *HE* 4.1. Sozomen, *HE* 8.13, says that they went to Scythopolis as there were many palm trees, the

leaves of which they used for basket making. The monks supported themselves by making baskets.

255. Isa. 27.1.

256. The letter is no longer extant.

257. στρατόπεδον, literally "army encampment," with the specialized meaning here of "imperial court." The theory of the imperator was that he was also commander-in-chief of the armed forces. The monks would naturally go to the capitol where the ecclesiastical courts and the civil courts cooperated. Cf. G. F. Reilly, *Imperium and Sacerdotium according to St. Basil the Great* (SCA7; Washington 1945) 88 ff.

258. Cf. Gen. 14.1–2.

259. Ps. 80.13.

260. St. Gregory Nazianzen began his ministry in this church and Chrysostom preached some of his sermons there.

261. The monks were self-sufficient in that they practiced the various crafts in their desert habitation. A mere perusal of Palladius' *HL* tells various trades: weaving, basket-making, mat-making, rope-making, spinning, linen-manufacture, tailoring, shoe-making, tanning, agriculture, horticulture, pig-raising, smithery. We have instances of their mental prayer as they worked at the more repetitive tasks. Cf. *HL* 12.12 which adds: "They all learn the Holy Scriptures by heart."

262. However Socrates, *HE* 6.9, and Sozomen, *HE* 8.13, both say that John had received them into communion and that this was one of the accusations falsely brought agaisnt him at the Synod of the Oak.

263. This letter is extant only here.

264. He charged them with Origenism. On Origenism, see DCC 993 f.

265. This letter is extant only here.

CHAPTER 8

266. This was the shrine of St. John the Apostle. Constantine had erected various churches and shrines at different places in Con-

stantinople. Cf. Eusebius, *Vita Constantini* 3.48. See also Baur 2.53, 55.

267. Elaphius is unknown outside the *Dial*.

268. ἀπὸ πριγκίπων, "from the principles," from the Latin, *princeps*, which was an imperial office. Cf. PGL 1131.

269. Is this some literary reminiscence or a proverb?

270. Theophilus had convened a synod to condemn Origenism and, according to Socrates, *HE* 6.9, 10, 15, and Sozomen, *HE* 8.14, 16, he journeyed slowly to Constantinople enlisting bishops on his side.

271. κάνθαρος, the dung-beetle of Egypt and southern Europe. The simile is a very striking one and strange language could be used of Theophilus coming laden with bribe money. For a classical account of this beetle, cf. J. H. Fabre, *Scènes de la vie des insectes* (Paris 1939) 106–135, "Le scarabée sacre." Schläpfer 236 says that the perfumes from India were intended for the women of the imperial court. Cf. also Baur 2.231.

272. τοῦ σαββάτου. As early as the Apostolic age, σάββατον could mean simply "week." Cf. PGL 1220; Arndt-Gingrich 746. See also Mark 16.9; Luke 18.12.

273. Sozomen, *HE* 8.17, says that when Theophilus entered the harbor of Constantinople none of the clergy went out to meet him for his enmity against John had been publicly known. Some sailors from Alexandria who chanced to be on the shore and some from the grain vessels as well as other ships gathered together and gave him a rousing welcome.

274. Phil. 3.19.

275. Cf. Job 21.23.

276. Ps. 84.11.

277. These were followers of Origen.

278. δαιμονιῶδες εἰς τὴν τοῦ δράματος ὑπερεσίαν. Cf. *HL* 16.4: ἀστοχήσας οὖν ὁ δαίμων τοῦ δράματος.

279. This was one of the charges brought against Chrysostom at the Synod of the Oak.

280. Acts 20.20.

281. Our chief authorities for the Synod of the Oak are Socrates, *HE* 6.15, and Sozomen, *HE* 8.17. The synod was held in the suburb of Rufinus, known locally as "The Oak," at Chalcedon,

across the sea from Constantinople. The presiding figure was Paulus, bishop of Heracleia in Thrace.

282. Cf. Matt. 26.14–16; 47–57. Palladius used this simile several times.

283. Again we have evidence of Palladius' actual presence at the synod.

284. 2 Tim. 4.6.

285. Phil. 1.21. Chrysostom used this quotation at the beginning of his *Homilia ante exsilium*.

286. ἐθρυλεῖτο παρρησίας. The same phrase occurs in *HL* 59.1

287. This is reminiscent of a fragment of Menander: "All the world's a stage; we come, we act, we are gone."

288. Cf. Jos. 1.1, 2, 5.

289. Cf. 1 Sam. 25. 1; 2 Sam. 5.3.

290. Cf. Josephus, *Antiquities* 10.9.

291. Cf. 2 Kings 2.9–15.

292. Cf. Eusebius, *HE* 2.25.

293. Cf. 1 Cor.16, 10–11; Phil 2, 19–23; 1 Thess. 3.2; 2 Tim. *passim*.

294. Cf. 2 Cor. 7.6–7, 13–15; 8.6, Gal. 2.1; Titus *passim*.

295. Cf. Cor. 3.4–5.

296. παιδάριον, "young child." Certainly Palladius is being very uncouth here. If the young man was soon afterwards to become bishop of Alexandria as some believe, we can hardly call him a booby. Was this possibly the great Cyril of Alexandria?

297. Rufinus before his death in 395 built a palace and a church near Chalcedon which was called after his name. Cf. Socrates, *HE* 8.17. For the life of Rufinus, cf. DCB *s.v.* Rufinus (2).

298. For the life of Tigrius, cf. DCB *s.v.* Tigrius.

299. This Dioscorus is unknown outside the *Dial.*

300. Paulus was bishop of Erythrum. For his life, cf. DCB *s.v.* Paulus (330).

301. Cf. Col. 1.18–22; Eph. 5.25–27; 1 Peter 3.18.

302. Cf. Gen. 4.8 (LXX).

303. κομιτᾶτος, the place where the *comes* is, imperial court, retinue; cf. PGL 767; Sophocles 677.

304. Cf. Sozomen, *HE* 8.10, Socrates, *HE* 6.11, for an account of the two bishops.

305. This letter is extant only here.

306. The members of Theophilus' synod are understood here; cf. Sozomen, *HE* 8.17.

307. Eugenius is unknown outside the *Dial.*

308. γεννάδες. A first declension masculine noun, γεννάδας, has been treated here as a third declensional form. Apparently all the manuscripts agree.

309. In his *Sermo cum iret in exsilium* 2, Chrysostom says that those who came to arrest him were like "spiders sent from a spider." He used this figure on several other occasions; cf. Coleman-Norton 168.

310. Literally, "what they had been weaving," continuing the figure of the spider and the web.

311. Sozomen, *HE* 8.17, says that Chrysostom was summoned four times and they degraded him.

312. Chrysostom had preached a sermon reproving women in general, but Eudoxia took this as a reference to her own way of life. Cf. Socrates, *HE* 6.15, and Sozomen, *HE* 8.16.

313. Possibly a reminiscence of Menander, *Epitrepontes* 385. The phrase occurs twice below.

314. Chrysostom referred to Jezebel in two of his sermons before his first exile: *Homilia ante exsilium* 2, and *Sermo cum iret in exsilium* 2. For the biblical references, cf. 1 Kings 16.31; 18.4, 13, 19; 19.1–2; 20.1–25; 2 Kings 9.7, 22, 30–37.

315. Cf. Dan. 6.1–23 (LXX).

316. Cf. also *HL* 18.28.

CHAPTER 9

317. Although John left the city three days later quietly, the people soon learned of his departure and there was such an uproar that the emperor was forced to order his return. Cf. Sozomen, *HE* 8.18; Socrates, *HE* 6.15 f.

318. This was across the Bosphorus, opposite Constantinople.

319. θραῦσις, a breaking, cracking; cf. PGL 634. Neither Sozomen nor Socrates mentions this "calamity," but Theodoretus, *HE* 5.34, says it was an earthquake.

320. Eudoxia herself sent a letter by a eunuch named Briso saying "she had taken no part in deposing John and she had always respected him as a priest and the initiator of her own children" (Sozomen, *HE* 8.18).

321. This is not mentioned in the other historians. I do not know why Coleman-Norton put it in brackets.

322. Theophilus is meant here of course.

323. This Paul of Libya has been mentioned in chapter 8.

324. Poimen is unknown outside the *Dial*.

325. This was in November 403.

326. For the life of Theodorus, cf. DCB *s.v.* Theodorus (50).

327. Rom. 1.8.

328. Pharetrius is mentioned by Chrysostom in *Ep*. 204. For his life, cf. DCB *s.v.* Pharetrius.

329. καθάπερ οἱ κομιδῇ παῖδεσ τὰ μορμολυκεία . . . . Cf. Plato, *Crito* 46C: ὥσπεο> παῖδαο ἡμᾶς μορμολύττηται, and *Phaedo* 77E: ὥσπερ τὰ μορμολύκεια.

330. For the life of Leontius, cf. DCB *s.v.* Leontius (8).

331. For this life of Ammonius, cf. DCB *s.v.* Ammon (2).

332. *Leodiceia combusta*, so called because of the volcanic nature of the surrounding country, is situated on the borders of Phrygia, Lycaonia, and Pisidia. Cf. Strabo, *Geogr*. 13.628 f., 663.

333. Palladius quotes very freely Canon 4 of the Arian Council of Antioch (341). There were ninety-seven bishops assembled there of whom forty were Arians. After the council had disbanded these forty remained behind to draft further canons of which this is one.

334. Arius (250–336) taught that "there was a time when the Son was not." St. Athanasius was his most famous opponent. For Arius life, see DCB; ODC 87.

335. This was in 343. About one hundred seventy bishops attended the synod of Sardica. The eastern bishops objected to the presence of Athanasius, but they were overruled. Palladius refers to

this event in *HL* 63.1: "Now it happened that the Arians were in conspiracy against Saint Athanasius, the Bishop of Alexandria, working through Eusebius whilst Constantius was Emperor."

336. St. Liberius was pope from 352 to 366. Cf. DCB *s.v.* Liberius (4); LTK 6.1015f.; NCE 8.714–716.

337. St. Julius was pope from 337 to 352. For his life, see DCB *s.v.* Julius (5); LTK 5.1203 f.; NCE 8.51 f.

338. Marcellus was bishop of Ancyra. For his life, see DCB *s.v.* Marcellus (4).

339. Cyrinus (ob. 403). For his life, cf. DCB *s.v.* Cyrinus (1).

340. Elpidius is addressed by Chrysostom in *Epp.* 25, 94, 131, 138, 142, and 230. For his life, see DCB *s.v.* Elpidius (8).

341. Tranquillus is unknown outside the *Dial.* but he may be the person addressed by Chrysostom in *Ep.* 37.

342. ἰλλιγσάντες . . . ἐλιττόμενοι, keeping the paronomasia of the original Greek.

343. Δεσποτικὴ νοστεία. This is apparently the Holy Week fast.

344. ἐπίσκοπος, one who looks over things, an overseer. So Cicero called Pompey "Episcopus of Campania." Palladius uses it in the double sense of bishop and overseer in *HL* 35.10: "I am bishop (overseer) in the kitchen and shops, over the tables and pots . . . ." Cf. note 19 above. On puns in general in the Fathers, cf. L. Spitzer, *Linguistics and Literary History* (Princeton 1948) 21, 35 ff.

345. Cf. Sap. 1.6; Prov. 15.3; Ecclus. 15.18; Esth. 15.2; Heb. 4.13; 1 John 3.20.

346. Cf. Exod. 10.7, 28; 14.5–9.

347. ὁ Σωτὴρ σταυρωθεὶς ἐσκύλευσεν τὸν Ἅδην. Cf. Philo Carpasianus, *Cant.* 126.

348. There were forty bishops as there are the forty days of the Lenten fast. The term for Lent in the Eastern Church is τεσσαρακοστή, "fortieth." Cf. Marcus Diaconus, *Vita Porphyrii* 102.

349. This Paul is mentioned only here. Crateia is a place in Bithynia.

350. Ecclus. 27.16.

351. Lucius is unknown outside the *Dial.*

352. χρυσέοις ῥήμασι. Moore conjectured that the first

two letters of the word for "gifts" (δωρήμασι) had been dropped out of the text here, and that the original meant "with golden gifts."

353. Cf. Gen. 32.6.

354. The labyrinth in Crete contained the Minotaur to whom were sacrificed every year seven Athenian youths and seven maidens until Theseus slew the monster.

355. Exod. 1.12, with some textual variants here.

356. So called because it was five miles from the city. The fifth mile = τὸ πέμπτον μίλιον.

Chapter 10

357. Moore 84 has a note here to the effect that the explanation of actual events leads to more expression than the demonstration of abstract thought. Palladius' language here is strangely reminiscent of Diogenes Laertius, *De vitis philosophorum* 1.9.

358. μαφόρια, veils worn by noble women, these were the forerunner of the nun's veil. Monks also wore them; cf. Cassian, *Inst.* 1.6. See Sophocles 737.

359. Eleutherus is unknown outside the *Dial.*

360. This was the period between Easter and Whitsunday. Socrates, *HE* 6.18, tells us: "For two months John did not go out in public, after which a decree from the emperor sent him into exile."

361. Cf. Dan. 2.21; Rom. 12.1–7; Titus 3.1; Heb. 13.17; 1 Peter 2.13, 17.

362. Cf. Matt. 27.25.

363. τῷ ἀγγέλῳ τῆς ἐκκλησίας. Cf. Chrysostom, *Oratio in synaxin archangelorum*: "Christ has placed guardian angels over every church . . . ."

364. ἱερατεῖον, "vestry, sacristy." Palladius sometimes uses the word in the earlier sense of "body of clergy," as here and in *HL*.

365. Olympias (c. 368–c. 408) is addressed by Chrysostom in *Epp.* 1–17. For her life, cf. DCB *s.v.* Olympias (2). Cf. *HL* 56.

366. Pentadia is addressed by Chrysostom in *Epp.* 94, 104, 185. For her life, cf. DCB *s.v.* Pentadia.

367. Procle may be the deaconess Amprucle addressed by

Chrysostom in *Epp.* 46, 103, 191. Otherwise she is unknown outside the *Dial*.

368. Silvina is unknown outside the *Dial*.

369. Nebridius (ob. c. 390) is mentioned in *HL* 56.1. He was a nephew of Emperor Theodosius. For his life, cf. DCB *s.v.* Nebridius (3).

370. Cf. Luke 22.37.

371. 2. Tim. 4.7.

372. Acts 20.25.

373. δυτικόν, the west, where the sun went down into darkness. Symbolically considered it is always relative. It signified evil, sin, ignorance, and darkness. The east signified light. In the time of Chrysostom those about to be baptized faced the west; after they had renounced evil they turned around to face the east. See Coleman-Norton 172, after Moore 87.

374. In true rhetorical style Palladius contrasts the powers of evil with the choirs of the celestial hierarchy.

375. The passage here in quotations is practically copied from Philo Judaeus, *Legatio ad Gaium* 46. It is not credited to Philo and Palladius may have taken it from a florilegium of rhetorical passages used in the schools of rhetoric in his day.

376. Acts 13.38.

377. Eccle. 27.15.

378. The fire was set by supporters of John, according to Socrates, *HE* 6.18. Sozomen, *HE* 8.22, says that the fire came from heaven. Each rival party blamed the other for the incendiary act. Palladius claims that it was because the "angel of the church" had left it when John was driven out. Palladius is confused here in his account. The church was burned at John's first expulsion.

379. Acts 1.18; 2 Peter 2.13, 15.

380. The church of St. Sophia built by Constantine in 360 was twice destroyed, but was rebuilt at great expense by Justinian in 532. Cf. *Cambridge Mediaeval History* 4.2 (Cambridge 1967) 316 f.

381. ἀνεχαίτιζεν. The figure is of a horse suddenly rearing and throwing back its mane.

382. According to Socrates, *HE* 6.18, this was on June 20, 404. Sozomen, *HE* 8.22, says the fire spread from late afternoon until morning.

CHAPTER 11

383. Socrates, *HE* 6.18, informs us that Chrysostom was carried into exile the very day of the fire. John, *Epp*. 10 and 221, tells us that he left Nicaea in Bithynia on July 4, 404.

384. This was a village in the Taurian Mountains on the edge of Cilicia. The journey took some seventy days. Chrysostom's letters describe the journey and its hardships in detail. It was apparently the Siberia of the Eastern Empire.

385. Arsacius (c. 325–405) was denounced by Chrysostom in *Ep*. 125. He was consecrated bishop on June 24, 404, when he was eighty years old. Socrates, *HE* 6.19, says that he governed the see quietly and Sozomen, *HE* 8.23, speaks well of him. For his life, cf. DCB.

386. Palladius made a mistake here, cutting Arsacius' rule short by three months. Socrates, *HE* 6.20, says he died November 11, 405.

387. What Palladius means here is that Arsacius was only waiting for Nectarius' death so he could become bishop of Constantinople. In those days the transfer of bishops from one see to another was a matter of grave scandal. Had Arsacius become bishop of Tarsus, he would never have had a chance to become bishop of Constantinople.

388. Atticus governed the see of Constantinople from 406 to 426. He is denounced in Chrysostom's *Liber ad eos qui scandalizati sunt* 20. For his life, cf. DCB *s.v.* Atticus; NCE 1.1030; LTK 1.1016 f.

389. Palladius makes a play on the words γραφή and ἀντιγραφή. I have tried to imitate the play in my translation.

390. Porphyrius was bishop of Antioch. Sozomen, *HE* 8.24, says that he joined with those who persecuted the followers of John.

391. Matt. 10.23.

392. Prov. 11.4.

393. The soldier's girdle showed his rank; in the case of military officers it was the sign of their commission.

394. Cf. edict of September 11, 404, in *Codex Theodosianus* 16.

395. ἐν τῷ ὑπαίθρῳ Cf. the Latin, *sub divo*, "under the wide and starry sky."

396. Cf. John 15.14–15.

397. John 14.6.

398. John 16.33.

399. Sozomen, *HE* 8.27, tells how the wealthy Olympias sent John money in his exile to help the poor. Many came to visit him from Cilicia and Syria to ask his advice. He was beloved by the Armenian people. This was autumn 405 to autumn 406.

400. Cf. Amos 7.11; Luke 4.25; 15.14.

401. Arabissus was a fortress town twenty leagues away from Cucusus. It was crowded with fugitives and open to attack from the Isaurians. Chrysostom spent the winter of 405–406 there and his letters (*Epp.* 4, 68–70, 128, 131, 135, 137) describe the hardships.

402. Matt. 5.14.

403. Cf. Matt. 5.15.

404. 2 Cor. 12.9.

405. εὐχάριστον φιλοσοφίαν. The phrase also occurs in *HL* 47.15. John showed the patience of Job in his trials and tribulations.

406. τὸ ζῆν ἀπρρῆξαι, a reminiscence of Aeschylus, *Persae* 507; Euripides, *Iphigenia Taurica* 974.

407. So also Chrysostom in his *Liber ad eos qui scandalizati sunt* 10: "Like David, a wanderer, an exile, disfranchised, homeless, I am exiled to a barbarous land."

408. Is ὄφισ ἐν σκηνῇ a reminiscence of some fable or a proverb?

409. This was on the easternmost shore of the Pontic (Black) Sea.

410. Cf. 2 Kings 2.23.

411. This was in June 407. He had travelled on the average only about two and a half miles a day. Cf. Baur 2.420.

412. This was a town in Pontus, the present Tokat.

413. For the life of Basiliscus (ob. 303), cf. DCB *s.v.* Basiliscus.

414. This was the general persecution of Diocletian, 303. For the life of Maximianus (246–305), cf. DCB *s.v.* Maximianus (1); RE 14.2.2486–2516; LTK 7.201.

415. For the life of Lucianus, cf. DCB *s.v.* Lucianus (12).

416. This is highly reminiscent of a passage in *HL* 60.1: "And the martyr of that place, Colluthus by name, stood over her and said:

'This day you will make the journey to the Master and see all the saints . . . .' "

417. This would have been less than two and a half miles by our present standards. Baur 2.421 would make it three and a half miles.

418. Chrysostom *Hom.* 116, had once said: "We clothe the dead in new garments to signify their putting on the new clothing of incorruption." Eusebius, *V. Const.* 4.62, says that Constantine wore white garments when preparing for death and refused to wear the royal purple.

419. νήφων. Bigot translated it *jejunus*, "fasting," but beginning with the New Testament writers it meant being self-possessed, exercising restraint, etc. Cf. Arndt-Gingrich 540.

420. The Eucharistic elements were taken along on journeys. Cf. Ambrose, *De obitu Sat.* 3.19.

421. Gen. 49.32. Cf. also *VA* 92: " . . . he drew up his feet."

422. Cf. Isa. 52.7.

423. Cf. Socrates, *HE* 6.21: "A man who in his zeal for temperance yielded to anger more than to respect, and for the sake of temperance all through his life allowed his tongue too much out-spokenness. I marvel how a man who practiced such zeal for temperance, taught men in his addresses to despise temperance."

423a. 1 Macc. 2.69. Socrates, *HE* 6.21, dates this as of September 14, 407.

424. Cf. Luke 10.11.

425. Job 5.26.

426. Prov. 13.2.

427. ἑορτάσθεις. Cf. GPL 504 for the various meanings of ἑορτάζω. Originally it meant any annual celebration. The *Apostolic Constitutions* 8.42 called for the relatives of Christians to meet for Psalms, hymns, and prayers on the third, ninth, and fortieth day after death. Cf. *HL* 21.14 f.: " . . . And in forty days Eulogius died, and in three days more the cripple also died. Now Cronius tarried a while about the regions in the Thebaid and then went down to the monasteries of Alexandria. And it so happened that the brotherhood was observing the forty days for the one and the third day of the other." The Copts kept a "month's mind," presumably a thirty-day period.

CHAPTER 12

428. Ecclus. 8.9. (LXX).

429. ὡμολόγηται, "it is confessed, admitted," This is one of those typically Palladian utterances that occurs often in both *Dial.* and *HL* and again seems to point to further proof of Palladius' authorship of both works.

430. 1. Cor. 8.8. The rest of the sentence is a paraphrase of the Scriptural passage.

431. Cf. Gal. 5.6.

432. See Socrates, *HE* 6.4.: "His reasons for not eating with others no one knows with certainty; but some persons in justification of his conduct state that he had a very delicate stomach, and weak digestion, which obliged him to be careful in his diet, and therefore he ate alone, while others thought that this was done to conceal his rigid and habitual abstinence. Whatever the real motive may have been, the circumstance itself contributed not a little to the grounds of accusation by his calumniators."

433. Acts 6.2–4, very freely quoted.

434. Matt. 25.35.

435. Luke 6.26.

436. Matt. 11.18 f.

437. Many of Chrysostom's letters date from his second exile.

438. Abraham is meant; cf. Gen. 18.1–33.

439. Lot is meant; cf. Gen. 19.1–3.

440. Abraham is meant; cf. Gen. 21.1–5.

441. Lot is referred to here; cf. Gen.19.12–28.

442. Heb. 13.2.

443. Cf. Matt. 10.16.

444. Luke 6.30.

445. Ecclus 11.31.

446. σαράβαρα. See Dan. 3.21. (LXX)., See also PGL 1222; Sophocles 979.

447. Cf. Gen. 13.18; 18.1–8.

448. Cf. Aristotle, *Ethica Nicomachea* 2.6.4. This may possibly be from a gloss, but the Church Fathers are fond of the doctrine of the mean.

449. Cf. Gen. 19.1–11.
450. Acts 6.2, 4.
451. Isa. 1.22 (LXX).
452. Cf. Matt. 14.15–21.
453. Cf. Matt. 5.1–2.
454. Cf. John 20.31; Rom. 1.16; Col. 1.5–6.
455. Amos 8.11.
456. Cf. Gen. 42.1–5; 46.5–7.
457. Amos 8.12.
458. ὕβρεις αἱ ὑπὸ γαστέρα, where ὕβρις is plural and could be translated, "acts of violence."
459. Cf. Gen. 3.1–6; 22–24.
460. Cf. Gen. 4.1–8.
461. Cf. Job 1.18–19.
462. Cf. Gen. 25.29–34. But cf. Gen. 27.1–40.
463. Cf. 1 Sam. 15.10–28, 28.15–18, 31.1–6.
464. Cf. Exod. 16.2–3; Ps. 94.8–11.
465. Cf. 1 Sam. 1, 3; 2.12–17; 4.11.
466. Deut. 32.15.
467. Cf. Gen. 13.13; Deut. 32.28, 32; Luke 17.28–29.
468. Ezech. 16.49.
469. Cf. Amos 6.3–8.
470. Amos 6.4–6.
471. Isa. 5.11–12.
472. Dan. 14.10–21. Daniel had spread ashes on the floor to prove that humans ate the feast put out for the idol Bel. Their footsteps on the floor were seen next morning.
473. Cf. Matt. 7.13–14.
474. Cf. Luke 16. 19–26.
475. Cf. Gen. 5.24; Heb. 11.5. Cf. also Clement of Rome 9.3.
476. διέδωσεν ἐν τῷ ξύλῳ. Justin Martyr, *Dial.* 138.2, points out that Christ too saved the world by dying on the tree (ξύλῳ).
477. Cf. Gen. 6.13–7.23; Heb. 11.7.
478. Cf. Gen. 9.20–23.
479. Cf. Gen. 14.8–16; Heb. 11.8–10.
480. Cf. Matt. 1.18–25.
481. Cf. Gen. 32.24–29.

482. Cf. Gen. 21.1, 17–21.

483. Gen. 31.40.

484. Gen. 28.20, 22, here quoted in the second person, though it is in the third person in the Vulgate and the Septuagint.

485. Cf. Exod. 19.17.

486. Cf. Exod. 17.1–6.

487. Cf. Exod. 12.37; 14.10 f.

488. Cf. Exod. 31.18; 32.15–16; 34.1, 4, 25–27.

489. This was the pheasant, named after the river Phasis in Colchis (Pontus) where the bird was first brought and from where it derives its name. Cf. J. B. Greenough-G. L. Kittredge, *Words and Their Ways in English Speech* (New York 1901) 129.

490. ἄρτους πλυτούς, loaves made of refined white flour in opposition to the barley loaves of the poor.

491. Cf. Exod. 16.14–15, 31; 17.1–6.

492. πνευματικῆς διδασκαλίας. Cf. *HL* 2.1: διδασκαλίας ἕνεκεν πνευματκῆς.

493. Cf. 1 Sam. 7.3, 4, 15–17. This was the biblical Ramatha.

494. David is referred to in Acts 2.29. Cf. Amos 6.5.

495. Ps. 102.10.

496. Cf. 1 Kings 17.1; 18.1–2; James 5.17.

497. Cf. 1 Kings 17.1–6.

498. Cf. Dan. 14.

499. Cf. Exod. 3.14: *God said to Moses: 'I AM WHO AM.'*

500. Heb. 13.7.

501. Cf. Mark 1.4.

502. Cf. Mark 1.6; Matt. 11.7–8.

503. This is highly reminiscent of the scene in *HL* 24.2, where Stephen of Libya undergoes an operation.

504. Luke 3.7–8.

505. Cf. Luke 3.8.

506. Cf. Gal. 2.2, 7, 9.

507. Cf. Rom. 2.25–29; Gal. 5.2, 6; 6.15; Col. 3.11.

508. Cf. Rom. 2.25–4.25.

509. Acts 9.25.

510. Cf. Rom. 1.14; Gal. 5.3.

511. Cf. 1 Cor. 5.11–13; 8; 10.20, 25–28.

512. 1 Tim. 4.13.

513. 2 Tim. 4.2.

514. The grammar is bad. Palladius has earned Tillemont's strictures that he indulges sometimes in "naughty rhetoric." Was this possibly a garbled account from some patristic commentary on the Epistles of St. Paul?

515. σεμνολόγημα. Cf. also *HL* 56.2. Chrysostom, *Hom. on John* 75.3: "Things which appear shameful (the cross) are the revered stories of our good things."

516. 2 Tim. 3.10.

517. Cf. 2 Tim. 3.11; 2 Cor. 11.23–30; 12.1–11.

518. Cf. Titus 1.1, 4, 5.

519. Titus 1.5, 13–14.

520. Titus 1.12. This quotation is from the *Minos* of Epimenides, a Cretan poet (c. 600 B.C.). Another poet, Callimachus (c. 300–240 B.C.), quotes the first half of it in his *Hymn to Zeus*, applying it to the Cretan legend that the tomb of Zeus was on that island of Crete. The phrase was no doubt a familiar one and cannot be used to prove that St. Paul or Palladius for that matter was acquainted with the writings of Epimenides.

521. γυναικοϊέρακες occurs only here and in *HL* 65.2. Cf. PGL 325; Sophocles 342. It is obviously Palladius' own coinage.

522. Exod. 32.6.

523. Exod. 32.1.

524. Mal. 2.7.

525. According to Gen. 10.10, Chalanne was one of the cities of Nimrod.

526. Cf. Gen. 9.20f.

527. Cf. Gen. 37.25–28.

528. Cf. Mark 6.21–28.

529. Cf. Acts 20.7.

530. Cf. Luke 21.7–20.

531. Cf. John 6.28–35, 48–58.

532. John 6.27.

533. 1 Cor. 8.8.

534. 1 Cor. 15.32.

535. 1 Cor. 15.33.

CHAPTER 13

536. Isa. 5.20.

537. Does this mean that John did not give great dinners because he who gives great banquets is "ambitious"? He serves a good meal, not for the sake of his belly so much as to make a good impression among the "right people," and also to show off his wealth. Certainly Petronius' *Cena Trimalchionis* is an excellent satire on a vulgar man who made an extravagant display of his wealth and even pretended to some degree of learning, ignorant as he was. (Was it possibly aimed at Nero?)

538. Cf. Mark 14.16–18.

539. παρ ὡραν ἢ παρ' ἡμέραν. Cf. *HL* 31.1; 61.6: μίαν παρὰ μίαν, "every other day."

540. μνηστευόμενος, "wooing, courting" It is used in the same sense in *HL* 30, where Dorotheus exhorts the women not to fight, and again in *HL* 63.4.

541. ἀνίπτοις . . . φύροντες. Cf. Aeschylus, *Prometheus Vinctus* 450: ἔφυρον εἰκῇ πάντα.

542. Ezech. 34.2, 4.

543. 2 Cor. 11.20.

544. Ezech. 34.3.

545. Jer. 12.10.

546. Matt. 5.11.

547. Luke 6.26.

548. Matt. 6.24.

549. φιλομαθέστατε. Cf. *HL* prol. 2.

550. Acts 6.2.

551. Matt. 19.27.

552. Cf. Matt. 7.22.

553. Matt. 25.41.

554. Luke 13.25.

555. Cf. James 1.22–24.

556. Cf. Heb. 1.13.

557. This was the so called *lithomania* mentioned in note 233 above.

558. *Eccle.* 2.4, 5, 11, 18.

559. But Sozomen, *HE* 8.6, says it was thirteen bishops, six in Asia and seven in Lycia and Phrygia. The charge at the Synod of the Oak was that he had illegally entered another province and ordained bishops there.

560. Cf. Num. 22.2–24.25.

561. So Moore keeps the play on words: γράφων καὶ καταγράφων.

562. Isa. 10.1.

563. ἐπινέμησις here for ἰνδικτίων, from the Latin, *indictio*, a period of fifteen years. This was taken over from the Roman West by Constantine in 312. It was to supplant the Greek Olympiad which was a period of four years. This then was 400 A.D. Cf. PGL 528; Sophocles 506, 600; NCE 7.467 f.; RE 9.2.1327–1332.

564. Theotimus was bishop of Tomi (392–403), a Goth who was missionary to the Huns. For his life, cf. DCB *s.v.* Theotimus (2); LTK 10.96.

565. Ammon was bishop of Adrianople. For his life, cf. DCB *s.v.* Ammon (1).

566. Arabianus was bishop of Ancyra. For his life, cf. DCB *s.v.* Arabianus (2).

567. See Moore 117, n. 4: "It was natural that at all times many bishops should visit the capitol of the Eastern Empire 'on ecclesiastical business'; these gradually formed a 'synodus endemusa'—a 'home' of 'floating synod'—meeting under the presidency of the archbishop. . . . Similar home synods existed at Rome and at Treves, during the residence of the emperors there."

568. This Eusebius is unknown outside the *Dial.*

569. Valentinopolis was a town in Asia Minor.

570. Antoninus is unknown outside the *Dial.*

571. It is apparent from this that Eusebius was not a regular member of the synod.

572. Basilina died in 331.

573. This was of course Julian the Apostate (331–363). For his life, cf. DCB *s.v.* Julianus (103); NCE 8.47; RE 10.1. 26–91.

574. In the Apostolic Constitutions only the lower orders of clergy were allowed to marry after their appointment to office. The Council of Trullo ordered that a bishop's wife should go to a convent, or become a deaconess. The Council of Caesarea declared that

a priest who married after ordination should be degraded. For Antoninus to resume relations with his wife was equivalent to marriage after ordination. See Moore 118–19.

CHAPTER 14

575. The *Dial.* apparently took place before a small audience.

576. 2 Cor. 12.11.

577. Paul of Heracleia had presided over the Synod of the Oak as the metropolitan. For his life, cf. DCB *s.v.* Paulus (34).

578. See Chrysostom, *Hom. in 2 Cor. 36*: "The bishop at his entry into the church says always: 'Peace be with you' as a proper salutation when he enters his Father's house."

579. Matt. 5.23.

580. ἀβολιτίων, from the Latin *abolitio*, a legal term. Cf. PGL 2; Sophocles 59. Possibly this is a hapax legomen.

581. 1 Tim. 6.10.

582. Ps. 15.5.

583. That is, until about two in the afternoon.

584. The third canon of the Council of Chalcedon (451) forbade bishops to be involved in secular business of any sort.

585. Gainas was a Goth who was in command of the army in Constantinople; see Socrates, *HE* 6.6. Gainas had enrolled in the army with many of his tribe and was supposed to defend the city against another Gothic tribe. But he joined forces with the enemy to conquer the city. When the Goths attempted to force the palace they were repulsed and fled into Thrace, where Gainas was killed in January 401. Chrysostom was himself favorably disposed to the Gothic peoples as he had sent missionaries to convert them. For his life, cf. DCB *s.v.* Gainas.

586. John was thinking of the cross examination of witnesses and "wearing them down" in their statements and contradictions. At first he had thought to save them the long journey with its expenses.

587. Syncletius is unknown outside the *Dial.*

588. Trajanopolis is a town in Southern Thrace. See RE 6.2. 2082–85.

589. For the life of Hesychius, cf. DCB *s.v.* Hesychius (7).

590. Parius is on the Propontis.

591. Thus Eusebius is himself guilty of the very crime he had so violently condemned.

592. It was the summer of 400.

593. ποιήσαντες ἀκοινώητον. Cf. *HL* 33.4, the story of several nuns who were forbidden to receive Communion for a period of seven years.

594. χρονοτριβούντων. Cf. *HL* 21.15, where the verb is used in a pun on the name of Chronius (Κρόνιος).

595. Probably this was to ask Chrysostom's help in selecting a successor to Antoninus.

596. This was early in 401.

597. The Proconnesus was a promontory on the south shore of the Sea of Marmora.

598. Apameia was a seaport on the Sea of Marmora.

599. This was Paul of Crateia, not of Heracleia.

600. Cyrinus was mentioned above in chapters 3 and 9. He was bishop of Chalcedon at this time and a friend of Chrysostom, later an enemy.

601. Palladius knew all the details at first hand, having been witness to what he reports.

602. Heracleides, one of Chrysostom's deacons, was consecrated bishop of Ephesus, according to Socrates, *HE* 6.11; Sozomen, *HE* 8.6. Three years later he was deposed and exiled.

603. Prov. 1.20.

604. Ps. 4.2.

605. When Chrysostom returned from Ephesus he preached a homily, preserved only in a Latin version printed in PG 42.421–24, in which he said the trip to Ephesus took more than 150 days.

CHAPTER 15

606. προσαντιλέγουσι. Cf. *HL* 32.7: προσαντιλέγοντος δὲ τοῦ Παχωμίου τῷ ἀγγέλῳ.

607. It is now late spring or early summer 402.

608. Constantine had exempted the clergy from all public offices, Cf. Eusebius, *HE* 10.7. Many men then offered themselves as candidates for the lower orders of the clergy to shun civic responsibility. Later on the law was changed, exempting only bishops.

609. We do not know to whom this refers. See also Moore 128 n. 3. After the fall of Jerusalem, Jewish "patriarchs" were set up at Tiberias and Babylon. References to these offices by early Christian writers stopped near the end of the fourth century.

610. Micah 3.11.

611. This is simony, the sale or purchase of spiritual things, named after Simon Magus. Cf. ODC 1278; R. A. Ryder, *Simony: An Historical Synopsis and Commentary* (Washington 1931); NCE 13.228f.

612. So Origen on John 2.7. Evil is στέρησις, "privation, loss." See Pseudo-Dionysius, *De div. nom.* 4, where "the non-existent" = "the evil."

613. Jer. 19.3. Cf. 1 Sam. 3.11.

614. φιλόθεος ὤν. Is this a play on words, contrasting Theodore with Theophilus?

615. Cf. Rom. 1.21; Eph. 4.18.

616. Cf. Acts 1.15–26; 6.1–6.

617. τὰ τῶν ἀνθρώπων ἐκτρώματα. Cf. 1 Cor. 15.8.

618. Job 30.1, 7.

619. Chrysostom, *Hom. in 2 Cor.* 18, tells of an "ordination which the initiated know, for all may not be revealed to the uninitiated." In *Hom. in 1 Cor.* 40 he will not speak of baptism because of the presence of uninitiated persons.

620. Cf. John 15.14 f.

621. John 13.23. St. John the Evangelist was regarded as the first bishop of Ephesus.

622. Matt. 24.15 (Dan. 9.27).

623. Victor is unknown outside the *Dial.*

624. The first Canon of Nicaea forbade the ordination of a eunuch. This fell under the general law laid down in Lev. 21.17 ff. forbidding anyone with any bodily blemish from offering sacrifice.

625. This was Heracleides who lived as a solitary in the desert.

626. ἐγκυκλίων ἠγμένον μαθημάτων. Cf. *HL* 21.3: ἐκ τῶν ἐγκυκλίων παιδευμάτων, and 58.2: τῶν ἐγκυκλίων μαθημάτων.

These were the liberal studies preparatory to professional training. They always included rhetorical training in both Greece and Rome. Cf. A. Gwynn, *Roman Education from Cicero to Quintilian* (Oxford 1926) 85 f., 145 ff., 177 ff., etc.; also H. I. Marrou, *A History of Education in Antiquity* (New York 1936) ch. 8 and notes 406 ff.

627. σιδηροκατάδικον. Moore 131 translated "jailbird" and in a footnote said that it was a word of Palladius' own coinage; he explained it literally as "condemned to be put into irons." However the word is not hapax as Moore thought over sixty years ago. PGL 1233 quotes other examples, always applied to eunuchs. I have followed the interpretation of PGL in my translation.

628. Dionysus was the god of wine and good cheer in Greek mythology.

629. The body as the temple of the Holy Spirit through baptism and confirmation, not to mention the reception of orders, is to be kept pure and chaste if we expect to rise on the Last Day.

630. Rom. 10.14.

631. Eph. 5.11.

CHAPTER 16

632. The earliest account of the consecration of a bishop (*Const. Apost.* 8.4.5) describes the ritual of placing the Gospels on the head of the ordinand while the bishops present touch it.

633. Cf. Mark 15.17.

634. Porphyrius was bishop of Antioch from 404 to 413. For his life, cf. DCB *s.v.* Porphyrius (4).

635. This letter has not survived.

636. Matt. 12.36, inexactly quoted.

637. Cf. Matt. 18.6.

638. ἀνεμόφθορος. Cf. Gen. 41.23; Jude 12. Cf. also *HL* 47.11.

639. Cf. the lengthy critical note *ad loc.* in Coleman-Norton 183 n. 94.12–14. See also Menander, *Epitrepontes* 566–69.

640. Cf. F. G. Allinson, *Menander: The Principal Fragments* (LCL 132; London 1921) 89–91.

641. Prov. 26.22.

642. Cf. Gen. 19.4 f.

643. This proverb has been attributed to Pythagoras. Stobaeus, a contemporary of Palladius, quotes it in his *Florilegium* 1.20.

644. Cf. Heb. 6.6.

645. This passage is not accepted as genuine by editors from Bigot to Migne.

645a. Judges 3.15.

645b. Apparently he was secretary of the synod.

646. Prov. 12.24.

647. τῶν πλεῖστον φαύλων. Cf. *HL*, Letter of Palladius to Lausus 2.

648. Prov. 12.24.

649. τὸ σκεπτικὸν ἀεὶ αἰνιττόμενος so Moore translates this passage, *op. cit* 136.

650. ἀπὸ γράμματος βασιλικοῦ Cf. Evagrius, *HE* 1.3: γραμμάτων βασιλικῶν.

651. Chrysostom addressed Cyriacus and Diophantus in *Epp.* 22, 62, 66, 107, 132, and 222. For their lives, cf. DCB *s.vv.* Cyriacus (9) and Diophantus.

652. For the labors of Hercules, cf. P. Hardy, *Oxford Companion to Classical Literature* (Oxford 1935) 203.

653. Daphne was a public park in the suburbs of Antioch.

654. Acts 17.9: Here the meaning is that they took their bribes and beat a hasty retreat.

655. This shows the ironic situation reflected in Palladius' own statement: the people returned from the circus to find that while they were away a similar theatrical performance had been enacted at home.

656. στρατοπεδάρχης. Cf. Arndt-Gingrich 778; Sophocles 1015.

657. Valentinus is unknown outside the *Dial.*

658. νυκτέπαρχος. Cf. PGL 927; Sophocles 787.

659. Nero was emperor of Rome, from 54 to 68 A.D. Cf. Tacitus, *Annales* 15.44 for this allusion.

660. Cf. Col. 3.22.

661. For the life of Nebridius (*ob.* 386), cf DCB *s.v.* Nebridius

(1). Palladius, *HL* 56.1, says that Olympias was the bride of Nebridius, who died shortly after their marriage, leaving her *virgo intacta*.

662. Similarly in *HL* 9 Melania is called the "female man of God."

663. Cf. John 17.18–23; 1 Cor. 1.10, 13; Eph. 5.25–27.

664. For his life (c.315–403), cf. DCB *s.v.* Epiphanius (1).

665. Damasus was pope from 366 to 384. Cf. ODC 374; LTK 3.136 f.; NCE 4.624 f.

666. Siricius was pope from 384 to 398. Cf. ODC 1261; LTK 9.793 f.; NCE 13.258 f.

667. χαμαὶ πιπτούσης. Cf. Homer, *Ilias* 13.530: χαμαὶ πεσοῦσα.

668. Cf. Matt. 13.53–58; Mark 3.21–22; Luke 7.34; John 6.41–42.

669. 1 Cor. 4.12.

670. Titus 3.10–11.

671. Cf 1 Tim. 3.1–7; Titus 1.7–9.

672. ἡ διάκονος, that is, Olympias. This form is used in *HL* 70.3. Later on ἡ διακόνισσα was used, but never by Palladius. See PGL 352.

673. Cf. John 6.5–13.

674. Barley was the staple flour of the poor.

675. Cf. John 6.26.

676. Cf. 1 Cor. 11.1.

677. Cf. John 6.25.

678. John 6.26.

679. Luke 5.31. Cf. *HL* 35.6, where John of Lycopolis quotes this verse to Palladius when he visited him.

680. Matt. 5.45.

681. Matt. 9.11; Mark 2.16. This passage is quoted in *HL* Prologue 12.

682. Cf. Dan. 12.3: "They that instruct others to justice shall shine like stars for all eternity."

683. δεισιδαιμονία. In ancient pagan religion this meant "fear of the gods," "due respect for the gods," and sometimes simply "religion." To the Christian as early as Acts 17.22 it meant "scrupulously religious." See the dissertation of P. J. Koets, Δεισιδαιμονία:

A Contribution to the Knowledge of the Religious Terminology in Greek (Purmerend 1929). Cf. Arndt-Gingrich 172; PGL 335; Sophocles 348.

CHAPTER 17

684. Hierax is mentioned in *HL* 22.1. There are several who bear this name in the monastic literature of Egypt. The name occurs in *Apophthegmata Patrum*.

685. This is St. Antony the Great (c. 250–355), the acknowledged founder of Egyptian monasticism. See C. Butler, *The Lausiac History of Palladius* 1 (Texts and studies: Contributions to Biblical and Patristic Literature 6, Cambridge 1898) 225 f.: "Whether in works which may claim to be history, or in the vaguer traditions enshrined in the *Apophthegmata*, or in the pure romances, a firmly set tradition ever looks back to Antony as the inspirer, nay even the creator, of that monastic system, which . . . had by the year 370 attained to vast proportion in Egypt and elsewhere." For a brief account of Antony's life, cf. DCB *s.v.* Antonius, St.; ODC 67 f.; NCE 1:594 f.; LTK 1.667 ff.

686. Ammonius was one of the "Tall Brothers." He and Dioscorus were mentioned earlier. The other two, Eusebius and Euthymius, are mentioned by Socrates, *HE* 6.7, and Sozomen, *HE* 8.12.

687. Valens was emperor of the Eastern Roman Empire from 364 to 378.

688. Aurelius is unknown outside the *Dial*.

689. Sisinnius was probably the Novatian bishop of Constantinople (395–407). Cf. DCB *s.v.* Sinnius (7).

690. This was the decree that banished Chrysostom.

691. φαντασίαι . . . νυκτεριναὶ. . . . Cf. *HL* 23.1: φαντασίας τὰς νυκτερινάς.

692. κυματώδη . . . ἐξηχοῦτας. Cf. Aeschylus, *Septem contra Thebas* 443: πέμπει γεγωνὰ . . . κυμαίνοντ' ἔπη.

693. ὀκταμηνιαίῳ . . . ἐταριχεύετο. Cf. *HL* 38.8: χρόνῳ ταριχεύσας.

694. Socrates, *HE* 6.19, tells of Cyrinus, bishop of Chalcedon, losing both his feet as a result of an accident, a terrible hail storm which ravaged Constantinople and its suburbs, and the dreadful death of Eudoxia shortly after John's expulsion from the city. Socrates did not know whether these were punishments, but states: "God only knows, He who is the discoverer of secrets and the just judge of truth itself. I have simply recorded the reports which were current at that time."

695. Cf. Luke 4.22.

696. Cf. Deut. 32.39.

697. Ps. 88.11.

698. Cf. Judges 5.39.

699. Most of the characters mentioned in this subsection are also to be found in the *HL*.

700. νόσους τὰς περὶ ῥῖγος ἐλαύνειν. Cf. also *HL* 11.5: θεραπεύων πάντας τούς ῥιγαζομένους. Now all the manuscripts of *HL* contain this passage, which is in all probability interpolated from the *Dial*. Cf. also J. Pargoire, "Rufinianes VI: Une tombe a Rufinianes," in BZ 8 (1899) 447 ff.

701. Socrates, *HE* 6.17, says he was given a magnificent funeral and was interred in the church at "The Oak" where the synod regarding Chrysostom had been held. According to Sozomen, *HE* 8.17, it was the church dedicated to St. Mocius.

702. The name means "falcon" in Greek. This person is possibly the Hierax mentioned in *HL* 22.1.

703. Mount Porphyrites is between the Nile and the Red Sea and is mentioned several times in monastic literature as the abode of hermits. Cf. Cassian, *Inst.* 10.24; *Coll.* 3.5, 7.26, 24.4. Cf. *HL* 34.3, 36.2, especially the latter where Posidonius says: "I dwelt in the place called Porphyrites for the space of a year in which I met no man, heard no conversation, and touched no bread . . . ."

704. Literally "without human breath," here taken in contrast to the breath of the Holy Spirit.

705. Cf. *HL* 4.1; 18.5; 29.3; 38.3, and 45.1 where the identical or very similar expression is used. For further examples cf. Coleman-Norton 186, note to 105.26–27. This again is proof of Palladius' authorship of both *HL* and *Dial*.

706. 2 Cor. 11.14.

707. Heb. 6.18.

708. πῶς καρτερήσεις; Cf. *HL* 5.3, where Melania asks Alexandra how she could persevere in the desert without seeing anyone.

709. Cf. *VA* 52, where Antony puts demons to flight, and they went as though whipped.

710. This was a state of spiritual weariness, boredom which was apt to cause monks to leave their ascetic life. It has been called the demon of the midday (Ps. 90.6). Spiritual writers of both the East and the West inveighed against it, and Chaucer called it the 'synne of accidie.' Aldous Huxley has an essay, 'Accidie,' in his *Essays New and Old* (New York 1927) in which he made a plea to bring the word back into good English usage. Cf. also *HL* Prol. 14; 5.3, 21.1.

711. Cf. Luke 9.62. See *HL* 35.9, where John of Lycopolis told Palladius that it was but a temptation of the Evil One that he should wish to leave the desert to look after his father and brother, and he quoted this passage from Luke 9.62.

712. This may well be the Isaac (28) of DCB.

713. Macarius (*ob.* 389) of Alexandria is the subject of a long chapter 18 in *HL*. For his life, cf. DCB *s.v.* Macarius (16), (17); LTK 6.1310.

714. Cf. Mark 16.18.

715. Cf. Luke 22.31.

716. This may be identical with Isaac (28 ii) in DCB.

717. For the life of Cronius, cf. DCB *s.v.* Cronius (2).

718. This is proof that the long *Dial.* extended over several days.

719. Cf. Luke 10.30 ff. Deacons are often referred to as Levites.

720. διάκονος θήλεια, literally "female deacon." Elsewhere Palladius uses the term ἡ διάκονος. Olympias is here referred to. Cf. the article "deaconess" in ODC 380 f.; NCE 4: 668–69; LTK 3: 327–28.

721. Cf. Luke 10.30, 33 ff.

722. Cf. *HL* 54.1, where Palladius speaks in much the same way of Melania and her distribution of wealth.

723. *HL* 56 is devoted to Olympias.

724. 1 Tim. 8.14.

725. 1 Tim. 1.9. Cf. *HL* 2.3.

726. δηλατορευθῆναι, from the Latin *delator*, "spy, accuser, informer." There is ample evidence that in late antiquity the Greeks had absorbed some of the worst of purely Roman vices.

727. Theodosius I was emperor of the Eastern Roman Empire from 379 to 395.

728. This Elpidius is unknown outside the *Dial.*

729. τὴν ἄνθρωπον. The woman Olympias was endowed with the courage and stability associated with men. Her marriage was never consummated because "she kept putting him off," according to the records. Cf also ch. 16 above, where she is said to be "man in life, words and in knowledge and in her patience under difficulties, man in everything but body."

730. According to *HL*, Melania the Younger, forced into marriage with a Roman of the first families, had two children, which died shortly after birth. She freed her husband Pinianus from the marriage bond by saying: "If God had willed us to have children, He would not have taken them away so soon." Pinianus went off to live with thirty monks reading and engaged in gardening and solemn conferences.

731. Cf. 1 Cor. 7.34.

732. Matt. 11.29.

733. ὕλην. Cf. *HL* 40.2, 41.3, and 54.1.

734. Maximus was a pretender to the Roman throne in 388. He did gain rule over Britain, Gaul, and Spain at a time when Rome was torn by internal factions.

735. Cf. 1 Kings 19.8.

736. Rom. 16.12.

737. Phil. 2.21.

738. St. Amphilochius was bishop of Iconium from 374 to c.397. For his life, cf. DCB *s.v.* Amphilochius, St.; NCE 1.455.

739. Optimus was bishop of Antioch in Pisidia. For his life, cf. DCB *s.v.* Optimus (1).

740. St. Gregory was bishop of Constantinople for but one month in 381. For his life, cf. DCB *s.v.* Gregorius (14).

741. Peter was bishop of Sebaste from 380 to 392. For his life, cf. DCB *s.v.* Petrus (41).

742. St. Basil (329–379) was bishop of Caesarea in Cap-

padocia. For his life, cf. DCB *s.v.* Basilius of Caesarea; NCE 2.143–146.

743. Sozomen, *HE* 8.9: "Seeing her bestowing her substance on all who asked for it, John said to her: 'I commend your purpose; but he who aims at the height of godly virtue must be a careful steward, while you, adding wealth to those who are wealthy, simply cast your goods into the sea. Of your own free will you have dedicated your substance to the needy, and, as you have been appointed to manage your money, you will have to render your accounts. Therefore regulate your giving by the need of those who ask it.' "

744. Cf. 1 Cor. 9.18; Acts 28.30.

745. Cf. *HL* 1.3, where Isidore wept at table, saying: "I am ashamed to partake of irrational food." Porphyry, *Vita Plotini* 1, says that Plotinus was ashamed even to have a body.

746. Cf. Ps. 123.2.

747. Ecclus. 21.15.

CHAPTER 18

748. 1 Tim. 5.18.

749. 1 Cor. 9.7.

750. 1 Cor. 9.12.

751. 1 Cor. 9.23.

752. 1 Cor. 8.9.

753. 1 Cor. 8.10.

754. 2 Cor. 5.15.

755. Ps. 25.12.

756. Rom. 8.15.

757. Ps. 25.8.

758. Cf. Rom. 8.15; Gal. 4.3–5; 1 Tim. 1.9.

759. Job 31.1.

760. Cf. Matt. 5.29–30 which comes to mind here.

761. Ps. 119.106.

762. Cf. Heb. 12.8.

763. Cf. *HL* 32.7, where it is stated: "the little ones (i.e., the novices) need the rule to guide them. Those advanced in the spiritual

life need no rule." So the *Regula Sancti Benedicti* 73 calls itself a "little rule for beginners" (*minima inchoationis regula*).

764. θωρακίσας ἑαυτοῦ τοῦ τῆς ψυχῆς ὀφθαλμόν. Cf. Plato, *Respublica* 533D: τὸ τῆς ψυχῆς ὄμμα.

765. Cf. Eph. 6.11, 13.

766. 1 Cor. 15.33.

767. Jer. 9.1.

768. Jer. 9.2.

769. *Ibid.*

770. Jer. 15.17.

771. Ps. 26.4 ff.

772. Cf. Ezech. 8.16.

773. Cf. Coleman-Norton note to 113.27, where he quotes parallel passages from Aeschylus.

774. Ezech. 8.7–10, 12–14, 16–17.

775. Gal. 2.6; 6.3.

776. 2 Peter 2.3.

777. Phil. 3.19.

778. Jude 12.13.

779. Ezech. 9.1–6.

780. Ezech. 1.1.

781. Ezech. 1.3.

782. Vespasian was emperor of Rome from 69 to 79 A.D.

783. The Romans captured Jerusalem in 70 A.D.

784. Cf. Acts 18.24–28.

785. A Jewish boy at the age of thirteen became a "son of the Law." Basil of Seleucia, *Orat.* 27, says, "Spiritual persons are the sons of the font."

786. 1 Cor. 10.11.

787. σιδηρᾶν ῥομφαίαν, the iron sword used by the Thracians. Cf. A. Fol - I. Marazov, *Thrace & the Thracians* (New York 1977) 59, 34, 147. PGL quotes *Max. schol. ap. Dion. Ar.*: ῥομφαία βαρβαρικόν ἐστιν ὅπλον.

788. Ezech. 33.2–6.

789. Chrysostom, *Sermo 64 de jejunio, ad init.*, said: "More clearly than a trumpet do I lift my voice." Cf. 1 Cor. 4.8.

790. Cf. Rom. 1.8.

791. Prov. 20.9.

792. πανοῦργος, "full of craft, cunning." The deacon's remarks are rather Rabelaisian and I could not resist the temptation!

793. Cf. Job 34.18; Eccle. 8.4; Heb. 13.17; 1 Peter 2.13–14.

794. Prov. 25.6.

795. Col. 4.5.

796. Prov. 25.6. Palladius here made a slip in assigning it to Ecclesiastes.

797. 2 Tim. 1.7. Cf. Acts 1.8.

798. Chrysostom, in his homily on Cor. 4.5, says: "The opportunity is not yours; you are strangers and pilgrims. Seek not honors and powers, but endure all things and so buy up the opportunity, as a man in a big house when attacked by robbers surrenders all, in order to buy himself from them."

799. Cf. Exod. 2.11–21; 3.1.

800. Cf. 1 Kings 19.2–5.

801. Cf. Justin Martyr, *Dialogus cum Tryphone* 120.

802. Cf. Dan. 6.10–16.

803. Cf. 1 Kings 22.1–28.

804. 1 Kings 22.27.

805. Matt. 11.11.

806. Cf. Matt. 14.3–11.

807. Cf. Heb. 11.10; Acts 17.24.

808. John 1.29, 36.

809. Cf. Matt. 18.18.

810. Chrysostom, *Hom. in Eph.* 3, had said that he was not speaking of Eudoxia when he referred to Jezebel and Herod's daughter.

811. 1 Cor. 10.25.

812. ἐκτραχηλίδαντες. Cf. *HL* 26.1, where the same verb is used of Heron who was thrown off balance by many labors. The verb is taken from the language of the horse race and means "to overthrow." It is used by the Greek fathers in a special spiritual sense.

813. "Though he speaks of Phoenicians, etc. by name, he is not attacking their personal faults, but using them as examples of faults common to all men" (Moore 163 n. 4).

814. Job 40.25 (LXX).

815. Deut. 4.20; Jer. 11.4.

816. Exod. 10.22; Ezech. 32.8.

817. Heb. 11.9. This phrase does not occur in the Old Testament as Palladius states.

818. Titus 1.12.

819. Gal. 3.1.

820. 1 Cor. 5.2.

821. Rom. 1.8.

822. Eph. 1.18.

823. 1 Thess. 4.9 f.

824. Cf. Rom. 7.15, 19, 21.

825. 1 Tim. 5.20.

826. Cf. 1 Cor. 11.16; 1 Peter 2.16.

CHAPTER 19

827. Cf. Rom. 1.30; 2 Tim. 3.2.

828. Cf. Mark 1.3, 5.

829. Matt. 5.1.

830. Matt. 8.18.

831. Cf. Rom. 1.30; 1 Tim. 1.13.

832. Matt. 8.19.

833. Matt. 8.20.

834. Cf. *HL* 9, where it is said of the monk Or: "In their stories they said that he neither lied, nor swore, nor cursed anyone, nor did he speak unless it was necessary."

835. Cf. John 2.24–25; 3.31; Eph. 1.20–21; Phil 2.9–11.

836. Cf. Matt. 12.39–41.

837. John 7.12.

838. Luke 11.15.

839. Luke 7.34.

840. Cf. John 8.48.

841. Matt. 16.18.

842. Matt. 16.14.

843. John 1.12.

844. Matt. 16.15.

845. Matt. 16.16.

846. Chrysostom, *Hom. 44–45 in Matthaeum* 2, thus comments

on Matt. 16.18: τουτέστι τῇ πίστει τῆς ὁμολογίας, "that is, in the faith of His confession."

847. Matt. 16.18.

848. Acts 17.6. Palladius is in error here. It was the Jews at Thessalonica, not the Ephesians, who made that statement.

849. Most of John's honors were posthumously conferred. His body was brought back from Armenia and buried in the Church of the Apostles on January 27, 438. Bishop Proclus won back to the Church those who had separated because of the deposition of John. Socrates, *HE* 7.45, says: "I marvel that ill-will touched Origen after his death and spared John. Origen, two hundred years after his death, was excommunicated by Theophilus; John, thirty years after his decease, was received into communion by Proclus." The Church has kept down through the centuries January 27 as the feast of St. John Chrysostom, but after Vatican Council II it was changed to September 13. For Chrysostom considered as martyr, cf. Baur 2.431–35.

850. John 7.12.

851. Matt. 16.16.

852. Cf. Luke 6.13–16; John 2.11.

853. Isa. 40.15.

854. This seems to be a practical application of the proverb quoted in *HL* 25.5: "Diseases are cured by their opposites."

855. Luke 3.7.

856. Acts 23.3.

857. Matt. 12.39.

858. Luke 24.25. It was not addressed to all the apostles as Palladius here states, but to two of them only.

859. Matt. 16.23.

860. Cf. 1 Cor. 2.15.

861. ἀπαιδεύτων, i.e, the uninstructed in Christian doctrine. Cf. 2 Tim. 2.23.

862. Cf. Gen. 21.3–10.

863. τῷ συνασμενισμῷ. Apparently the word occurs only here and in *HL* 66.2.

864. Cf. Gen. 27.41–44; 28.1, 2, 5.

865. Cf. Gen. 19.1, 12 f., 15.

866. Heb. 11.24.

867. Cf. Exod. 2.15.

868. Cf. Exod. 3.15–18; 4.29 ff.

869. Heb. 11.38.

870. Cf. Aristotle, *Ethica Nicomachea* 1165B; also 1155B, where a similar saying is attributed to Empedocles. Note our own: "Birds of a feather flock together."

871. Ecclus. 13.19.

872. 2 Cor. 6.14.

873. 1 Cor. 9.20 f.

874. 1 Cor. 9.20.

875. Cf. Phil. 3.5.

876. τὰ δόγματα τοῦ Σωτῆρος. Cf. *HL* prologue 1: τοῖς δόγμασι τοῦ Σωτῆρος.

877. Cf. Acts 13.1 ff.; 17.1 ff.

878. Plato, *Respublica* 408D, said that skillful physicians should have had all manner of diseases in their own persons to make them truly efficient.

879. In the spiritual life an important aspect was the discernment of spirits, the knowledge of good and evil. In the natural order the teacher was to meditate on discernment of character, the morality of acts, and so educate their pupils. It was a moral education taught through the medium of the ancient classics, and later the Scriptures and some early Christian writers.

CHAPTER 20

880. Cf. *HL* prologue 1: "This book is written for the emulation and imitation of those who wish to succeed in the heavenly way of life and to take the journey which leads to the kingdom of heaven."

881. Cf. Chrysostom, *Hom. in Acts* 3: "The bishop cannot sin unobserved. Let him be angry, let him laugh, let him dream of a moment's recreation, and many are offended, scoff, call to mind previous bishops, and abuse the present one. Yet if he enters the palace, who is first? If he goes to visit ladies or the houses of the great, none is preferred before him. I do not speak wishing to put bishops to shame, but to repress your hankering after the office."

882. Moore 174 says it could have been Eunuchus of Ephesus. Migne and others of the editors have considered it a proper name.

883. Heb. 13.3.

884. Ps. 116.15.

885. ἐν ταῖς βαρβαρικαῖς ζώναις. PGL does not note this meaning for ζώνη. Pring 78 defines "girdle, belt, cordon, zone."

886. Emesa was on the east bank of the Orontes. See RE 5.2496–97.

887. Bostra was south of Damascus, in the oasis of the Syrian Desert. See RE 3.789–91.

888. The Blemmyes, mentioned in *HL* 32.10, were a turbulent tribe of Ethiopian nomads living in the Upper Nile country. Apparently the earliest literary mention of them is in Theocritus, *Idylls* 7.114, and we are indebted to the *scholia* on that passage for much of our knowledge of them as well as for some information on the pagan worship of Pan. Strabo, *Geogr.* 17.786, and Eusebius, *V. Const.* 1.8, also mention them. In about 450 A.D. they invaded the Thebaid and were then driven into the area between the Nile and the Red Sea where they are still represented by five tribes speaking their own language. Cf. RE 5.566 ff.

889. Syene is the present day Assam. Cf. *HL* prologue 2: ". . . of those I had lived with in the Egyptian desert and Libya, in the Thebaid and Syene . . . ."

890. Serapion was sent back to Egypt. He had been consecrated bishop of Heracleia in Thrace by John Chrysostom (Socrates, *HE* 6.17) and fled from there to take refuge among the Goths. Sozomen, *HE* 8.9 f., says that Serapion was intensely opposed to John at a later date.

891. We have no information which see was occupied by Hilarius. He is mentioned by Chrysostom in *Ep.* 14. For his life, cf. DCB *s.v.* Hilarius (12).

892. Antonius is unknown outside the *Dial.*

893. Timotheus is unknown outside the *Dial.*

894. Maroneia is in Thrace; cf. RE 14.1912–13.

895. This John may be the Lydian who was later consecrated bishop of Proconessus (Socrates, *HE* 7.36). For his life, cf. DCB *s.v.* Joannes (329).

896. Rhodon is unknown outside the *Dial.*

897. Gregory is unknown outside the *Dial*.

898. Brisson is mentioned only here and in Chrysostom, *Epp*. 190 and 234.

899. Lampetius is unknown outside the *Dial*.

900. Eleutherus is unknown outside the *Dial*.

901. Cf. *HL* 30, the story of Dorotheus who looked after the monastery of women, living upstairs in a building next door, overlooking the women and exhorting them not to fight. "He grew old in the upper story. No women came up to him, and he did not go down, for there was no ladder placed there." W. H. MacKean, *Christian Monasticism in Egypt to the Close of the Fourth Century* (London, 1920) 124, finds this chapter an "amusing picture."

902. Anatolius is unknown outside the *Dial*.

903. Tigrius was a priest of Constantinople, distinguished for his moderation and meekness of disposition and known for his charity to the poor. Sozomen, *HE* 8.24, says he was stripped of his clothes, scourged, bound hand and foot, and stretched on the rack.

904. Philip is unknown outside the *Dial*.

905. Theophilus is mentioned by Chrysostom in *Ep*. 210 and addressed in Epp. 115, 119, and 212. For his life, cf. DCB *s.v.* Theophilus (11).

906. John is unknown outside the *Dial*.

907. Stephanus is unknown outside the *Dial*.

908. Sallustius is mentioned by Chrysostom in *Epp*. 210 and 212 and addressed in *Ep*. 203. For his life, cf. DCB *s.v.* Sallustius (3).

909. Philip is addressed by Chrysostom in *Ep*. 213. For his life, cf. DCB *s.v.* Philippus (11).

910. They were probably like the cathedral Latin school in the West where poor boys were educated for the priesthood in their elementary stages. Those schools were eminently religious and practical; the pagan classics had no place in the curriculum.

911. Sophronius is unknown outside the *Dial*.

912. Paul is unknown outside the *Dial*.

913. This Paul is likewise unknown outside the *Dial*.

914. Helladius is mentioned by Chrysostom in *Ep*. 14. For his life, cf. DCB *s.v* Helladius (18). Migne prints palace with a capital letter making him son of Palatius. He may have been a chaplain at the court. Sozomen, *HE* 8.6, says that Helladius, bishop of Caesa-

rea, had ordained Gerontius because he had been influential in obtaining for his son a high appointment in the army. Was this Helladius his son?

915. Silvanus is unknown outside the *Dial.*

916. Stephanus is unknown outside the *Dial.*

917. There is no previous mention by name of anyone who brought letters from Rome.

918. τῶν περὶ τὸν βασιλέα σχολῶν. σχολή, "school," was a late term given to the royal body guard. Cf. PGL 1361; Sophocles 1064. Note the usage in *schola cantorum* or even "a school of fish."

919. Provincalius is unknown outside the *Dial.*

920. For the life of Elpidius, cf. DCB *s.v.* Elpidius (28).

921. The whole account is given in Sozomen, *HE* 8.21, who adds that the culprit was seized and taken to the prefect, who put him into custody and assured the people that justice would be done.

922. For the life of Eutropius, cf. DCB *s.v.* Eutropius (18).

923. ψάλτης, a singer or cantor. There was in the early Church an order of singers, beginning in the fourth century. They were appointed by the priest rather than the bishop.

924. Cf. Mark 15.15–37.

925. This section related the trials of the Eastern bishops who joined the embassy from Rome. We last saw them at Lampsacus in chapter 4.

926. ζιβύνη, with a spear or javelin. Former editors treated this as a place-name, Zibyne, which does not exist. Bigot conjectured βιζύη. Only Coleman-Norton has it as a common noun, and he pointed out that the word exists in Isa. 2.4; and Jer. 6.23.

927. Palladius here invents the "fellow soldier" to record his own prophecy at the time. In this way he also made oblique references to himself in *HL.*

928. Was this possibly Palladius himself speaking? Both Moore and Coleman-Norton thought it highly probable.

929. Cf. 2 Thess. 1.10.

930. What he means here is that the philosopher (let us say, both sage and saint) should find an opportunity to derive good from evil circumstances.

931. 2 Cor. 2.15.

932. 1 Cor. 4.9.

933. This may very well have been Palladius referring to himself in the third person.

934. The bishop of Tarsus was Phalerius, 392–c.415.

935. Porphyrius was bishop of Antioch at that time.

936. Eulogius (died c. 417) is addressed by Chrysostom in *Ep.* 87. When he wrote that letter he did not realize that Eulogius was opposed to him. For the life of Eulogius, cf. DCB *s.v.* Eulogius (5).

937. Leontinus was bishop of Ancyra. He has been mentioned in ch. 9.

938. For the life of Ammonius, cf. DCB *s.v.* Ammon (3).

939. The Catholic (Universal) Epistles were so called because they were addressed to everyone in the Church, not directed to a particular person or group. They were the two Epistles of St. Peter, the first of St. John, and the Epistle of Jude.

940. 3 John 1–4; Philem. 7.

941. 3 John 9–11.

942. δευτέρας Καππαδοκίας. Cappadocia consisted of two provinces. Father Schläpfer translates: "Die Bischöfe der zweiten Provinz Kappadozien."

943. Only Palladius mentions that Bosporius was a bishop for forty-eight years. For his life, cf. DCB *s.v.* Bosphorius.

944. Sarapion is unknown to us outside the *Dial.*

945. 1 John 2.18.

946. 2 Thess. 2.3.

947. John 2.18. Cf. also *HL* 54.5, where Melania said: "*Little children*, it was written over four hundred years ago, *it is the last hour*. Why are you fond of the vain things of life? Beware lest the days of the Antichrist overtake you and you not enjoy your wealth and your ancestral property."

948. Matt. 20.6.

949. Matt. 20.1.

950. ἐξαιτοῦντος αὐτοὺς τοῦ διαβόλου. Cf. Didymus, *Comm. in Job* 1.7: ὁ διάβολος . . . τοὺς ἐχθροὺς ἐξαιτούμενος. This was the famous Didymus the Blind whom Palladius says he met four times at various intervals in the desert.

951. Luke 22.31 f.

952. Phil. 3.19.

953. Hos. 4.12.

954. Cor. 6.10.

955. Cf. Col. 3.5.

956. John 2.9.

957. Prov. 15.1.

958. Ps. 119.28.

959. Ecclus. 2.14.

960. Ps. 52.6.

961. James 4.10; 1 John 2.16.

962. Ps. 119.51.

963. Aristotle, *Nic. Eth.* 4.1, says that prodigality and stinginess are the two extremes. But liberality is a virtue which is the happy mean between these two vices.

964. This is Moore's conjecture (182) reading φόνος adopted by Coleman-Norton. It makes more sense than φθόνος, "envy," which all other editions show including the *cloaca maxima* of the Abbé Migne.

965. Cf. Matt. 15.19; Mark 7.21–22; Rom. 1.29–31; 2 Cor. 12.20; Gal. 5.19–21; Col. 3.5, 8; 1 Peter 2.1.

966. Cf. Gal. 5.22–23; 1 Tim. 6.11; Col.3.12.

967. James 4.6.

968. Ps. 74.3.

969. Ps. 94.2.

970. Matt. 12.33.

971. Matt. 7.16.

972. Cf. Rom. 9.22; 1 Peter 3.19–20.

973. Cf. Exod. 34.6; Num. 14.18; 2 Esdras 19.17; Ps. 7.10; 86.15; 103.8; 145.8; Sap. 15.1; Ecclus. 5.4; Isa. 57.15; Joel 2.3; Jonah 4.2; Nahum 1.3; Rom. 2.4,11; 2 Peter 3.9, 15.

974. Cf. Ecclus. 2.1–11; 2 Macc. 6.12–17; 1 Tim. 1.16; Heb. 11.32–38; 12.1–2.

975. Cf. James 5.11.

976. Job 21.4–14.

977. Ps. 101.1.

978. Ps. 73.1. f.

979. Ps. 73.3.

980. Ps. 144.13, 12.

981. Ps. 144.14.

982. Ps. 144.13.

983. Ps. 146.5.

984. Hab. 1.2.

985. Hab. 1.2. ff.

986. Jer. 12.1 f.

987. Sophonias is the LXX name for Zephaniah. Palladius is mistaken again in placing his quotation. What follows is really from Mal. 3.13–16.

988. Chrysostom, *Hom. in Acts* 28, tells of those who denied that providence extended to all things beneath the moon. "Does a charitable person meet with disaster? A laborer who receives his food gets less wages at the end; so does the charitable man who receives blessings in this world" (*In 1 Cor.* 43). "If you see an evil man prosper, know that he once did some good, and receives his reward here, and loses his claim on that which is to come" (*Or.* 65).

989. Mal. 3.13–16.

990. Cf. 1 Tim. 2.2; 3.16; 4.7–8; 6.3, 5–6; Titus 1.1.

991. 2 Tim. 3.13.

992. 1 Cor. 4.9, 11 ff.

993. Cf. 1 Cor. 9.24 ff.; Phil. 2.16; Heb. 12.1 f.

994. Deut. 30.15; cf. Ecclus. 15.18.

995. Cf. Rom. 11.33 f.

996. Ps. 51.7.

997. Cf. Heb. 13.8; James 1.17.

998. Cf. *HL* 24.3, where Stephen is undergoing a severe operation and addresses those who pity him: "My children, do not be hurt by this . . . It may well be that my members deserve punishment and it would be better to pay the penalty here than after I have left the arena." Chrysostom, *Hom. in Mart.* 2.799, said: "Today is the time for wrestling; you have come to learn how to strive manfully, to take part in every contest. No man coming to the training school lives in luxury; nor in the time of conflict does he seek for tables."

999. Coleman-Norton accepts the conjecture τόπων, "of the places" offered by Bigot, meaning "position in the Church" (cf. Acts 1.25; 1 Cor. 14.16). This is against all the manuscripts and the other editions where τοίχων, "of the buildings," is to be found. When we recall Palladius' own feeling about the inanity of great church edi-

fices both here and in the *HL* we must surely accept τοίχων as the true reading. The Church consists in the people and not in great stone edifices.

1000. M-G. de Durand believes that this shows definite influence of Palladius' own teacher Evagrius of Pontus. Cf. his article "Evagre le Pontique et le *Dialogue sur la vie de Saint Jean Chrysostome*," *Bulletin de littérature ecclésiastique* 77 (1976) 191–206.

1001. θερμότερος πυρὸς ἔχων τὸν ζῆλον Cf. *HL* 54.1: ἐν τῳ θείῳ ζήλῳ καθάπερ πυρὶ φλέξασα.

1002. Eph. 4.30.

1003. Matt. 25.15–28.

1004. ἐν ὀλίγῳ καιρῳ πληρώσας πολυχρονίᾳ χρέῃ. Cf. Wisd. 4.13 which is quoted in *HL* 38.1 speaking of his teacher Evagrius.

1005. διαθήκην ὕλης οὐ γράφει. Cf. *HL* 1.4: οὐ διαθήκην ἔγραψε τελευτῶν: "Very rich and exceedingly generous, he made no will when on the point of death, and he left neither money nor property to his own virgin sisters, but rather he entrusted them to Christ." Antony also (VA 3) left his sister with a group of holy virgins when he went off to the desert.

1006. Cf. John 14.31.

1007. Ps. 120.5.

1008. Matt. 25.21.

1009. Matt. 12.34; Luke 6.45.

1010. Cf. Ps. 116.11.

1011. According to ancient *scholia* on Aristophanes, *Aves* 768, the partridge was wily and full of treachery to the hunters. Cf. also T. Gaisford, ed., *Paroemiographi Graeci* (Oxford 1836) 44 (B) 392; D. W. Thompson, *Glossary of Greek Birds* (Oxford 1895) 137–39.

1012. δηνάριον, from the Latin *denarius*. Cf. Matt. 20.2.

1013. Cf. Matt. 25.14–30.

1014. κατὰ καιρόν, "for the time being, the present," in contrast to the eternal.

1015. 2 Tim. 1.18.

1016. There is no record of any such Western synod. Sozomen, *HE* 8.26, reports two epistles from Pope Innocent in which he said: "It is necessary that there be a synodical investigation, and a synod we said long ago should be gathered."

1017. κοινὸν τῆς φύσεως. Moore translated: "unselfishness of the Christian character," which may be a better rendering, since the deacon is imagining himself as addressing bishops who should have these qualities to a higher degree than any other Christians. Moore refers to 1 Tim. 6.18: "ready to communicate."

1018. Matt. 5.23 f.

1019. Matt. 5.39.

1020. Ps. 133.1.

1021. Prov. 17.17 (LXX).

1022. Prov. 18.19 (LXX).

1023. τρὶς καὶ οὐχ ἅπαξ ἄθλιοι. Moore translates: "wretched to the third degree." This is in direct opposition to the phrase τρὶς μακάριοι applied to the saints. Cf. PGL 1409 f.

1024. τὴν τιθηνοκόμον καὶ κουροτρόφον. This same phrase occurs in the essay of Philo, *Quod deterius potiori insidiari solent* 31.

1025. Amos 1.11. (LXX).

1026. Cf. Titus 3.8.

1027. Mal. 2.10.

1028. Cf. Acts 17.28.

1029. Hos. 9.8.

1030. Cf. Sophocles, *Trachiniae* 139–140.

1031. ὁμοδιαίτους . . . ὁμοσπόνδους, ὁμοτραπέζους τε καὶ ὁμολέκτους, a rhetorical device called *homoearchon* (a similar beginning in a series of words).

1032. Cf. Aeschylus, *Choephorae* 391–92.

1033. Cf. Ps. 64.4.

1034. 2 Tim. 4.14.

1035. 1 Peter 5.4. The ancient Greeks crowned the victors of the race with a crown of ivy which would fade very soon. This never-fading crown is the crown of eternal life. Chrysostom gained immortality by his holiness of life and good works as well as by his writings which are still read.

1036. μετὰ ἔξοδον τοῦ σταδίου. Cf. *HL* 24.3: μετὰ τὴν ἔξοδον τοῦ σταδίου.

1037. Deut. 33.8, 13.

1038. John in his active life resembled Joseph, but in his prayers and meditations he was not unlike Levi. However, the practical side of John's life was directed by his contemplation which preceded action and so made his works effective.

1039. Deut. 33.13–17.

1040. Deut. 33.8–11.

1041. θηρευτὰ νοημάτων. The deacon was an avid student of Sacred Scripture as his abundant quotations show.

1042. Matt. 13.52.

1043. John had benefited from his earlier instruction in the "old" pagan learning under Libanius and others. His "new" learning came from the Scriptures which are inspired by the Holy Spirit.

1044. Cf. Lev. 18.21.

1045. John 16.2, freely quoted.

1046. Ps. 9.27.

1047. This accusation may have been made in a letter from Theophilus to Pope Innocent. However, that letter is no longer extant, if indeed it was ever written.

1048. Cf. Wisdom 7.23.

1049. Ps. 104.24.

1050. λαμπάδες, literally "lamps." It will be recalled that oil-burning lamps were applied to some being tortured on the rack, earlier in this chapter.

1051. κρουνοὶ αἱμάτων, literally, "streams of blood," so translated by Moore 197.

1052. Exod. 5.2.

1053. The punishments described in chapter 17 above are referred to here.

1054. εἰδότες had been conjectured by Bigot and seems to be required here to make sense.

1055. Cf. Matt 6.19. Chrysostom, *Orat.* 71: "Do you boast of your silken robes? They are the spinnings of worms, the invention of barbarians."

1056. παραχαράξαντες. The word παραχαράσσω meant in classical Greek to "restamp, devalue currency, to debase or counterfeit money." The Jews in Hellenistic times applied the term to breakers of the Sabbath. Here the meaning is that the Temple had been made into a common market-place.

1057. Cf. Lev. 19.30; 26.2.

1058. John 2.13–16.
1059. Apoc. 19.15.
1060. Heb. 10.28–31.
1061. Some of the manuscripts and some of the printed editions omit this colophon.

INDEXES

1. OLD AND NEW TESTAMENT

2. PEOPLE

3. PLACES

4. GREEK WORDS

5. GENERAL INDEX

Abba, 161
abolitio, 196
accidie, 204
accusation, 179, 220
actor, tragic, 176
advice, from Job, 188
age, Apostolic, 180
altar, 'to swear by,' 178
anchorites, 171
angel, of the church, 188; guardian, 185
antithesis, 172
apostasy, 157
Apostles, church of, 210
archdeacon, 164; distributes church revenues, 167
army, 196, 214
Asceterion, 171
ashes, 191
Augustial prefect, 45
aureus, 176

banishment, of Chrysostom, 157
baptism, 178, 198, 199; font of, 163; by heretics considered valid, 171; withheld until old age, 171
barbarians, 220
barley, 201
basket-weaving, monks engaged in, 179
bathing, 175
baths, public, 175
beetle, 180
bishop, 160, 161, 164, 183, 187, 192, 212, 214; accompanied by deacon, 162; Arian, 183; must be circumspect, 211; consecration of, 172, 197; ordination of, 193; exempt from public office, 198; list of exiled bishops, 157; expels the bad, 108; first bishop of Ephesus, 198; metropolitan, 196; 'of the mountain,' 178; to distribute church revenues, 166;

ordination of, 193; pastoral care of, 175; not to engage in business affairs, 196; highly respected, 162; transfer of, 187
Blessed Sacrament, 178
body, chaste, 195; temple of the Holy Spirit, 199
bodyguard, royal, 214
booby, 181
boredom, 204
bribes, 180, 200
business, ecclesiastical, 195; secular, 196
buskins, worn on stage, 176

caloyer, 160
candidates, for clergy, 198
cantor, 214
care, pastoral, 178; of souls, 172
catechumens, 163; wear white robes, 172
cathedral, Latin schools, 213
character, 203; Christian, 219; discernment of, 211
charity, 176, 213
choir, 81, 186; of saints, 79
Christ, 52; Church of, 62; saved the world, 191
Christians, 1, 169, 170, 201, 219; doctrine of, 30, 210; give witness, 211; in good standing, 164; non-Christian, 163; persecution of, 157; relations of, 189
Christ-loving, 53
church, 6, 154, 161, 163, 165, 172, 174, 190, 215; the Apostolic, 210; at Chalcedon, 181; of Christ, 25; in Constantinople, 161; law of, 164; dedicated to St. Mocius, 203; offenses to, 144; peace in, 111; does not consist of the buildings, 218; of St. Sophia, 165; the suckling, 144; tempest within